PERGAMON GENERAL PSYCHOLOGY SERIES

Editors: Arnold P. Goldstein, *Syracuse University*
Leonard Krasner, *SUNY, Stony Brook*

Smoking:
A Behavioral Analysis
PGPS-12

Smoking:
A Behavioral Analysis

Bernard Mausner and Ellen S. Platt
Beaver College, Glenside, Pa.

With the assistance of

Judith S. Mausner
The Medical College of Pennsylvania

Pergamon Press
New York • Toronto • Oxford
Sydney • Braunschweig

92143

PERGAMON PRESS INC.
Maxwell House, Fairview Park, Elmsford, N.Y. 10523

PERGAMON OF CANADA LTD.
207 Queen's Quay West. Toronto 117, Ontario

PERGAMON PRESS LTD.
Headington Hill Hall, Oxford

PERGAMON PRESS (AUST.) PTY. LTD
Rushcutters Bay, Sydney, N.S.W.

VIEWEG & SOHN GmbH
Burgplatz 1, Braunschweig

Contents

Preface

This is a book about cigarette smoking by two experimental social psychologists. We were attracted to the study of smoking because it seemed an ideal problem within which to pursue a general interest in social interaction, a specific interest in the interrelation of attitudes and behavior, and a concern with the way in which the community at large applies or fails to apply scientific advances.

The book falls into two parts. The first describes a series of investigations into the natural history of cigarette smoking; the second describes an experimental attempt to induce change in smoking habits. The initial studies in the first part consist of analyses of descriptive material drawn from interviews, questionnaires, and diaries furnished by a variety of groups of smokers. In two of these studies we examined the interrelations of different kinds of reports from individual smokers. The next step was intensive analysis of questionnaire data on the role played by smoking in the lives of a group of young men and their beliefs about the consequences to themselves of continuing to smoke or stopping. These data on beliefs and patterns of support for smoking were related to measures of personality traits.

The material on the natural history of smoking will, we hope, be of interest to social scientists working with health-related behavior, to professionals in public health and preventive medicine struggling to implement the insight that prevention of many illnesses now lies in the hands of the patient, and, lastly, to psychologists interested in an ecological approach to the study of behavior. We suggest the last because we found that an ecological model is necessary for a meaningful discussion of the sources of a complex behavior like smoking. In addition, since all three of these groups are interested in change, the study of the natural history of smoking should be salient because a detailed and comprehensive analysis of the behavior itself is needed for the understanding of outcomes of any attempts to influence this behavior. The response of cigarette smokers to attempts at persuasion would surely be affected by the way in which smoking was intermeshed with their total pattern of habits, perceptions, and motives.

The second section of the book reports an experiment which tested the effect of role playing on smoking behavior. Role playing is being widely studied by experimental social psychologists because of the apparent readiness of people who play a role to be influenced by the content of their role-playing experience. We hope that the data reported and the interpretations offered will furnish some useful insights to practitioners in public health and preventive medicine. It may be that information developed about change in smoking could serve as a model for the more general study of innovation and for the design of control programs in other areas in which people must give up immediate gratification for long-range good.

Smoking is clearly dependent on the complex interrelations of a variety of biological, physical, and social factors. Our work has focused on psychological aspects of the problem even though we realize that this represents only a partial view. We are not competent to study the biochemistry of tobacco or the physiological and anatomical systems affected by smoking. We are also poorly equipped to deal with the political and economic systems which provide important sources of support or discouragement for smoking. Perhaps some of our readers, grounded in the necessary disciplines, will be moved to go beyond the investigations of the behavior of the individual smoker which we have done. We hope that our sketch of an ecological model, even if we have not been able to fulfill all of its demands, will encourage others to attempt multifaceted research which would include aspects of the ecology of the smoker other than those we have examined.

It has been our intention to write a book which would be meaningful to any educated person interested in the problem of cigarette smoking, either for its own sake or as an example of the pervasive problem of the impact of scientific discovery on attitudes and behavior. Of necessity, our work has to be reported through the use of a vocabulary probably familiar only to a limited group of specialists. We hope that nonspecialists will skip the presentations of factor analyses, analyses of variance, and multiple regressions, and read the verbal translations which we have tried to include at every stage.

The current volume represents work in progress. We began with a model and closed with a series of unanswered questions. To stop and report one's work at almost any stage in a program of scientific investigation is almost as agonizing as the experiences of Ogden Nash's hero, who runs to the laundry to wear his woolen socks as they go shrinking by. It would always be wonderful to do just one more experiment, to include one more sample, to replicate a tantalizing finding. We are presenting our material at this point because we feel that we have gained some useful insights into the problem of cigarette smoking. We hope that this will be only the first step on a long road.

Bernard Mausner
and Ellen S. Platt
Beaver College
January 1970

Acknowledgments

This volume is the result of nearly eight years' work on the problem of cigarette smoking. The work began at the Graduate School of Public Health of the University of Pittsburgh in 1961 under a grant from the National Institute of Mental Health (M-5061 c). The following year the two of us began working together at Beaver College under a grant first awarded by the National Institute of Mental Health (MH-06684) and later transferred to the new research program of the Division of Chronic Disease of the United States Public Health Service (CD-00039). A grant from the Pennsylvania Tuberculosis and Health Association enabled us to begin work on the problem of role playing. Most of the studies reported here were carried on with the support of the United States Public Health Service under demonstration project Grant Numbers 4037 and 29429. The American Cancer Society has provided support for the final stages of the treatment of the data reported here and for the preparation of the manuscript. This work was carried on as a prelude to continued studies of role playing.

Preliminary versions of many parts of this book were presented at various meetings. We benefited from the opportunity to discuss our ideas at all three of the conferences on behavioral aspects of smoking sponsored by the National Clearinghouse on Smoking and Health. Some of the material in this volume was presented at the first conference, held at Beaver College in 1965, as part of the introductory remarks delivered by one of us (B.M.). An earlier version of part of the first three chapters was read at the third National Research Conference on Smoking and Health held at Madison, Wisconsin in May 1967. This material was also presented as part of a symposium entitled "Psychological Factors in Cigarette Smoking" at the meetings of the Eastern Psychological Association in Washington, D.C. in April 1968. During this same symposium one of us (E.S.P.) also presented a summary of the findings of the role-playing study reported in Part II of this volume.

Many individuals collaborated in the gathering and treatment of these data. Ellen Krassen Rosen designed and carried out the interviews with high school students described in Study I and gathered the data on adult males for Study II.

Margaret Cronin assisted in the analysis and treatment of the sociometry study in Chapter 2. Clara Fishburn and Harriet Weldon assisted in the gathering and analysis of the data of Studies IV and VII; they also assisted in assembling the data and preparing the manuscript. Jerry Toporek served as an invaluable guide through the mazes of the computer center at the University City Science Center in Philadelphia where the analyses were carried out. He prepared original programs and modified standard programs for our use. We are grateful to Daniel Horn, director of the National Clearinghouse for Smoking and Health, for permission to use items from the Horn-Waingrow scale in our Test of Patterns of Support for Smoking. Dr. Horn was the scientific officer monitoring our two major grants from the Public Health Service. He was especially instrumental in assisting us to obtain support for the role-playing study.

The manuscript was transcribed, assembled, and turned into usable form through the devoted efforts of Clara Fishburn and Margaret Lee; Mrs. Fishburn was especially helpful in the preparation of the tabular material. Classification of the adjectives used by respondents in Study IV was carried out by Ronald Green and Samuel Cameron of the Department of Psychology and by Norman Johnston and Richard Juliani of the Department of Sociology at Beaver College.

We are pleased to acknowledge the invaluable assistance given us by the many people who helped recruit the subjects without whom our work could not have been done. The Cheltenham High School has been generous in permitting us to talk with their students. Members of the Holy Name Society of the Seven Dolors Catholic Church in Springfield Township, Montgomery County, Pennsylvania, gave us their time, and the Society itself assisted us in organizing the work of our project. Any number of students at Beaver College helped uncomplainingly in the task of trying out our instruments and procedures. The smokers in the class of 1966 were particularly helpful in making possible the diary project reported in Chapter 2. We would never have been able to do the extensive role-playing study reported in the second part of this volume without the help of the administration and staff of the Ogontz Campus of Pennsylvania State University, in particular Jeanne Smith of the Department of Psychology. Of special assistance were J. William Johnston, Assistant Dean of Student Affairs, and F. Lynn Christie, Registrar, who helped us organize the first contact with subjects during registration. We are grateful to Leon Festinger (1957) for permission to quote from *A Theory of Cognitive Dissonance* (pp. 5-6).

The manuscript benefited from the comments of a number of readers. Leonard Krasner encouraged us to write the book after seeing a small part of it, and made some helpful suggestions. Clifton Read, of the American Cancer Society, reminded us of the necessity for avoiding jargon and brought us a perspective on the broad social forces engaged in the battle against smoking. Alice Isen contributed psychological sophistication from her viewpoint as an experimental social psychologist. Irving Janis read and reacted to Chapter 5.

We owe an incalculable debt to Howard Leventhal, who read the manuscript carefully and commented on almost every page. His reactions were invaluable in forcing us to think through the theoretical implications of our work.

Lastly, but of the highest importance, was the assistance given by Judith S. Mausner which is noted on the title page. She contributed to the epidemiological aspects of the research and the definition of an ecological approach to the problem of smoking. In addition, she edited the final version of the book. If this manuscript has any lucidity, it is probably due to her editorial influence.

Part I:
The Natural History of Smoking

1
Introduction

As social psychologists we are interested in the way in which knowledge and feeling interact as determinants of decision, and, eventually, of behavior. Cigarette smoking seemed a most appropriate area within which to explore these interests, for here is an apparent discrepancy between knowledge and behavior. Except for a tiny minority of skeptics, scientists have arrived at a consensus that smoking is harmful, and yet about half the adult males and one-third of the adult females in the country continue to smoke.

The Report of the Surgeon General's Committee on Smoking and Health (1964) and the succeeding publications by the United States Public Health Service (1967, 1968, 1969) are powerful indictments of cigarette smoking which need no restatement here. Apart from the increasing toll from cancer of the lung, smoking has been found to be associated with coronary artery disease, emphysema and chronic bronchitis, and a host of other ailments. It has been estimated that two to three hundred thousand deaths a year occur prematurely because of cigarette smoking. The prematurity of these deaths is a matter of great moment. The man who dies of a coronary at the age of 45, or of lung cancer at the age of 50, has lost for himself and for society some of the most productive years of his life.

The response to date in this country to the indictment of cigarette smoking has been measurable but small. According to the Public Health Service, in 1968 the per capita purchase of cigarettes in the United States by persons 18 years of age and above was approximately 210 packages. This was three to four packs less than the per capita rate for 1967. The total number of cigarettes sold in 1968 was 571.5 billion; in 1967 it was 572.5 billion. Thus, there has been a slight drop, a drop which according to current estimates seems to be continuing through 1969.

The presumed drop in consumption of cigarettes inferred from the figures on sales is consonant with the results of a Gallup poll released on September 4, 1969. This survey showed that 40% of the national sample of adults polled smoked cigarettes. One-third of the non-smokers had previously smoked at some time. The proportion of smokers was 5% lower than that found in a survey carried out by Gallup in 1958. Seventy-one percent of the 1969 sample agreed that smoking is a cause of lung cancer, 60% that it is a cause of heart disease. The smokers among them were asked whether they had cut down on cigarettes; 41% replied that they had. However, as we shall see later, generalized reports from smokers that they have reduced their consumption of cigarettes are quite unreliable.

The limited extent of the drop in consumption of cigarettes may not reflect accurately the actual effect of the knowledge that cigarettes are dangerous. With the increase in population and the changed mores legitimizing smoking by women, one might anticipate that cigarette smoking should be climbing rapidly. And, indeed, projections based on the rate of increase in smoking during the forties and early fifties show such a climb. Thus the essentially steady level of consumption may represent a decrease from "expected" levels due to widespread acceptance of the thesis that smoking is harmful. However, there is no question that cigarette smoking still represents an enormous problem in public health; although many smokers do stop, the rate of recidivism is high and the number of young people taking up smoking continues to be impressively large.

The problem is clear. In the face of overwhelming evidence that smoking is harmful, neither the individuals who continue to smoke nor society as a whole have engaged in what seems to be appropriate action. Although it is true that no individual smoker can be sure that he will be adversely affected, the smoking of cigarettes represents a form of Russian roulette in which the odds for a long and healthy life are markedly reduced. A disinterested observer committed to rationality might find any survival of smoking incredible.

It is beyond the scope of this volume to discuss in detail the active anti-smoking programs carried out in other countries, notably Great Britain, Italy, and Norway. But since our work has dealt entirely with Americans, a brief summary of the strangely mixed response of the American government to the need for action against smoking has been included as potentially useful for understanding the experience of our subjects over the past few years.

Many individuals and governmental agencies in this country have an honorable history of involvement in attempts to control smoking. Former Senator Maureen Neuberger was a pioneer in calling attention to the menace of smoking (Neuberger, 1963). The late Robert F. Kennedy saw the problem in its widest perspective; his powerful address to the World Conference on Smoking and Health (1967) was a stirring call to social action. Chief among the agencies concerned with smoking has been the United States Public Health Service. Each Surgeon General since 1959 has spoken out vigorously on the issue. The limited anti-smoking activity which has been generated by governmental agencies has primarily been centered in one or another section of the Public Health Service. The Federal Trade Commission has been concerned since 1955 with advertisements for cigarettes which made claims related to health. More recently (1968) this Commission has taken a leading role in attempts to include warnings on the consequences of smoking not only on cigarette packages but also in advertising. The Federal Communications Commission, when pressed by a young lawyer named John F. Banzhoff III, passed a ruling which led to the widespread appearance on television of anti-smoking messages.

The contrast between the response of regulatory agencies and public health groups and that of the Congress is painful. An influential group of legislators with considerable seniority is, of course, committed to the support of the tobacco industry because of its importance in the economies of their states. But beyond this, the large number of Congressmen and Senators with interests in broadcasting and newspapers may account for the fact that the history of legislation concerned with smoking is a grim reflection of the primacy of self-interest over the good of the community. One of the few legislators who have responded to the problem of smoking is Senator Frank E. Moss (Democrat, Utah). In commenting on the influence of the broadcasting and tobacco lobbies on Congress, he said in November 1969, "There are times when service in this body leaves one cynical and depressed."*

In summary, the heavy social and economic investment in the growing and processing of tobacco and in the manufacture, promotion, and sale of cigarettes continues. The sale of cigarettes is still a source of 4.4 billion dollars in tax revenues each year. At the present writing, apart from the devoted efforts of a handful of public leaders and voluntary agencies in health, the response of American society to the information that smoking of cigarettes is lethal has been essentially one of denial.

The mechanism of denial, as described by Freud, is a virtually universal device for insuring psychological comfort in the face of danger. A man can tolerate life in a city under aerial attack if he does not really believe that he himself can be hit by a bomb. If this denial does not lead him to take foolish risks, it may, indeed, be a useful device for the maintenance of sanity and of an organized life in otherwise impossible circumstances. If, however, the denial of danger destroys prudence, it becomes thoroughly maladaptive.

For individuals, the continuation of smoking illustrates a *maladaptive* form of denial. True, some smokers claim that they do not deny the dangers; for them continuing to smoke may represent a reasoned acceptance of risk. These smokers may really believe that smoking is hazardous to themselves but may continue to smoke because the rewards seem worth the possibility of danger. However, we are convinced that most smokers really do not feel personally vulnerable, despite their almost universal verbal assent to the proposition that smoking is harmful.

For society, the casual neglect of the dangers of smoking is a minor illustration of the placing of easy rewards above long-range good. It is minor compared to the toleration of a deteriorating environment, of a restless and underemployed underclass, of an international polity in which the total destruction of life on the planet is casually discussed as an option for governmental policy.

---

*For a full survey of the legislative history of smoking, see Fritschler, 1969.

Thus, behavioral studies of cigarette smoking are legitimate not only in themselves as a part of the attack on a serious problem of public health, but for their potential contribution to an understanding of what may be the most critical issue faced by mankind. It is a truism that man must learn to forego momentary pleasure, immediate gains, and personal rewards for the overall long-range good of the race. It is hard to imagine an organized society of billions of people surviving for long on this crowded planet unless that lesson is learned.

An Ecological Model for the Study of Smoking

The basic premise of our work is that cigarette smoking is not only a complex act in itself, but that it is the final common path for forces resulting from a variety of factors both in the smoker's environment and in his internal psychological and physiological states. For the study of smoking, therefore, an approach is needed which encompasses this complexity. An ecological orientation, which deals with the interactions of organisms and their total environment, was chosen as the starting point for our formulation of the problem of cigarette smoking.

FIGURE 1

An Ecological Model for the Determinants of Behavior

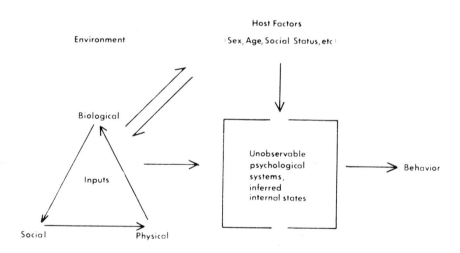

Our model was derived in part from one used in epidemiology to study the determinants of disease and in part from analyses of complex determinants of behavior (Fig. 1). Ongoing characteristics of the environment and of the person constitute inputs which act as determinants of unobservable mediating systems (i.e., events in the head). These in turn determine behavior. Each instance of behavior may create feedback which could modify the individual's internal states and/or his environment. The total pattern of inputs, mediating states, and behavior may be characterized as an ecological system.

There are, of necessity, semantic problems in the assignment of an individual factor to a given area of the environment, i.e., physical, biological, or social, or to an aspect of a mediating state. Is a smoking car in a railroad a part of the physical or the social environment? Obviously, it is both. Can the biochemical properties of the cigarette be separated from the physical impact of hot tarry smoke? The sex of a smoker, a characteristic of the individual, affects the nature of interactions in the social environment as well as the character of mediating responses within that individual.

Fortunately, it is not really necessary to assign factors to individual sectors of the ecological system for purpose of analysis since the main point of the diagram is to serve as a reminder of the complexity of the "web of causation," to use MacMahon's expressive term (1960). For the epidemiologist as for the psychologist there are no simple "causes." Any disease process or any behavior is inevitably related to the interactions among all sectors of the environment as they affect the intrinsic character of the organism.

In studying a behavioral system the psychologist who wishes to adopt an ecological approach must analyze the determining factors, state laws relating these factors to observable behaviors, and make inferences about mediating systems. The inferences should lead to a coherent body of theory. If the point of reference is a particular behavior such as cigarette smoking, the psychologist would relate the initiation, maintenance, and decay or elimination of that behavior to the complex network of determining factors. It is necessary as a first step to specify what these factors are and to search for ways of measuring them with precision. This may first be done descriptively; the descriptive matrix of determinants may then be used as a basis for hypotheses testable in experiment.

In this section of the volume, we will review the literature on cigarette smoking, including some of our own early studies, to develop a model based on the pattern of Fig. 1. The model in conjunction with the contributions of many investigators concerned with smoking will be shown to yield a number of working hypotheses. A series of exploratory studies relating a variety of data to the model will then be presented.

THE INITIATION OF SMOKING

Experiments with smoking occur very early, but most smokers begin to smoke regularly shortly before, during, and immediately after puberty. The most comprehensive information about the initiation of smoking comes from a survey carried out by Lieberman Research, Inc. for the American Cancer Society in March and April 1969. This survey, based on a nationwide sample of 1562 adolescents, showed that the median age of first experiments with smoking is 12, but that one-quarter of those who tried cigarettes did so before they were ten. The proportion of "regular" smokers, defined as those consuming one cigarette in the 30 days before the survey (a somewhat unusual criterion), rose from 14% at ages 13-14 to 24% in the 15-16 year age group and 42% among 17-18 year olds.

Many studies support the notion that smoking is linked to a complex of behaviors associated with the transition from childhood to adulthood; among these behaviors are the driving of automobiles, the exploration of heterosexual relations, the consumption of alcohol and other drugs, and increasing freedom in the making of personal decisions. Obviously, not all adolescents include cigarette smoking among their newly acquired quasi-adult behaviors. There seems to be some evidence that those boys and girls who do begin to smoke are more rebellious than non-smokers (Stewart & Livson, 1966), have poor relations with authority figures (Salber & Rochman, 1964), date frequently, drive early and use alcohol (Pumroy, 1964), and tend to have accidents when they drive (Ianni & Beck, 1958). The Lieberman report to the American Cancer Society shows lower grades in school for smokers than non-smokers; 60% of the students with D averages smoked, compared to an 8% level of smoking among those with A averages. These generalized descriptions of the "young smoker" must be viewed with caution since they are based on comparisons of groups and represent trends which may be statistically significant despite much overlap. We shall comment at length later on the weakness of formulations of "the character of smokers." Our point here is that the onset of smoking is a part of the peculiar *"rites de passage"* of the adolescent. It would hardly be surprising that adolescents for whom the transition into adult status comes hard should turn to cigarettes more frequently than others.

As yet there is little confirmed knowledge of the reasons that cigarette smoking has always been rejected by so many people despite its many attractions. After all, over half the adult population did not smoke even before the hazards to health were known. They were not attracted past the unpleasant experience of smoking their first cigarette. While some marginal differences between smokers and non-smokers in individual experiences and in exposure to the smoking of others have been noted, the low level of differentiation suggests that some unknown, possibly biological, factors may be operating. At present, however, there is nothing but speculation to support the notion (Eysenck, 1965; Fisher, 1959) that non-smokers and smokers are biologically different.

While we know relatively little about the factors which inhibit smoking, there is a growing body of theory and data dealing with the factors which support the initiation of smoking. In the following section we shall describe three mechanisms which seem important. These are the use of smoking for role definition, for social affiliation, and as a source of emotional rewards.

Role Definition as a Factor in the Onset of Smoking

Psychologists and sociologists use the term "role" to describe the pattern of expected behavior associated with a particular social status. Thus, a teacher, a truck driver, a mother are all expected to engage in certain socially prescribed acts. Most people perceive themselves in terms of the role or roles they play; much of their behavior consists of acts designed to demonstrate to others and, indeed, to themselves that they really carry out the demands of their roles. For the child and adolescent the task of creating a role and drafting a set of role-defining behaviors is especially important. The source of much role-defining behavior is imitation of other people after whom the child models himself, the "role-models." For example, as Bandura and Walters (1963) have shown so elegantly, children tend to engage in aggression after they have viewed films in which role-models act aggressively. In fact, the chief reinforcement for the aggression is the performance of that act by the role-model; the aggression needs no other reward.

Cigarette smoking can be an important source of role-defining behavior. The act of smoking has symbolic significance; it is associated with adult status, with freedom, with daring, with attractiveness. Television commercials have enhanced the image but, even before television, there was a folklore associated with smoking. And so it is understandable that young smokers say that smoking makes them feel more grown-up, more sophisticated, more a "part of things." The national sample of teenagers in the Lieberman study reported perceiving smokers as adventurous and socially advanced but neurotic and alienated. In contrast non-smokers were considered sensible, cautious, and hardworking.

The fact that each adolescent chooses his role-models on the basis of the particular circumstances of his own life means that no universal relation can be expected between smoking among adolescents and smoking among any one set of role-models. Thus, the finding that smoking in children is associated with smoking in parents (Higgins, Kjelsberg & Metzner, 1967; Horn *et al.*, 1959; Salber & MacMahon, 1961) may be contrasted with studies in which no association between the smoking of children and parents has been reported (Pervin & Dalrymple, 1965a; Straits & Sechrest, 1963). The Lieberman report showed that a slightly higher proportion of the teenagers whose fathers smoked, 29%, were themselves smokers, as compared to 22% smokers among the children of non-smoking fathers. The mother's smoking yielded sharper differences, 32% as opposed to 23%. Today, older brothers and sisters are apparently more influential than parents. Of teenagers whose older brothers or sisters smoke, 43% were themselves smokers compared to 20% among those whose older brothers or sisters did not smoke. This confirms earlier reports that smoking in children is associated with smoking in older siblings (Higgins et al., 1967; Lampert, 1965; Salber & Abelin, 1967). Lastly, Lieberman found that friends are extremely influential. Among smokers, 56% reported that most of their friends smoked, as compared to 14% among non-smokers. The world of adults in general is seen as a world of smokers. When the respondents were asked to estimate the proportion of grown-ups who smoke, the median estimate was 72%, considerably more than the actual figure of approximately 40%. And 75% of the teenagers who smoked said that teachers were likely to smoke, as compared to 64% of the non-smokers.

There are some indications in the literature about factors which differentiate populations in which the parents' smoking does or does not seem to influence the smoking of their children. Pervin and Dalrymple (1965a) suggest that the relationship of parents to children's smoking may hold only for those starting to smoke during early adolescence. College students who are no longer living at home would find other influences more potent. In a follow-up of the 1959 study of Newton, Mass., school children, Salber and Abelin (1967) found that, if both parents smoked, children up to the age of 15 were twice as likely to be smokers as children whose parents did not smoke. After that age, the smoking habits of the parents were apparently unrelated to the child's starting to smoke. Age of starting to smoke, social class of family, historical period of starting, presence of other smokers in the family (older siblings, grandparents) are all variables which may interact with the influence of parents' smoking and which must be studied if conflicting evidence is to be resolved. For example, Salber, Welsh, and Taylor (1963) noted that, although emulation of adult smokers is given as a major reason for smoking by high school students, this was more true for upper-class than lower-class students. The finding makes sense; upper-class adolescents in as class-bound a society as that of a Boston suburb are probably under greater pressure to model themselves after adult exemplars than are lower-class boys and girls.

Probably the most interesting body of data concerning role definition as a factor in the initiation of smoking comes from the program in studies of psycho-social correlates of smoking behavior and attitudes at the University of Arizona (Zagona, 1967). Questionnaires were completed by a large number of adolescents in three ethnic groups resident in Arizona: Anglos, Indians, and Mexican-Americans. Smoking was clearly portrayed as a reflection of emancipation for members of the subordinate groups, especially among the girls. The smoker saw his or her smoking as an indication of defiance of parental disapproval, of assimilation towards Anglo culture. Even among the members of the dominant group there was some evidence that smoking was tied in with self-concept and had symbolic value.

Intensive study of the process by which smoking is integrated into the pattern of role-defining behaviors during the first years of smoking requires something more than retrospective data. Perhaps the techniques used by Barker and Wright (1951) in continued and careful observation of the behavior of a seven-year-old boy could be adapted to the study of smoking. Time-sampling procedures, in which periods of observation are systematically chosen, could also be employed in conjunction with the more usual interviews and questionnaires. Such techniques of systematic observation would be especially useful in looking at the way in which the rituals of smoking in young persons develop as a reflection of the smoking of role-models. Does the young smoker imitate not only the general act but also the specific gestures of lighting up, puffing, holding, extinguishing? Are these imitated acts perceived by the smoker and others as symbolic of role? Unhappily, we do not know.

Social Factors

A second source of support for the early smoking of adolescents can be found in the social forces which tie individuals to their peer groups. Social factors in promoting smoking may be of two kinds. Smokers may be aroused by the smoking of others because the sight and smell of cigarettes act as stimuli to their own smoking habits. In addition, smokers may derive emotional support from each other. Groups of smokers may use smoking as a source of increased cohesion. It is frequently observed that when one member of a group lights a cigarette there is a tendency for cigarettes to be passed around and for other smokers to begin to smoke. The mutual giving of pleasure from the communal sharing of cigarettes and matches, and the very fact of smoking together may account for the apparent social contagion in smoking. There may be some parallel in this to the use of tobacco and other similar drugs as a part of social ritual in American Indian and other societies.

The power of pressures towards conformity to group norms is evidenced in the reports by Salber and her colleagues (Salber, Welsh & Taylor, 1963) that high school students gave a desire to be one of the gang, a fear of seeming "square" or "chicken," and a wanting to be liked as leading reasons for smoking. This was especially true for girls. Interestingly enough, both social and role-defining factors may have seemed somewhat shameful since they were attributed to others more often than accepted for themselves. Respondents were more likely than not to report that their own smoking was based on pleasure. Salber's findings from Massachusetts were confirmed in a study of high school students in Montana (Lampert, 1965). In a replication of Horn's Portland study, Creswell (Creswell *et al.*, 1967) noted that light smokers were more likely to smoke in groups than not, whereas heavy smokers paid little attention to the context in which they smoked. It may be that light smokers are still at the beginning stage in which social supports for smoking are predominant, whereas heavy smokers among teenagers have learned the tension-reducing effects of cigarettes and, indeed, may have developed a craving for them.

Smoking as a Source of Emotional Rewards

Most young smokers discover very quickly that cigarette smoking can be pleasurable and pacifying even though the first cigarettes are uniformly reported to be unpleasant. Probably the pharmacological and neurological effects of smoking are also quickly learned, i.e., the stimulation from the nicotine and the "information-giving" consequences of the irritation of the mucosa from hot smoke. The power of a need for "information," i.e., varied stimulation, has been established through a wide variety of experimental studies. (For a discussion of the literature on this issue see Cofer & Appley, 1964, pp. 278 ff.) It is highly probable that the irritating character of cigarette smoke and the contact of the cigarette with fingers and mouth provide relief from boredom as well as pleasurable stimulation. The Lieberman report indicated that the preponderance of young teenagers in their national sample gave social reasons for smoking while older respondents stressed the relaxing and tension-reducing effects of cigarettes. It is likely that the young smokers in this sample are largely very recent smokers. In one study of junior high school students, even 12-year-old smokers reported finding cigarettes extremely pleasurable (Mausner & Mischler, 1967). In fact, some of these very young smokers even claimed that they craved cigarettes (i.e., they reported symptoms of psychological addiction).

Unfortunately, little is known about the process by which the pleasurable and tension-reducing effects of smoking are discovered. Both Horn (unpublished paper) and Tomkins (1966a,b) have attempted to conceptualize the stages by which young smokers develop specific affective uses for cigarettes, i.e., those related to emotional rewards. Normative data are lacking on the time needed for these discoveries, the level of smoking required, and individual differences in environment and constitution which determine the learning process.

There is almost no information about the forces affecting those who begin to smoke in college, in the army, or during their first experiences at work. It seems that virtually no one starts smoking after the early twenties. Why this should be so is not known.

Summary

Virtually all adolescents are exposed to a variety of forces which both stimulate and inhibit a tendency to smoke. Our ecological model suggests that these external forces interact with a variety of internal systems; the final common path for some is the acceptance, for others the rejection, of smoking.

We have proposed that the forces which favor smoking are role identification, social affiliation, and affective rewards. Presumably, in addition to possible inhibition by biological factors, smoking is inhibited by social pressures of adults and by the virtually universal knowledge among young people today of the harmful effects of smoking (see Lieberman report). The net effect of stimulating and inhibitory factors has been the daily recruitment of an awesome number of new smokers.

THE MAINTENANCE OF SMOKING

The initiation of smoking has been ascribed to the operation of three psychological systems in adolescents exposed to an environment which encourages the use of cigarettes. Presumably the same psychological systems continue to operate as smokers mature, although their relative importance may change. Certainly the character of the environment becomes increasingly conducive to smoking. Internally based needs join with external cues to create what is, for most adult smokers, a remarkably constant and stable set of responses. Of course, it is well known that factors such as unusual stress, a holiday season, or an illness will interrupt the usual pattern of smoking. However, smokers tend to be highly aware both of the pattern they follow and of any interruptions.

The following sections will discuss briefly the environmental supports for smoking as well as the evidence that each of the three psychological systems, i.e., role definition, social affiliation, and emotion, which support the initiation of smoking, persist to varying degrees as aspects of the complex pattern of determinants of smoking in adults.

The Environment of the Smoker

Data on the influence of the physical environment are meager. Trends in smoking have not been related to such factors as climate or altitude. One can only speculate to what extent crowding in the slums, apart from other characteristics of slum life, is responsible for the uniformly high level of smoking reported among lower-class adolescents. The physical environment of virtually all adults is filled with invitations to smoke: ashtrays, vending machines, special areas reserved for smokers.

The cigarette as a biological agent is certainly a potent factor in the initiation and maintenance of smoking. Cigarette smoking leads to a variety of physiologic effects. Nicotine is a sympathomimetic agent (Knapp *et al.*, 1963); 20 minutes after smoking the smoker's heart rate accelerates and there is a sympathetic-like constriction of the peripheral vascular bed. Simultaneously, the irritation of the mucosa induces a neural stimulation, an effect to which we have alluded above as satisfying a need for "information."

In contrast, the tension-*reducing* effect of smoking suggests the results of parasympathomimetic activity, perhaps initiated by handling and oral activity. It is also possible that some as yet unknown biochemical fraction of the complex substance labeled "cigarette smoke" may have a pacifying effect.

The techniques of psychopharmacology, as developed in the study of tranquillizers and psychic energizers, have not, to our knowledge, been applied to the analysis of the effects of smoking. The literature on the influence of smoking on learning, perception, and attention is surprisingly meager. Given the lack of knowledge about the psychopharmacology of cigarette smoking, it is hardly surprising that there is much confusion about the identification of smoking as an "addictive" act. A committee headed by C. M. Fletcher which was part of the World Conference on Smoking and Health (1967) concluded that the term "dependence" could be used for smoking but that, in the absence of secure evidence on withdrawal symptoms, the term "addiction" had best be avoided. The committee made a plea for an intensive research effort on both the nature of habituation and the character and duration of symptoms of deprivation.

Factors in the social environment are more readily defined; they range from the awesome power of the tobacco and broadcasting industries and their congressional allies to immediate influences from individual role-models, peers, and social groups. The social groups which the smoker enters continue to stimulate his use of cigarettes, and the larger society is filled with social symbols legitimizing the cigarette, if not actually encouraging smoking. All act to increase the likelihood that those individuals who are susceptible will begin to smoke and will continue once they have begun. Countervailing influences in the social environment which tend to discourage smoking may be found among forces in the society at large, i.e., public agencies, voluntary associations, and in more immediate personal influences, such as some doctors, teachers, parents, and peers.

Intra-individual Factors Supporting Smoking

Smoking as role-defining behavior. The notion has already been presented that adolescents begin to smoke as a part of the process by which they develop behaviors appropriate to their perceived social roles. Along with the use of smoking as public behavior, being a "smoker" is probably an integral part of the smoker's self-concept. Most psychologists would accept the proposition that each individual has a set of mediating responses, or cognitions, which add up to a picture of the "real me." It is probably justified to assume that most behavior has some relation, even if remote, to this picture, i.e., the self-concept. This is another way of stating the notion, so aptly described in Allport's classical work on expressive behavior (1937), that an individual's idiosyncratic behavior, his gait, speech, handwriting, posture, express his character. The fact that a person smokes and the way in which he smokes should be added to the list of expressive behaviors. But expressive behavior is not only used to play a role for others; just as an observer judges a person by his style of action, each individual makes an interior picture of himself utilizing, in part, feedback from his own expressive behavior.

Formal support for the concept that smoking is an important part of self-defining behavior is difficult to achieve. Horn (personal communication) has found that subjects respond differently to TAT plates in which the protagonist is smoking than to pictures in which the protagonist is not smoking. The cigarette-smoking girl, for example, is viewed as being less moral and more adventurous than a non-smoker.

Weir (1967) photographed two male and two female models in candid poses with a cigarette; in another set of pictures the photos were retouched to eliminate the cigarettes. Each subject was shown a picture of two smokers, one male and one female, and a picture of two non-smokers. An extensive check list of adjectives was provided for characterizing the models in each photo. Weir reported only the descriptions of the photographs of the male smokers. As compared to descriptions of the same model without a cigarette, the presence of the cigarette produced a significant decrease in the frequency of use of adjectives such as gentle, awkward, timid, shy, and quiet, and a marked increase in the use of adjectives such as adventurous, rugged, daring, energetic, and individualistic. Weir concluded that his subjects' descriptions of a smoker could reflect the image they hope to project by smoking. He also stated, "To the extent to which these data reflect qualities of self, which may be expressed by cigarette smoking, an increase in the quality **ADVENTUROUS** and a decrease in the quality **TIMID** could be important social gains for many teenagers" (p. 155).

Vitz and Johnston (1965) noted that individuals who score high on masculinity on the Mf scale of the MMPI tend to prefer a cigarette which they themselves perceive as being more "masculine." Forrest (1966) reported that students in a women's college gave a stereotyped picture of a female smoker as attractive and sociable and partaking of alcohol. Not surprisingly, in Forrest's study, non-smokers gave much more negative stereotypes of the female "smoker" than did smokers. For the non-smoker, the typical smoker was perceived as empty and only apparently sophisticated while for the smoker she was well-groomed and likable.

The suggestion that the manner in which one smokes as well as the very *fact* of smoking is an aid in defining the self-concept arose from an analysis of comments made during the course of a smoking clinic conducted by one of the writers (Mausner, 1966b). A group of college girls engaged in the task of trying to stop smoking described some of the things which smoking did for them. Among other themes, there was much discussion of the use of cigarette smoking to create for the college girl the image of herself as a bright, sophisticated, career-oriented young woman. The almost total failure of the smoking clinic was undoubtedly due in part to the sense of social isolation faced by the students, many of whose friends continued to smoke. But probably it was also due to the inability of these young women to redefine their picture of themselves, to eliminate the idea that they were "smokers" and that to be a smoker was eminently desirable.

These data show that many people would agree that smokers are different kinds of people from non-smokers. This however may not mean that smokers themselves actually utilize their smoking behavior as an important part of their own self-defining response systems. It is possible that adult smoking may have very little to do with role definition. It may very well be that smoking represents an example of Allport's functional autonomy (Allport, 1937). If this were so, then smoking which began as a gesture of role definition could turn into either a purely habitual response, a response based solely on social stimulation, or a response supported by its pleasurable or tension-reducing characteristics. On the other hand, it is possible that support for the self-concept is one of the most powerful gains from smoking. Testing these alternative hypotheses will certainly tax the ingenuity of social psychologists to the utmost.

Social supports for smoking. The fact that smoking is stimulated by many aspects of the social environment has already been noted. But the social environment is effective because it is mediated by an individual's need for social affiliation and his learned reactions to social stimulation. It is readily apparent to even a casual observer that smoking can be an elaborate social ritual. As noted in the discussion of initiation of smoking, smoking behavior is probably contagious. It is a cliché of "human relations" training that it is a safe gesture for a superordinate to offer a cigarette to a subordinate. The gesture is guaranteed to put the recipient at his ease. The offer of a cigarette or the quest for a light is a well-known icebreaker in circumstances where it is difficult to penetrate the reserve of strangers. Lastly, the high level of smoking in social gatherings where alcohol and conviviality go together is well known.

The functions of social stimulation in the initiation of smoking have been noted above. It is possible that smoking continues to act as part of the cement which increases the cohesiveness of groups of adult smokers. It is not only the gestures of offering cigarettes, ashtrays, and matches which pull people together; the very sight and smell of another person's smoking create feelings of warmth and closeness. In more formal terms, the sights and smells may be heavily reinforced discriminative stimuli to affiliative responses.

Tomkins (1968) has suggested another function for smoking in social groups. For many people, interacting with others generates tension. Tomkins feels that much of the smoking which occurs as people begin to interact may be a consequence of this tension and may function as a pacifier. It would be a matter for empirical test to determine the relative importance of tension reduction, social affiliation, or pure cue value to the smoking which is stimulated by social intercourse.

In a series of interviews with smokers and ex-smokers, McKennell (1968) sought to classify the main occasions for smoking and the emotional states associated with taking a cigarette. A factor analysis of the data revealed five factors pertaining to "inner need" and two factors of social relevance. The first of the two social factors contained items indicating that the respondent particularly likes to smoke when in company, when talking, or when at a party. The second was a social confidence factor and contained items which indicate that smoking makes the respondent feel more sure of himself, have confidence with other people, fit in better with a group, be more relaxed in a group, and be happier when with other smokers.

The relevance of the social factors supporting smoking probably differs considerably among individuals. It may also vary from time to time for any single individual. One indication of the strength of social supports for smoking is the degree to which the presence or absence of these supports affects the success of attempts to modify smoking behavior. Schwartz and Dubitzky (1968b) have reported that male smokers who were successful in stopping were less likely to have wives who smoked and less likely to "smoke with loved ones" than those who were unsuccessful. Horn (1968) has indicated that the strength of social supports is one of the most important factors in determining the success with which people who attempt to stop smoking are able to carry out their intentions. In a study of the influence of a physician on smoking behavior, Mausner, Mausner, and Rial (1968) reported that individuals who were married to smokers showed no change in smoking behavior in contrast to individuals whose husbands or wives were not smokers.

On the basis of even these limited data we feel secure in suggesting that a sense of affiliation towards other smokers is an important support for adult smoking in some people and that the degree of its importance could be assessed by various methods, including resistance to anti-smoking influence.

The affective consequences of smoking. The most systematic discussion of smoking as a measure for the control of affect has been presented by Tomkins (1966, a,b; 1968). In his most recent statement, Tomkins describes three major types of smokers, those for whom smoking is a source of pleasure (positive-affect smokers, in his language), those for whom smoking is used to reduce tension or other unpleasant feelings, and those who are psychologically addicted. He uses the term "psychological addiction" to indicate that the smoker reports a craving for cigarettes and that he smokes to reduce the pain of not smoking rather than to alleviate externally induced tension.

Horn and Waingrow (1966a) have constructed a questionnaire consisting of items based on Tomkins' typology. Factor analysis of responses to these items has yielded factors patterned after Tomkins' types. In the widely used Smoker's Self-Testing Kit (Horn, 1969) there are six factor scales. Three represent varieties of positive affect, i.e., Stimulation, Handling, and Pleasurable Relaxation. The other three include one scale for tension reduction (Smoking as a Crutch), one for psychological addiction (Craving), and one representing affect-free smoking (Habit).

In informal discussions with smokers, the writers have been impressed by the possibility that the affective factors presented by Tomkins, Horn, and Waingrow are not actually independent, but form a gradient of emotionality. Our hypothesis is that their affective supports for smoking represent a continuum with smoking for pleasure at one extreme and addiction at the other. Most smokers seem to engage in some smoking which has no particular affective character, smoking which is purely habitual. Such smoking is cued off by the taste of coffee, by the presence of other smokers, by behaviors such as driving, typing, or reading which have become a source of discriminative stimuli for smoking. Similarly, most smokers seem to find some cigarettes quite pleasurable. It is true that very heavy smokers will report that much of their smoking, especially late in the day, is no longer very enjoyable. But virtually all smokers indicate that the first cigarette of the day or the cigarette taken with after-dinner coffee is intensely pleasant. Fewer smokers, but still a large number, use smoking as a way of relaxing after tension-filled moments as well as a source of sensual pleasure. Lastly, the minority of smokers who are psychologically addicted also show each of the other affective patterns. The question of the scaled or independent nature of the components of the affective dimension of smoking behavior will be tested in some of the studies reported in this volume.

Summary

An ecological view of the maintenance of smoking was presented in which both environmental and intra-individual supports were delineated. The possibility was suggested that crowding could be a source of tension which encouraged a tension-reducing behavior like smoking. The stimulating and pacifying properties of tobacco as a biological agent were outlined. Factors in the social environment encouraging and discouraging the use of cigarettes were presented briefly.

Three major intra-individual factors supporting smoking were discussed. These are the degree to which smoking is valuable as a source of strength to the smoker's self-image, as a component of the cohesive forces attracting individuals to groups composed of other smokers, and as a means for achieving a variety of emotional rewards. Tomkins' concept of types of smoker categorized according to the nature of the emotional rewards derived from smoking was described and rejected in favor of the concept of an affective gradient ranging from simple enjoyment of the taste or other sensory aspects of cigarette smoking, through the use of the cigarette as a pacifier, to psychological addiction. The next step in our inquiry is to present data from our own studies illustrating the heuristic value of the ecological model and providing support for its components.

2
Descriptive Studies of Environmental and Intra-individual Supports for Smoking

For the past several years the writers have been engaged in empirical studies of smoking. Most of them have been attempts to assess the impact of interventions designed to encourage the reduction or elimination of smoking. As part of each study, however, descriptive data were obtained, usually before the experimental manipulations. In addition, several investigations were specifically designed to yield pictures of the natural history of smoking. The following chapter is devoted to presentation of materials from both sources. Except in one or two minor instances the research was exploratory rather than hypothesis-testing. The aim was to furnish raw material with which to clothe the skeletal structure of the ecological model presented in the previous section.

Reference will be made at a number of points to a "three-dimensional model." This refers not to the overall ecological approach to smoking but to the picture of intra-individual supports described above. The three intra-individual factors or dimensions are (1) affective supports with subcategories defining positions on the dimension ranging from purely hedonic support through the use of smoking to reduce externally caused tension to the extreme of psychological addiction; (2) social supports, including both social contagion and the use of smoking to increase a sense of affiliation to social groups; (3) role definition, the use of smoking as part of a pattern of role-defining behavior.

RETROSPECTIVE REPORTS FROM SMOKERS: STUDIES I AND II

Factors Maintaining Smoking Among Adolescents: Study I

The goal of this study was a descriptive account of factors in the environment and within the individual which maintain smoking behavior among adolescents. We felt the need to know more than could be learned from the literature about the way in which smoking behavior is woven into the pattern of their lives. Some material of this kind had been obtained from a smoking clinic conducted with college students the year before (Mausner, 1966). In the present study we decided to extend our investigation to high school students in order to explore the factors maintaining smoking among individuals who are relatively new to the habit.

A standard technique for delineating such factors is the use of fixed-alternative questionnaires with large populations. However, the general character of most fixed-alternative items creates severe limitations to their usefulness. The tendency of respondents to give socially desirable answers is enhanced by the necessity for choosing among generalizations. In addition, the general statements to which respondents must react rarely reflect the subtle nuances of individual experience.

One of the writers had previously participated in a study of attitudes towards work (Herzberg, Mausner & Snyderman, 1959) which overcame the difficulties of fixed-alternative questionnaires by asking respondents to give anecdotal accounts of specific incidents in their lives. The technique, derived in part from Flanagan's work on "critical incident" procedure (Flanagan, 1954), yielded data which provided rich material for theoretical analysis. In an analogous approach, the current study employed an interview designed to encourage respondents to give detailed accounts of the circumstances in which they smoked particular cigarettes and of the rewards they expected and derived from those cigarettes.

Subjects and Procedures. The population chosen was the group of students attending the 1966 summer session of a suburban high school. Thirty of the 67 smokers among the 216 students were interviewed at the school (see Appendix I for the interview form). They were first asked to rate on a 7-point scale the degree to which each cigarette smoked the previous day was "wanted." Subjects were then asked to choose one cigarette they wanted very much, one they wanted moderately, and one they wanted relatively little. The interviewer asked a series of questions to determine what was happening at the time each of these three cigarettes was smoked, what cues led to smoking, the mood of the subject, his or her feelings at the time, expectations about smoking the cigarette, and the degree to which these expectations were fulfilled. Further open-ended comments were also collected. The protocols from these interviews were subjected to content analysis with an *a priori* analytical scheme to determine the degree to which each of the three major dimensions of support for smoking described previously could be identified.

Findings. Quantitative analysis of the protocols from these interviews revealed some mention of each of the major components of the affective dimension, i.e. enjoyment, tension reduction, etc. (see Table 1). "Habit" appeared most frequently in the description of the most wanted cigarettes, next most frequently for the moderately wanted cigarettes, and with lowest frequency for the least wanted cigarettes. The fact that cigarettes described as "most wanted" could be classified as responses to habit is hard to reconcile with Tomkins' concept of habitual smoking as emotionally neutral. It may, rather, mean that, although smoking was "habitual" in the sense that it was elicited by some external cue at a time when the respondent usually smoked, it still provided a great deal of satisfaction.

Not surprisingly, tension release was mentioned somewhat more frequently in connection with cigarettes wanted most compared with those wanted moderately or least. There were few other differences in the frequency with which other factors were mentioned for the cigarettes desired to different degrees. The infrequent mention of role definition and the frequent mention of social factors in smoking may reflect either the relative importance of these two areas in the population being studied or, more likely, the difficulty with which these adolescents identified role-defining behavior and the ease with which they could identify social factors.

TABLE 1

Frequency of Occurrence of Themes from Interviews[†] (30 High School Students)

Pattern of Support	Cigarette Wanted Most	Cigarette Wanted Moderately	Cigarette Wanted Least
Habit	15	12	7
Affective:			
Enjoyment	7	5	4
Manipulation	1	2	3
Stimulation	9	10	8
Tension Release	15	12	10
Addiction (Craving)	1	0	0
Social:			
Others smoking	11	11	8
Others stimulating	2	5	2
Others present	5	4	7
Alone	12	10	13
Role Definition	1	1	2

[†] *The occurrence of a given theme was tallied as present or absent in each respondent's protocol for each of the three cigarettes.*

About a fifth of the respondents gave records in which, to use Tomkins' terminology, only positive affect was associated with smoking (Table 2); a similar proportion described only reduction of tension. Almost three-fifths of the group, however, reported a mixture of the two patterns. The one subject whose protocol gave evidence of psychological addiction also reported the use of smoking to reduce externally induced tension and indicated a certain degree of pleasure from the act of smoking. Although the data in Table 2 do not support the concept that most smokers base their smoking on only one source of support, they also fail to give evidence of a scaled dimension in which the use of cigarettes for tension release represents a position which invariably also includes smoking for enjoyment or stimulation.

TABLE 2
Frequency of Themes Relating to the Affective Dimension of Cigarette Smoking[†]
(30 High School Students)

Enjoyment or Stimulation only	6
Tension Release only	5
Enjoyment or Stimulation plus Tension Release	18
Enjoyment or Stimulation plus Tension Release plus Addiction (Craving)	1
Total	30

[†] *Each theme in the entire record from each subject recorded as present or absent.*

Table 3 gives a somewhat bloodless picture of the situations in which respondents smoked. There did not seem to be any clear tendency for smoking in any given situation to be associated with a particular pattern of support, except that both social recreation and study (i.e., solitary non-recreational activity) apparently generated enough tension so that cigarettes were frequently described as necessary for relief. It should be pointed out that these young smokers were, indeed, under considerable tension. They were academically marginal students attending summer school to repeat courses they had failed during the preceding year.

TABLE 3
Frequency[†] of Various Patterns of Support for Cigarette Smoking in a Variety of Contexts

Contexts	Supports			
	Habit	Pleasure	Tension Reduction	Social
Solitary recreational activity	0	0	3	0
Solitary nonrecreational activity	10	5	16	0
Social recreation	6	8	13	0
Unorganized social	7	11	11	4
Work, school	1	0	0	1
Travel	10	3	11	2
Meals	9	7	7	1
Coffee	0	0	0	0
Work break	0	0	0	0

[†] *Sum of responses on three cigarettes rated "Wanted Most," "Wanted Moderately," and "Wanted Least."*

The interviews portray the character of their smoking far more vividly than any quantitative analysis. The following summaries of individual protocols are condensed versions of the interviews primarily in the respondents' own language.

1. Female, 20 cigarettes per day.

Cigarette wanted most was smoked when subject was alone and extremely angry. Subject expected cigarette to absorb some of the anger. This cigarette was also first of the day — one that she always wants.

Cigarette wanted moderately was smoked with another who was not smoking. Subject was in bad mood and angry. She only expected cigarette to give her something to do with her hands and claims she would have felt no different if she could not have it.

Cigarette wanted least was smoked alone when subject was in calm, good mood. She expected cigarette to increase her appetite and it did. Subject reports smoking more alone than with others.

2. Female, 22-25 cigarettes per day.

Cigarette needed the most was smoked out of a combination of habit (after meals) and desire for stimulation and pick-up. She expected the cigarette to wake her up and claims that it did.

Cigarette moderately wanted was smoked with another person when subject was bored. She expected the cigarette to relieve her boredom and it did. She was also following the cue of the other who was smoking.

Cigarette wanted least was smoked alone when subject was bored. Subject reports that it tasted so horrible it made her nauseous. She sees smoking as a repulsive habit that sometimes sickens her, but also claims that once she begins thinking about a cigarette an intense craving to smoke builds up within her.

She smokes alone more than with others because she thinks she is too young to smoke in public.

3. Female, 12 cigarettes per day.

Cigarette wanted most was smoked with friend. Subject in good mood. Expected little from cigarette.

Cigarette wanted least was smoked when subject was alone and in good mood. Expected nothing from cigarette.

Claims she would feel no different if not allowed to smoke any of the three cigarettes on which she reported. Subject admits that she smokes because "all my friends do." Since she is not permitted to smoke, she seems to see smoking as something daring and will smoke whenever she has an opportunity. She believes that smoking makes her look older and wants this very much. Her moods do not seem to be active cues for her smoking behavior.

4. Male, 27 cigarettes per day.

Cigarette wanted most was smoked alone when subject had just gotten up. He claims that he habitually smokes when he gets up. He expected satisfaction and his expectations were fulfilled.

Cigarette wanted moderately was smoked with others when subject was a little tense. Subject expected enjoyment from cigarette and his expectations were only mildly fulfilled.

Cigarette wanted least was smoked when subject was with others and in need of something to do. Subject expected release from boredom and his expectations were fulfilled. Subject smokes more alone. He thinks smoking gives a bad impression of him to others.

He claims that tension and boredom are his prime cues to smoking.

5. Male, 28 cigarettes per day.

Needed cigarette most in morning when with others and bored. Expects cigarette to taste good and to give him something to do.

Needed cigarette less in afternoon when with others and bored. Cigarette's good taste wears off in afternoon.

Needed cigarette least when alone in evening. Cigarette does not taste good. Claims that he probably wouldn't notice bad taste if with another.

Cigarette smoking depends on expectation of good taste (governed by time of day) and the presence of others. Feels like he is "somebody" when smoking. This feeling seems to keep him smoking when taste has worn off and friends have gone.

Summary. Interviews were conducted with 30 high school students who were asked to describe the circumstances under which they smoked each of three cigarettes during the previous day. For these students, both social stimulation and affective factors were important sources of support for smoking, but affective factors seemed more important. Role definition was mentioned only infrequently. The word "habit" was often given as a reason for smoking, but its frequent use in connection with cigarettes "wanted most" indicates that habitual smoking was probably not affectively neutral for these adolescents.

Factors Supporting Smoking in an Adult Population: Study II

A replication of the study of high school students with an adult population would have been very desirable. However, the use of interviews was not practicable for the next group of subjects in our series of investigations. In the study of attitudes towards work it has been found (Herzberg, 1966) that information about critical incidents similar to that derived from interviews can be obtained by written open-ended questionnaires. Therefore we decided to use this method.

Subjects and Procedure. The respondents were members of the Holy Name Society of a suburban Catholic Church. Subjects were recruited by the Society for a study of "attitudes towards health" (Platt, Krassen & Mausner, 1969). The men ranged in age from the early twenties to the sixties, with a median age in the forties. Most were craftsmen, small businessmen, or professionals, i.e., lower to middle strata of the middle class. Virtually all had completed high school; a few were college graduates.

A randomly chosen sample of 354 members of the Society were called and asked whether they smoked. Those who smoked one-half pack of cigarettes or more a day, 114 in all, were invited to come to the church for a battery of tests. Sixty of the men attended the test sessions, but not all gave usable data; six were no longer smoking and some of the others found portions of the battery too difficult to complete. Therefore the number of subjects varies for the different tables in this section.

Part of the test battery was the "critical incident" questionnaire (Appendix II). In this the subject was asked to list five cigarettes he wanted most, five he wanted moderately, and five he wanted least during the previous day. He gave the times at which he smoked these cigarettes, indicated what was happening before, during, and immediately after the smoking of the cigarette, and "what made him want the cigarette." Following this he chose the one cigarette he wanted most, one of the cigarettes he wanted moderately, and one he wanted very little, and answered an extended questionnaire on each of these three. This questionnaire explored the degree to which he was stimulated to smoke in the presence of other smokers, his mood at the time he smoked, the degree to which his mood was affected, the expectations he had of the cigarette, and the degree to which these expectations were fulfilled.

A content analysis of this material was carried out to identify and classify material from the reports relevant to each of the major dimensions of support for smoking. Table 4 shows the frequency with which evidence for each of the patterns of smoking can be found in the extended comments on the three cigarettes wanted most, moderately, and least.

For the men, "habit" was clearly the most frequently reported term used to describe their smoking. This contrasts with the high school students, for whom other themes were more commonly used. However, the gradient noted for the high school students in which "habit" was associated with the most wanted cigarettes was reversed for these adult men. The cigarettes they really wanted were more likely to be related to something other than pure habit, either enjoyment or tension release. The men rarely described their smoking as due to craving. This, of course, could be due to a genuine absence of craving or to a possible stigma attached to the use of words such as "craving" or "addiction." Although a fairly high proportion of the cigarettes, especially those wanted most, were smoked in a social context, there were few indications that the men felt that being with other smokers stimulated them to smoke. Role identification was not mentioned in any of the protocols.

The analyses of each protocol were examined to determine the degree to which Tomkins' "types" would be manifest. Five of the 45 respondents reported pleasure only, 17 reported tension reduction only, 16 reported both patterns, and 7 reported neither. The last group either used the word "habit" exclusively or indicated social factors as a reason for smoking. Although the number of "pure types" was somewhat larger than that shown by the high school group, almost 40% of the respondents did not exhibit a single pattern of support for smoking. Since attrition among the target population was so great, it is hard to know whether the high frequency of tension release as a support for smoking represents a true picture for this stratum of the male population or results from sampling bias.

TABLE 4
Frequency of Occurrence of Themes from Protocols[†] (45 Adult Males)

Support	Cigarette Wanted Most	Cigarette Wanted Moderately	Cigarette Wanted Least
Habit	16	19	20
Affective:			
Enjoyment	13	5	4
Manipulation	1	5	5
Stimulation	0	4	4
Tension Release	9	8	7
Addiction (Craving)	2	0	0
Social	9	5	4
Role Definition	0	0	0

[†]*The occurrence of a given theme tallied as present or absent in each respondent's protocol for each of the three cigarettes.*

In a further analysis, the nature of the context in which people smoked was related to the character of the supports for smoking (Table 5). Habit was reported frequently in virtually all contexts. However, the relative proportion of other components varied considerably with the context. For example, tension reduction was much higher for cigarettes smoked at work or in school than in other contexts. (Some of the respondents were night school students.) Interestingly, the reduction of tension was reported commonly for cigarettes smoked in connection with solitary recreational activities. Pleasure was relatively high for cigarettes smoked with meals. It should be noted that the same respondent often cited both pleasure and tension reduction, even though not in the same context.

Although the open-ended material gave no indication that these men used smoking as role-defining behavior, we have one piece of evidence suggesting its importance. In the pretest questionnaire, the subject was asked whether he would "recognize himself" if represented in various ways (see Appendix III). Two of these questions related to smoking. The first asked the subject to indicate whether a snapshot taken with a cigarette would show the "real you." Another question asked the reverse, i.e., about a snapshot without a cigarette. A fairly high proportion of the subjects indicated that they would not really be "themselves" without a cigarette (Table 6). As with other material on role identification this does not necessarily indicate that subjects actually use smoking to create a role. It may merely be a realistic assessment by moderate to heavy smokers of the frequency with which they actually are visible with or without a cigarette. However, given the phrasing of the question ("the real me"), these answers probably reflect the subjects' feeling that smoking a cigarette is expressive behavior for them.

TABLE 5

Frequency of Various Patterns of Support for Cigarette Smoking in a Variety of Contexts[†] (45 Adult Males)

Contexts	Supports			
	Habit	Pleasure	Tension Reduction	Social
Solitary recreational activity	38	8	24	1
Solitary nonrecreational activity	20	7	16	0
Social recreation	1	0	4	6
Unorganized social	2	0	2	1
Work, school	87	17	45	7
Travel	29	6	16	2
Meals	44	20	14	0
Coffee	17	3	6	2
Work break	14	7	0	4

[†]Sum of responses on 15 cigarettes: 5 rated "Wanted Most," 5 rated "Wanted Moderately," 5 rated "Wanted Least."

TABLE 6

Responses to Questionnaire Items on Role Identification as a Support for Smoking (46 Adult Males)

Response	Number of Subjects	
	Is a snapshot of you *with* a cigarette the "real you"?	Is a snapshot of you *without* a cigarette the "real you"?
Completely	17	1
Almost completely	13	8
Moderately	14	17
Weak	2	13
Not at all	0	7
Total	46	46

A COMPARISON OF SOCIOMETRIC CHOICES IN SMOKERS AND NON-SMOKERS: STUDY III

There is abundant evidence that smoking is socially stimulated, i.e., that many people smoke more frequently when they are with other smokers than when they are alone or with non-smokers. This may represent nothing more than a kind of behavioral contagion. The sight, sound, and odor of cigarettes being smoked probably do act as cues to the smoker. However, it was proposed earlier not only that people smoked in groups, but that smoking actually promoted the forces holding groups together and therefore increased cohesiveness. This implies that the individual smoker should feel attracted towards other smokers, both individually and in groups. The next study to be described provides a partial test of this proposition by examining the degree to which sociometric choices are affected by smoking status. Specifically, it was predicted that smokers should tend to choose other smokers more frequently than they would choose non-smokers as partners for various activities. Similarly, non-smokers would be expected to choose other non-smokers as partners more frequently than they would choose smokers. While it is true that such choices do not necessarily prove that it is the smoking itself which makes people more attractive or unattractive to each other, they lend credence to the informal comments by smokers which suggest that this is so.

The prediction concerning sociometric choice and smoking was tested with the sophomore class of Beaver College as subjects. Those students present at a regular class meeting, 115 of the 175 women in the class, were asked to indicate on a questionnaire their choice of a fellow student with whom they would most like to share each of the following three activities: (1) a social or cultural activity off campus; (2) an extracurricular activity on campus; and (3) a study session. The choices were not restricted to other members of the sophomore class. In addition to making these choices the students completed a questionnaire on smoking habits, identified their major area of study, and indicated whether they lived on or off campus.

Seventy-six students who were named as choices in one of the three categories, but who had not originally participated in the study, were reached and asked to complete all the instruments listed above except for the choices of fellow students with whom they would like to share activities (i.e., the sociometric choices). College records were consulted and average grades for the previous semester were recorded for each of the students participating in the study and for all students chosen as a partner for any one of the three activities.

If all students named by the participants in the study had in turn been asked to make sociometric choices, it might have been necessary to expand the survey to include virtually all of the 700 students in the college. Since this was not practicable, the 115 students who attended the original meeting were considered the population whose choices constituted the basic data. The lack of a complete set of mutual choices made it impossible to carry out an analysis using the standard techniques of sociometry (for those interested in what could have been done with more complete data, see Lindzey & Aronson, 1969, Vol. 3, Chapter 14).

The chief analysis was a comparison of choices made by smokers and non-smokers (Table 7). Smokers were defined as all those who indicated regular smoking of cigarettes at any level. It is clear that a majority of smokers chose fellow smokers and, conversely, a majority of non-smokers chose other non-smokers for all three activities. A tally of the choices made by these 115 young women reveals that 68% of them chose different companions for the social and study activities, 78% for the social and campus activities, and 73% for the campus and study activities. The remarkable similarity among the patterns of choice revealed in Table 7 is, therefore, not due to choices of the same partners in the three settings.

TABLE 7
Smoking Habits of Subjects and of Sociometric Choices (College Women)

Smoking Habits of Subjects	Smokers	Non-smokers	Total	χ^2
Smoking habits of girl chosen to share social or cultural activity				
Smoker	29	19	48	
Non-smoker	18	45	63	
Total	47	64	111	11.38, $df=1$, $p<.01$
Smoking habits of girl chosen to share campus activity				
Smoker	27	19	46	
Non-smoker	16	45	61	
Total	43	64	107	11.46, $df=1$, $p<.01$
Smoking habits of girl chosen to share study session				
Smoker	27	21	48	
Non-smoker	18	43	61	
Total	45	64	109	7.9, $df=1$, $p<.01$

A further analysis was carried out to determine the degree to which students would tend to choose others in the same dormitory. Table 8 shows that smokers tended to choose others in the same dormitory to a greater extent than non-smokers. The difference was significant for two of the three activities. Each dormitory has both smoking and non-smoking lounges and study rooms. The smoking lounges were frequently described in smoking clinic discussions at Beaver (Mausner, 1966b) as places to which one went to participate in the fellowship of interesting and attractive people. It is likely that the act of smoking helps to create this mutual attraction and that non-smokers tend to scatter their social contacts more widely about the campus, choosing individuals with whom they share interests.

There was no relation between friendship choices and the subject area of concentration in the curriculum. This may be due to the fact that the sophomore group spends much of its time in basic courses taken by students from the entire college. It is possible that friendships sort out on disciplinary lines in the upper two years when students specialize more than they do as freshmen and sophomores.

TABLE 8
Smoking Habits of Subjects and Dormitory Location of Sociometric Choices
(College Women)

Smoking Habit of Subject	Same Dorm Location[†]	Different Dorm Location	Total	χ^2
Residence of girl chosen to share a social or cultural activity off campus				
Smoker	33	16	49	
Non-smoker	36	28	64	
Total	69	44	113	1.45, df=1, N.S.
Residence of girl chosen to share a campus activity				
Smoker	31	18	49	
Non-smoker	28	36	64	
Total	59	54	113	4.2, df=1, p $<$.05
Residence of girl chosen to share a study session				
Smoker	34	14	48	
Non-smoker	34	29	63	
Total	68	43	111	3.3, df=1, p $<$.10 $>$.05

[†] *Same dorm, floor, and wing.*

There was one incidental finding related to grades which parallels results reported by Salber and MacMahon (1961) for high school students, by Mausner and Mischler (1967) for junior high school students, and by Lieberman (1969) for his national sample of teenagers. Non-smokers had higher average grades than smokers. The difference is small; on a scale in which 1 = C, 2 = B, 3 = A, the mean grade of smokers was 1.41, of non-smokers, 1.62 (t = 2.62, p $<$.01). Certainly the overlap in grades between the two groups is large; many of the smokers were outstanding students. However, virtually no students with really low averages were found among the non-smokers. There was no correlation between the subjects' average grades and the average grades of students chosen for any of the three activities. Both smokers and non-smokers chose girls whose grades were higher than their own for the sharing of study, but not for social or extracurricular activities.

In summary, a study of the choices of partners made by a group of college women confirmed the hypothesis that smoking is associated with patterns of social interaction and provided some support for the concept of smoking as a source of cohesiveness in social groups.

THE USE OF A DIARY TO STUDY SMOKING BEHAVIOR: STUDY IV

The limitations of retrospectively collected data are serious. Subjects may easily forget critical materials, either as a matter of simple decay or selectively via the well-known Freudian mechanisms. An attractive possibility for overcoming at least some of the handicaps created by the retrospective method is to obtain records of behavior which are contemporaneous with the behavior itself. These could be obtained through the observations of unbiased witnesses or through reports by subjects themselves recorded at each occurrence of the behavior being studied. Each of these methods has its own merits and drawbacks. Self-reports, i.e., diaries, have obvious flaws. The very fact that the diary must be completed may affect the frequency of occurrence as well as the character of the behavior. And the data are always subject to the limitations of self-insight. However, for exploratory work, the use of diaries seemed promising for the investigation of supports for smoking. There are a few precedents. Allport (1961) mentions the use of diaries in his discussion of personal documents. Schonbar (1959) and Singer (1966) have asked subjects to keep logs of events, dreams, and fantasies. Hersey's technique (1929, 1931, 1932) comes closest to the kind of "log" in which we were interested. He asked industrial workers to record their moods periodically and studied the relation between mood and productivity.

In this study, then, we decided to use a diary (a "log-inventory" in Allport's term) in which smokers could inform us about the events surrounding the smoking of each cigarette during the course of several days. In addition to a description of externals, we hoped to obtain a record of the subjects' feelings and attitudes.

There were several motives for the study. The first was a desire to obtain descriptive material which was not retrospective. This could be analyzed to determine whether the themes found in retrospective accounts of the patterns of support for smoking would also occur in contemporaneous descriptions of the smokers' feelings, the events which accompanied smoking, and the consequences of smoking. The second was a need to determine the degree of consistency among various measures of patterns of support. We were primarily interested in using the diaries to validate a paper-and-pencil measure which could then be used in research with large populations. We added an interview to our protocol for an additional source of information to be related to data from the diaries and the questionnaires.

A third goal was the testing of a number of hypotheses. Although the study was primarily exploratory, we wanted to answer a number of questions. The first was the extent of the relation between patterns of support for smoking and grades. We expected that students who were doing poorly at college would probably report smoking for the release of tension more frequently than those who were doing well. Secondly, we planned to follow the group to determine whether change in smoking could be predicted from patterns of support, from expressions of plans for change, or from a measure of fatalism or belief in control over one's own destiny (Test of Internal/External Control, Rotter, 1966). Our expectation was that students who were fatalistic, i.e., externally oriented, would be unlikely to stop smoking after they left college but that students who were internally oriented would, if they chose, be able to stop. Lastly, in analyzing the material of the diaries, we planned to see whether there would be a relation between the character of the circumstances in which smoking took place and the smokers' reports on the nature of the support for smoking at that time.

Procedure: Study IV

At a routine class meeting seniors at Beaver College were asked to complete a smoking history and the Liverant-Rotter I/E test. Students who reported smoking more than 10 cigarettes a day were invited to maintain a diary which would give information about the events accompanying the smoking of cigarettes, and the diarist's feelings at the time she was smoking each cigarette. The students were offered a five-dollar fee for the four-day period in which the diary would be kept. They were assured that the project was designed to find out why people smoke, not to influence them to stop. Of the 137 students in the class, 57 were non-smokers, 7 were former smokers, and 18 smoked fewer than 10 cigarettes per day; 15 could not be reached and 4 refused to reply to the question on smoking. This left 36 moderate and heavy smokers of whom 32 agreed to participate in the diary project. Thirty-one students actually completed the necessary records.

The participants came to the psychology department in groups of five for a briefing and a battery of pretests. They were then given the diary to be described below, and asked to use it during four consecutive days, two regular school days, and two weekend days. The diaries were turned in by 11:00 A.M. of the day following that on which they were completed. Weekend diaries were returned on Monday. Several days later subjects returned to the laboratory for a post-test and a brief interview (for interview items see Appendix IV). The interview was observed through a one-way screen and the subjects' responses to the interview items recorded.

The study was carried on during the month of May, the last month of the spring semester. During the following September all of the subjects were reached by mail; they were asked to report on their current smoking levels, to comment on circumstances which might have led to change in their smoking, and the relation of these changes, if any, to the experience of completing the diary.

Pretest and post-test battery. Before and after they completed the diaries, subjects were given an expanded version of a test of patterns of support for smoking originally devised by Horn and Waingrow (private communication). The items in that test are given below. Sections A through F show those items prepared by Horn and Waingrow grouped under the rubrics derived from their factor analyses. The items we added, testing the degree to which smoking is used to define the self-image and as an aid to social affiliation, are shown in sections G and H respectively. Numbers in parentheses indicate the order in which the items were presented in the test. For each item subjects were asked to circle the appropriate number from 1 to 5. The low end of the scale indicates that a given support is totally irrelevant to their smoking, the high end that it is always characteristic.

The entire test, Horn and Waingrow's items plus ours, will be referred to as the Test of Patterns of Support.

Test of Patterns of Support for Smoking

A. Habit

(2) *I've found a cigarette in my mouth and I don't remember putting it there.*

(8) *I smoke cigarettes automatically without even being aware of it.*

(15) *I light up a cigarette without realizing I still have one burning in the ashtray.*

(22) *I smoke cigarettes just from habit, without even really wanting the one I'm smoking.*

B. Psychological Addiction

(3) *I am very much aware of the fact when I am not smoking a cigarette.*

(10) *I get a real gnawing hunger for a cigarette when I haven't smoked for a while.*

(17) *Between cigarettes, I get a craving that only a cigarette can satisfy.*

(24) *When I have run out of cigarettes, I find it almost unbearable until I can get them.*

(31) *I do not feel contented for long unless I am smoking a cigarette.*

C. Tension Reduction

(4) *When I feel blue or want to take my mind off cares and worries, I smoke cigarettes.*

(12) *When I feel uncomfortable or upset about something, I light up a cigarette.*

(19) *I light up a cigarette when I feel angry about something.*

(25) *When I feel ashamed or embarrassed about something, I light up a cigarette.*

(33) *Few things help better than cigarettes when I'm feeling upset.*

D. Sensory motor

(30) *When I smoke a cigarette, part of the enjoyment is watching the smoke as I exhale it.*

(36) *Part of the enjoyment of smoking a cigarette comes from the steps I take to light up.*

(39) *Handling a cigarette is part of the enjoyment of smoking it.*

E. Pleasure

(7) *I find cigarettes pleasurable.*

(13) *Smoking cigarettes is pleasant and relaxing.*

F. Stimulant

(20) *I smoke cigarettes to stimulate me, to perk myself up.*

(28) *I smoke cigarettes in order to keep myself from slowing down.*

(34) *I smoke cigarettes to give me a "lift."*

G. Self-image

(1) *I think that smokers are basically different kinds of people from non-smokers.*

(9) *When other people think of me, they think of me as a smoker.*

(16) *Part of my enjoyment of smoking comes from knowing that I look "right" with a cigarette in my hand.*

(18) *If I suddenly stopped smoking, people would hardly recognize me without a cigarette.*

(21) *Smoking a cigarette helps me to show what kind of person I am.*

(26) *When I think of myself, I picture myself with a cigarette in my hand.*

(35) *I feel more like "myself" when I am smoking a cigarette.*

H. Social

(5) *If someone I am with takes out a cigarette to smoke, I offer a light.*

(6) *When I am with friends who are not smoking, I tend to smoke less than I usually do.*

(11) *If a friend recommends a different brand than the one I am smoking, I would try it.*

(14) *I offer cigarettes around when I am with other people.*

(23) *When I am with friends who are smoking heavily, I tend to smoke more than I usually do.*

(27) *I prefer to smoke when I am by myself rather than when I am with other people.*

(29) *If all the people in a crowd smoke, they feel a little closer to each other.*

(32) *When I go somewhere where others are not smoking, I don't smoke.*

(37) *Part of the enjoyment of smoking a cigarette comes from lighting up and smoking with someone else I like.*

(38) *I enjoy a cigarette more if it is offered by someone I like.*

(40) *If I see others smoking, I want to light up too.*

Format of the diary. The form of the diary was a pad slightly larger than a pack of cigarettes which could easily be kept in a student's purse. Figure 2 shows a sample page from the pad reproduced to scale. The subject was requested to fill out the sheet as soon after the smoking of each cigarette as possible. The time she smoked each cigarette and the events just before she started smoking were elicited through open-ended questions. The first 17 checklist statements in the diary are based on items from the Test of Patterns of Support. The last four statements were designed to determine the presence or absence of social stimulation to smoking. The subject checked those statements applicable to the cigarette just consumed.

Since we had had difficulty in the past in determining through generalized statements the extent to which smoking is used for role definition, we included a section specifically designed to determine the degree to which each cigarette contributed to role-defining behavior. The subject was requested to write any three adjectives describing how she felt while smoking and any three describing how she looked to others while smoking. A list of adjectives was reproduced on the stiff cover of the diary package (see Appendix V). The subjects were told that the adjectives furnished were intended only as suggestions and that they should feel free to use any adjectives they cared to. They were also invited to make any additional comments on the reverse side of the sheets.

The Treatment of Data: Study IV

The analyses in this study were chosen to examine environmental influences on smoking and to test the adequacy of the three-dimensional model of intraindividual supports for smoking. This problem was approached in two ways. The first was the use of multivariate procedures, primarily factor analysis, to search for internal consistencies and relate these to the previously defined theoretical constructs. In this way it is possible to see whether the factors which emerge from a study of the actual intercorrelations of responses correspond with those predicted by the model. The second approach was the application of an *a priori* classificatory scheme to the subjects' responses to study internal consistencies and to predict behavior.

Although the first approach is methodologically the more elegant, most psychologists would question the propriety of inferences from multivariate analyses in which the number of measurements far exceeds the number of subjects. In light of this we used factor analysis, but only as a descriptive tool. A program for factor analysis developed at the University of Miami was available. This computes principal components and then sequentially carries out Varimax rotations which increase the number of factors in stepwise fashion. The factor analyses were examined, and an analysis was chosen which yielded factors whose patterns of items made the most sense.

Because the number of subjects in the study was too small to permit the use of scales based on the factor analyses, the data from the Test of Patterns of Support were scored according to an *a priori* classification. The categories of affective items which we used were those derived by Horn and Waingrow from their original factor analysis. The titles for groups of items under categories A - F of the Test of Patterns of Support indicate the character of the various affective scales (page 31). The items relevant to self-image (category G) and social sup-

FIGURE 2
Sample Page from Smoking Diary Given to 31 College Women

Time I smoked this cigarette _____ Just before I started smoking, the following was happening _____

While I was smoking this cigarette . . . (Check any statements that apply.)

___ 1. I got a lift
___ 2. I was just happy to be having a cigarette.
___ 3. I was alone.
___ 4. It was the time of day I usually smoke.
___ 5. I was with others who were not smoking.
___ 6. I felt more lively.
___ 7. I had a good feeling.
___ 8. I had no particular feeling.
___ 9. I felt less tense than just before.

___ 10. I felt closer to the people I was smoking with.
___ 11. I enjoyed the cigarette—that's all.
___ 12. I was with others who were smoking.
___ 13. I felt less nervous than just before.
___ 14. I lit up at the same time as someone else.
___ 15. I felt no better or no worse than just before.
___ 16. I felt calmer than just before.
___ 17. I felt less depressed than just before.

Just about the time I started to smoke this cigarette

___ 18. Someone offered me a cigarette.
___ 19. Someone offered me a light.

___ 20. I offered someone a cigarette.
___ 21. I offered someone a light.

Choose three adjectives which best describe how THIS cigarette made you FEEL.

22._____23._____ 24. _____

If others had seen you smoking, choose three adjectives which best describe how this cigarette would have made you LOOK to others.

25._____ 26. _____ 27. _____

Additional Comments: (Use reverse side of paper.)

ports for smoking (category *H*) were grouped into two scales, one for each of these categories. Each subject was given a score on every scale by averaging her ratings on the items grouped to form the scale. Thus every subject was placed on scales defining each of eight patterns of support.

The fixed-alternative items from the diary were grouped in accordance with their relevance to the eight scales of the Test of Patterns of Support. Thus the first item ("I got a lift") was considered related to the stimulant scale (category *F*). Each subject was given a series of scores on the diary material based on the average number of cigarettes for which items relevant to each scale had been checked.

The adjectives used in the diary were also treated on an *a priori* basis. A list was made of all adjectives used by the subject to describe how she felt and looked to others while smoking. This list was then presented to four of the writers' colleagues: two psychologists and two sociologists. They were also given the following capsule descriptions of each of the major dimensions:

Factor *S*: *Social*

Adjectives indicating that the smoking of others is a cue to smoking, that smoking with others leads to increased feelings of closeness to them, to warmth and interchange. Does not deal with the use of smoking to project one's self-concept.

Factor *R: Self-Image* (Role)

Adjectives indicating that the smoker uses the act of smoking or the gestures of smoking to define her identification of herself in a social role, the character of her "persona," "who I am," "what kind of person am I."

Factor *A: Feelings* (Affect)

Adjectives indicating that smoking is purely habitual, i.e., that it is cued off by some internal or external stimulus (no affect); that smoking is enjoyed and/or pleasurable; that smoking leads to the release of tension; that smoking leads to a diminution of craving for cigarettes.

The judges were asked to categorize each adjective into one of the three groupings, to indicate that they fit more than one of the groupings, or to describe them as not classifiable. All those adjectives in which there was virtual consensus among the judges were labeled and a count was made of the frequency with which each subject used adjectives in each of the three categories as well as in some of the mixed categories. This was then entered as a score into the subject's record. The categorization of the adjectives used was included in the various treatments of data from the diaries, including the factor analysis.

The post-diary interviews were analyzed. A record was made of responses on each of the questionnaire items and of spontaneous comments given during the interview. Comments written on the diary booklets were also transcribed and coded.

Finally, the circumstances described as accompanying the smoking of each cigarette were classified into a number of categories and an attempt was made to relate the context of smoking to patterns of support for smoking described in the checklist, the adjectives, and the spontaneous comments.

Findings: Study IV

The data will be presented in terms of both administrations of the Test of Patterns of Support, the diary material itself, the interview carried out after the completion of the diary, and, finally, the interrelation of the entire body of information about smoking behavior to the follow-up survey conducted five months after subjects had completed the diaries.

The Test of Patterns of Support. The absolute levels of response on each of the scales in this test and changes from pre- to post-test are shown in Table 9. A mean difference t was calculated for each item to see whether the experience of writing the diary would systematically affect responses on the test. Although 16 of the 40 items showed significant mean difference t s when first and second administrations were compared, the actual amount of change was relatively small. In no instance did the average scale score shift as much as one position, and most of the changes, even the significant ones, represent an average of less than half a scale position. For six of the items the shift was upward, i.e., the item was viewed as more representative of the subject's patterns of smoking; for the remaining ten the shift was downward. The upward and downward shifts seemed to be randomly distributed among the various factors.

TABLE 9

Patterns of Support for Smoking Average Scale Positions and Correlations — First and Second Administration[†] (31 College Women)

Support	Average Scale[††] Position		r[‡]
	1st Admin.	2nd Admin.	
Habit	2.2	1.9	.74
Pleasure	3.9	3.6	.43
Sensory Motor	2.0	2.2	.89
Stimulation	1.7	2.6	.61
Tension Reduction	3.0	3.1	.73
Addiction	2.7	2.5	.75
Social	2.9	3.1	.70
Self-image	2.1	2.1	.84

[†]*Fixed alternative paper-and-pencil test,* [††]*Scale ranges from 1 through 5, with 5 signifying maximal relevance to the subject's smoking,* [‡]*Pearsonian r.*

It may be concluded that the Test of Patterns of Support is reasonably reliable and that the activity of writing a diary after each cigarette does not systematically alter a person's report of the pattern of his own psychological supports for smoking. The reliability of the test is further evidenced by the fact that scores for the first and second administration on all but one of the scales are highly correlated (Table 9). However, as we shall show below, the post-test did differ from the pretest in one respect. The way in which items could be grouped together, as demonstrated by factor analysis, was simpler and more meaningful for the post-test than for the pretest.

The use of an *a priori* scheme for the classification of items on the Test of Patterns of Support provides a crude picture of the average strength of the various supports for smoking. As noted above, scores on these *a priori* scales could vary from 1.0, representing absolute rejection of the relevance of a given support, to 5.0, representing total acceptance. Table 9 shows that none of the supports was totally rejected. The items describing smoking as a source of stimulation were the least frequently chosen as relevant. Those referring to habit and to self-concept were also relatively rarely chosen. The highest values were ascribed to cigarettes as sources of relaxation, of reduction of tension, and of social affiliation. In view of the subjects' youth, it is perhaps surprising that the items referring to psychological addiction were assented to as frequently as they were.

Factor analysis was carried out on data from the first and second administrations of the Test of Patterns of Support. Fifty percent of the variance in the responses from the first session was taken up by eight factors (Table 10). Five of these make some sense even though some of the items fit the overall pattern of each factor poorly; three were nonsense factors. The factor which carried the highest amount of variance (13.2%) included all five of the addiction items, one of the "reduction of tension" items, the two "pleasure" items, and negative loadings on four of the social items. This suggests that addicted smokers see themselves as smoking regardless of the social context and view release of the tension generated by not having a cigarette as a great reward. Subjects low on this factor probably do much of their smoking in a social context or, if solitary, view smoking as a pleasure rather than a release from pain. The second factor includes two of the items dealing with self-image. It also includes one item related to unconscious or habitual smoking and one which expresses a tendency to smoke when the subject feels embarrassed or ashamed. The two social items in this factor deal with affective relations between the smoker and the people with whom she smokes. The third factor relates primarily to the reduction of tension and to stimulation. The fourth factor has self-concept material of a nonsocial nature, and the fifth relates to the pleasurable characteristics of smoking.

As shown by Table 11 the factor analysis of the post-test is considerably simpler. Clear factors emerge which describe self-concept, the reduction of tension, habit, pleasure, and stimulation. An additional factor reflects the fact that subjects who report psychological addiction reject the notion that their smoking is dependent upon other people and therefore tend to have negative loadings on the social factor. While it is impossible to be certain, it seems likely that the subjects' intensive exposure to the diary items and their constant focusing on the reasons for their smoking during the period in which they worked on the diary were responsible for the greater clarity of the factor matrix in the second administration.

The diary itself. All but one of the subjects were able to carry out the diary exercise successfully. They were highly cooperative and good humored. Several did tell us informally as they turned in the packets that they were somewhat irritated by the necessity of filling out the diary items but felt that the effect on their level of smoking was modest. Following are some specific analyses of the material of the diary:

a. The fixed-alternative material. Each item (Table 12) was checked if the respondent thought it applied to the circumstances under which she was smoking a given cigarette, her needs at the moment, or the consequences of smoking. Table 12 shows the average percent frequency with which each of the items was checked. Some of the items reflect the environmental circumstances of smoking, for example, the frequency with which the subject smoked while she was with others who were smoking. Other items show the relevance to this particular population of each of the factors supporting smoking. The following discussion is based on averages for the group, but it should be noted that the dispersions on many individual items are quite high. Obviously the subjects varied considerably in the frequency with which each item was used. This reflects the fact that individuals differ in the degree to which the patterns of support reflected by these items are relevant to their smoking.

About half of the cigarettes were smoked in a social context (item 10), but relatively few of these incidents involved sharing cigarettes or matches (items

TABLE 10
Factor Analysis of Test of Patterns of Support for Smoking (31 College Women) (Pretest)

Items	Psych. Addict. 13.206	Sensory Motor 8.917	Tension Reduct. & Stim. 12.225	Self-Image 9.130	†7.710	†6.894	†7.968	Pleasure 5.721
% of Variance . . .								
(2) Found cigarette in mouth—didn't remember putting it there	0.238	-0.065	-0.286	0.185	0.171	-0.224	-0.384	-0.030
(8) Smoke automatically without being aware of it . .	-0.037	-0.095	-0.050	0.256	0.792	-0.199	-0.134	0.072
(15) Light cigarette without realizing one is still in ashtray	0.226	-0.163	0.154	0.315	0.124	-0.410	-0.006	-0.169
(22) Smoke cigarettes from habit, without really wanting one	-0.073	-0.120	0.092	0.810	-0.046	-0.029	-0.035	0.111
(3) Very aware of fact when not smoking a cigarette	0.391	0.078	-0.124	-0.083	-0.144	0.119	-0.740	0.033
(10) Get real gnawing hunger for a cigarette	0.829	-0.126	-0.281	-0.199	-0.061	-0.064	0.028	0.116
(17) Get craving only a cigarette can satisfy	0.823	-0.042	-0.220	0.150	-0.081	-0.072	-0.322	0.094
(24) When out of cigarettes, it's almost unbearable	0.891	0.046	-0.218	0.121	-0.162	-0.148	0.056	0.089
(31) Not contented for long without smoking	0.602	0.107	-0.033	0.165	0.060	0.309	-0.417	-0.044
(4) When blue or worried, I smoke cigarettes	0.244	-0.260	-0.748	0.036	0.072	0.300	-0.177	0.119
(12) When uncomfortable or upset, I smoke cigarettes	0.396	-0.044	-0.661	0.109	-0.034	0.327	-0.238	0.120
(19) I light a cigarette when angry	0.199	0.119	-0.644	0.278	-0.135	0.170	-0.165	-0.229
(25) When ashamed or embarrassed, I light cigarette	-0.069	-0.095	-0.388	0.572	-0.071	0.017	-0.047	0.573
(33) When upset, few things help better than cigarette	0.008	-0.229	-0.682	0.014	-0.202	-0.037	-0.425	0.038
(30) When smoking, watching smoke as exhale is part of enjoyment	-0.077	0.525	0.064	-0.052	-0.022	0.032	-0.219	-0.609
(36) Part of enjoyment comes from steps I take to light up	0.002	0.906	0.068	-0.140	0.083	0.132	-0.094	-0.052
(39) Handling cigarette is part of enjoyment	-0.270	0.534	0.388	-0.329	0.290	0.012	-0.111	-0.173
(7) I find cigarettes pleasurable	0.558	-0.038	0.118	0.167	0.054	0.085	-0.016	0.585
(13) Smoking cigarettes is pleasant and relaxing	0.344	0.136	-0.230	-0.155	0.101	-0.207	-0.304	0.590
(20) I smoke to stimulate, to perk myself up	0.085	0.075	-0.749	0.166	0.102	-0.124	-0.165	-0.138
(28) I smoke to keep myself from slowing down	0.011	0.466	-0.599	-0.158	-0.204	0.213	-0.012	0.111
(34) I smoke to give me a "lift"	-0.008	0.226	-0.751	-0.013	-0.021	-0.128	0.014	0.197
(1) Smokers are basically different from non-smokers	-0.059	0.425	-0.023	0.257	0.034	0.094	-0.388	-0.228
(9) People think of me as a smoker	0.304	0.028	-0.240	0.742	-0.046	-0.062	0.069	-0.202
(16) Part of enjoyment is knowing I look "right" smoking	0.059	0.730	-0.242	0.048	-0.061	-0.173	-0.132	-0.088
(18) If I stopped, people wouldn't recognize me without cigarette	0.075	-0.081	-0.171	0.723	0.187	-0.215	0.064	-0.018
(21) Smoking helps me show what kind of person I am	-0.029	0.317	-0.206	0.311	0.009	-0.252	-0.748	-0.072
(26) I picture myself with a cigarette in my hand	0.027	0.121	-0.095	0.235	-0.673	-0.456	0.011	-0.337
(35) I feel more like "myself" when smoking	0.196	0.205	-0.299	0.484	-0.478	-0.191	-0.234	0.071
(5) I offer a light to someone who takes out a cigarette	0.060	0.436	0.039	0.137	-0.169	0.121	0.058	0.123
(6) I smoke less when with friends who are not smoking	-0.724	0.005	0.086	-0.070	-0.380	0.163	0.086	-0.076
(11) If friend recommends different brand, I would try it	-0.062	0.117	-0.126	0.350	-0.238	0.819	0.065	-0.114
(14) I offer cigarettes when with other people	-0.379	-0.309	-0.278	-0.029	0.056	0.466	0.146	0.174
(23) Smoke more when with friends who are smoking heavily	-0.085	-0.123	-0.094	0.005	0.633	-0.002	-0.139	0.258
(27) Prefer to smoke when alone rather than with other people	-0.078	0.140	-0.024	0.214	-0.844	-0.339	-0.423	0.172
(29) When all in crowd smoke, they feel a little closer	-0.417	0.158	-0.088	-0.138	-0.179	-0.002	-0.212	-0.468
(32) When others are not smoking, I don't smoke	-0.735	-0.003	-0.123	-0.106	0.096	0.144	-0.078	0.008
(37) Part of enjoyment is smoking with someone I like	-0.091	0.604	-0.583	-0.118	0.038	-0.146	-0.078	0.097
(38) Enjoy cigarette more when offered by someone I like	-0.291	0.229	-0.328	-0.118	-0.091	-0.030	-0.768	0.095
(40) If I see others smoking, I want to light up too	0.272	0.001	0.109	-0.518	-0.052	-0.617	-0.038	0.105

†Unused factors.

TABLE 11
Factor Analysis of Test of Patterns of Support for Smoking (31 College Women) (Post-test)

Items:		Rotated Factor Loadings – Varimax Rotation							
% of Variance . . .	Self-image 9.049	Sensory Motor 11.129	Psych. Addict. 12.672	Tension Reduct. & Stim. 15.876	† 5.899	Habit 6.410	Pleas. 6.609	Social Stim. 5.651	† 4.311
(2) Found cigarette in mouth-didn't remember putting it there	0.195	-0.048	0.310	-0.241	-0.127	0.648	0.310	0.037	-0.155
(8) Smoke automatically without being aware of it	-0.127	0.113	0.189	-0.127	-0.156	0.806	0.112	0.204	-0.106
(15) Light cigarette without realizing one still burns in ashtray	-0.019	0.054	-0.191	0.122	0.081	0.890	-0.120	-0.030	0.009
(22) Smoke cigarettes from habit, without really wanting one	-0.294	-0.051	-0.047	0.009	-0.104	0.181	0.075	0.106	-0.753
(3) Very aware of fact when not smoking a cigarette	-0.328	0.042	0.323	0.104	-0.007	0.127	0.081	0.693	0.274
(10) Get real gnawing hunger for a cigarette	-0.328	0.180	0.526	-0.051	-0.157	0.287	-0.364	0.203	0.134
(17) Get craving only a cigarette can satisfy	0.066	-0.084	0.817	-0.158	0.200	-0.049	-0.112	0.087	-0.021
(24) When out of cigarettes, it's almost unbearable	0.047	0.105	0.677	-0.286	0.146	-0.049	-0.250	0.364	-0.232
(31) Not contented for long without smoking	-0.377	-0.132	0.625	-0.233	0.280	0.323	-0.053	-0.061	-0.036
(4) When blue or worried, I smoke cigarettes	-0.165	0.049	0.221	-0.835	0.079	-0.075	0.102	0.022	0.150
(12) When uncomfortable or upset, I smoke cigarettes	-0.255	0.099	0.323	-0.801	0.077	0.181	0.199	-0.001	-0.002
(19) Light cigarette when angry	-0.359	-0.129	0.284	-0.682	0.008	0.064	0.082	0.051	-0.048
(25) When ashamed or embarrassed, I light cigarette	-0.286	-0.057	0.159	-0.752	0.172	0.014	-0.009	0.097	0.027
(33) When upset, few things help better than cigarette	-0.255	-0.116	0.232	-0.730	-0.062	0.064	-0.047	-0.050	-0.230
(30) When smoking, watching smoke as exhale is part of enjoyment	0.031	-0.882	0.068	-0.142	0.036	-0.021	0.051	-0.199	0.028
(36) Part of enjoyment comes from steps I take to light up	0.024	-0.887	0.029	0.196	0.036	-0.020	-0.094	-0.010	0.083
(39) Handling cigarette is part of enjoyment	-0.128	-0.856	-0.041	0.116	-0.077	-0.185	-0.167	-0.013	0.056
(7) I find cigarettes pleasurable	-0.178	-0.017	0.111	-0.174	-0.036	0.079	-0.841	-0.041	0.037
(13) Smoking cigarettes is pleasant and relaxing	0.081	-0.006	0.262	-0.748	0.008	-0.123	-0.820	-0.199	0.075
(20) I smoke to stimulate, to perk myself up	-0.019	-0.007	-0.156	-0.658	-0.329	-0.026	-0.396	0.148	0.197
(28) I smoke to keep myself from slowing down	0.024	-0.262	-0.059	-0.672	-0.182	0.191	-0.427	0.037	-0.141
(34) I smoke to give me a "lift"	-0.161	0.040	-0.122	-0.251	-0.378	0.082	-0.390	-0.176	-0.093
(1) Smokers are basically different from non-smokers	-0.040	-0.527	-0.248	-0.325	0.163	0.099	0.174	0.273	-0.375
(9) People think of me as a smoker	-0.686	-0.784	-0.058	-0.133	0.352	0.236	-0.107	0.110	-0.285
(16) Part of enjoyment is knowing I look "right" smoking	-0.236	0.081	-0.261	-0.331	-0.068	0.084	0.020	0.127	-0.201
(18) If I stopped, people wouldn't recognize me without cigarette	-0.025	-0.031	0.119	-0.497	-0.147	-0.024	-0.099	-0.029	-0.209
(21) Smoking helps me show what kind of person I am	-0.808	-0.463	-0.022	-0.195	-0.252	-0.020	0.225	-0.109	-0.161
(26) I picture myself with a cigarette in my hand	-0.877	-0.091	-0.048	-0.213	-0.093	-0.045	-0.005	0.159	0.012
(35) Feel more like "myself" when smoking	-0.737	-0.230	0.188	-0.361	-0.004	-0.053	-0.031	0.182	-0.056
(5) I offer light to someone who takes out a cigarette	0.103	-0.221	-0.220	0.137	0.091	0.043	-0.099	-0.034	0.352
(6) Smoke less when with friends who are not smoking	-0.037	-0.099	-0.798	0.405	0.141	0.095	0.051	0.231	-0.168
(11) If friend recommends different brand, I would try it	0.032	-0.185	-0.010	-0.231	0.776	-0.169	-0.049	-0.117	0.097
(14) I offer cigarettes when with other people	0.045	0.177	-0.202	-0.002	0.698	-0.130	0.285	0.088	0.179
(23) Smoke more when with friends who are smoking heavily	0.098	0.039	-0.554	0.015	-0.029	0.081	0.031	0.677	-0.185
(27) Prefer to smoke when alone rather than with other people	0.008	-0.031	-0.472	-0.235	-0.541	-0.062	0.164	-0.045	0.273
(29) When all in crowd smoke, they feel a little closer	0.005	-0.390	-0.578	0.104	0.225	0.330	0.101	-0.009	-0.163
(32) When others are not smoking, I don't smoke	0.243	-0.160	-0.804	-0.597	0.231	0.069	-0.049	0.104	0.153
(37) Part of enjoyment is smoking with someone I like	-0.099	-0.446	-0.342	-0.462	0.104	-0.160	0.209	-0.004	0.130
(38) Enjoy cigarette more when offered by someone I like	-0.030	-0.519	-0.128	-0.104	0.151	-0.093	0.144	0.316	0.250
(40) If I see others smoking, I want to light up too	-0.277	-0.006	-0.037	-0.104	0.007	0.145	0.158	0.755	-0.210

†Unused factors.

39

16-19). About half were described as smoked at a usual time of day (item 3), and so can be viewed as "habitual" smoking. The primary psychological support reflected in these data is the pleasure derived from smoking (items 1, 2, 4, 5, 9). Individual cigarettes were rarely recorded as leading to a reduction of anxiety or tension (items 7, 11, 14, 15). It was not anticipated that the fixed-alternative material would reflect the role-defining properties of smoking; that was the function of the adjectives. Therefore no items dealing with self-image or role definition were included.

b. *Use of adjectives:* absolute levels. Table 13 shows the frequency with which various adjectives were used on the diary form in answer to the questions, "How did you *feel?*" and "How did you *look?*" while smoking a particular cigarette. Most of the adjectives were related to the affective or to the role-defining aspects of smoking. Adjectives dealing with the social aspects of smoking were used relatively little despite the fact that so much of the smoking took place in a social context. The one exception was the word "sociable." This word, which was considered by the "experts" to relate both to social rewards from smoking and to role definition, was among the most frequently chosen in answer to both questions.

TABLE 12
Mean Percent Use[†] of Items on Diary (31 College Women)

Statement About Smoking	Percent Use	
	Mean	S. D.
1. I got a lift.	11	17
2. I was just happy to be having a cigarette.	43	31
3. It was the time of day I usually smoke.	48	32
4. I felt more lively.	10	11
5. I had a good feeling.	25	19
6. I had no particular feeling.	32	22
7. I felt less tense than just before.	7	6
8. I felt closer to the people I was smoking with.	6	9
9. I enjoyed the cigarette — that's all.	38	28
10. I was with others who were smoking.	56	20
11. I felt less nervous than just before.	3	5
12. I lit up at the same time as someone else.	18	15
13. I felt no better or no worse than just before.	24	24
14. I felt calmer than just before.	5	6
15. I felt less depressed than just before.	1	3
16. Someone offered me a cigarette.	6	8
17. Someone offered me a light.	13	10
18. I offered someone a cigarette.	5	6
19. I offered someone a light.	4	4

[†]*The total frequency with which subjects checked each item was divided by the number of cigarettes smoked. Figure cited represents the average for 31 subjects.*

The adjectives describing affect indicate that the subjects most frequently felt and thought they looked relaxed, calm, and content while smoking a ciga-

TABLE 13
Frequency of Use of Adjectives on Diary (31 College Women)

Adjective	How did you *feel* while smoking? Number of Subjects	Number of Times Used	Mean % Use	Adjective	How did you *look* while smoking? Number of Subjects	Number of Times Used	Mean % Use
			Affective				
relaxed	31	671	21.6	relaxed	31	782	25.2
calm	30	322	10.7	calm	29	358	12.3
† good	16	130	8.1	† content	17	126	7.4
† satisfied	14	109	7.8	† usual	5	33	6.6
† content	21	159	7.6	pleasant	22	129	5.9
† happy	22	127	5.8	quiet	27	138	5.1
† quiet	23	132	5.7	† tired	15	73	4.9
pleasant	25	140	5.6	† bored	13	56	4.3
† bored	7	30	4.3	† happy	20	85	4.3
pleasure-seeking	6	23	3.8	† at ease	11	35	3.2
† tired	14	49	3.5	tense	17	51	3.0
† comfortable	13	43	3.3	† cool	9	25	2.8
† enjoyed	6	19	3.2	† pensive	8	22	2.8
† awake	15	40	2.7	† comfortable	10	27	2.7
nervous	17	43	2.5	unemotional	17	44	2.6
† sick	6	15	2.5	nervous	20	47	2.4
unemotional	15	37	2.5	† enjoyed	5	12	2.4
† less tense	7	17	2.4	anxious	12	28	2.3
tense	14	34	2.4	† uneasy	5	11	2.2
† lively	9	20	2.2	irritable	9	18	2.0
† at ease	7	15	2.1	† collected	9	18	2.0
efficient	12	25	2.1	† sleepy	5	10	2.0
† great	7	15	2.1	† satisfied	9	16	1.8
† excitable	7	14	2.0	† excitable	12	19	1.6
† pensive	8	16	2.0				
anxious	13	25	1.9				
† nauseous	5	9	1.8				
weak	5	8	1.6				
touchy	6	9	1.5				
† relieved	7	9	1.3				
irritable	8	10	1.2				
† peaceful	5	6	1.2				
			Social				
friendly	25	107	4.3	† friendly	25	162	6.5
† talkative	9	19	2.1	† involved	5	29	5.8
				† talkative	7	11	1.6

†*Not on list of suggested adjectives.*

rette. This tallies with the fact that the most important support for smoking given in the Test of Patterns of Support was relaxation. The degree to which smoking a given cigarette led to pleasure or calm following a feeling of emotionality is not clear from the use of adjectives. The reduction of tension was ac-

TABLE 13 cont.

	How did you *feel* while smoking?				How did you *look* while smoking?		
Adjective	Number of Subjects	Number of Times Used	Mean % Use	Adjective	Number of Subjects	Number of Times Used	Mean % Use
				Role			
† casual	12	81	6.8	informal	30	403	13 4
informal	28	189	6.8	† casual	13	164	12.6
active	17	63	3.7	† normal	14	111	7.9
suggestible	5	18	3.6	conventional	19	136	7.1
curious	5	13	2.6	frank	7	35	5.0
† busy	8	19	2.4	† busy	11	31	2.8
† normal	8	19	2.4	poised	10	27	2.7
independent	6	13	2.2	active	15	38	2.5
sensitive	5	10	2.0	feminine	6	15	2.5
adventurous	5	9	1.8	independent	8	20	2.5
conventional	10	18	1.8	mature	6	14	2.3
frank	5	9	1.8	sophisticated	11	25	2.3
good-natured	12	22	1.8	masculine	5	11	2.2
uninhibited	9	15	1.7	responsible	8	17	2.1
mature	5	8	1.6	self-confident	12	24	2.0
† thoughtful	8	12	1.5	good-natured	14	28	2.0
† interested	7	10	1.4	sensitive	7	14	2.0
responsible	5	7	1.4	uninhibited	9	17	1.9
self-confident	9	13	1.4	immature	5	9	1.8
† aggressive	6	8	1.3	† interested	12	21	1.8
				† thoughtful	9	15	1.7
				Unassigned and Mixed			
† no change	24	406	16.9	sociable	30	342	11.4
sociable	27	220	8.1	easy-going	24	102	4.3
† alert	5	30	6.0	† no change	12	50	4.2
† passive	6	33	5.5	† passive	7	24	3.4
energetic	13	40	3.1	† intent	6	20	3.3
easy-going	18	52	2.9	self-controlled	12	32	2.7
eager	16	37	2.3	energetic	11	28	2.6
† intent	5	11	2.2	eager	13	32	2.5
† confident	7	15	2.1	unexcitable	8	19	2.4
enthusiastic	13	27	2.1	† confident	8	18	2.3
warm	16	34	2.1	† studious	8	17	2.1
† studious	5	10	2.0	moody	7	14	2.0
restless	11	19	1.7	enthusiastic	9	17	1.9
self-controlled	15	26	1.7	restless	15	27	1.8
unexcitable	9	14	1.6				
moody	7	10	1.4				

† *Not on list of suggested adjectives.*

cepted as being an important support for smoking on the Test of Patterns of Support. The failure of the checklist material on the diary to show a quantitative substantiation of "reduction of tension" as a consequence of smoking among these college girls leaves the importance of this factor moot. Furthermore (see Table 17 below) there was no significant tendency for girls who reported high scores on the Tension Reduction scale of the Test of Patterns of Support also to use "affective" adjectives or to check items related to tension reduction on the diary. The problem of consistency among the different data on tension reduction

TABLE 14
Summary of Factor Analysis of Diary Items, Adjectives, and Interview Scales
(31 College Women)

	Loading		Loading
Tension Reduction & Pleasure — 13%[†]		Social — 11.2%[†]	
felt less nervous	.91	felt close to other smokers	−.75
felt calmer	.79	someone offered me a light	−.67
felt less tense	.78	feel adjective — social	−.67
enjoyed the cigarette	.69	someone offered me a cigarette	−.66
felt less depressed	.66	look adjective — social	−.59
happy to have a cigarette	.62	interview — social	−.59
		lit up same time as other	−.53
Social & Role — 10%[†]		with others smoking	−.50
feel adjective — social/role	−.75		
interview — red. neg. aff.	−.74	Habit — 9.6%[†]	
look adjective — social/role	−.69		
interview — role	−.67	felt no better, no worse	.84
		had no particular feeling	.80
Felt Good — 8.2%[†]		look adjective — affective	.50
		feel adjective — no change	.49
feel adjective — affective	.61		
happy to have a cigarette	.48	Stimulant — 6.7%[†]	
offer a light	−.84	felt more lively	.65
offer a cigarette	−.68	had a good feeling	.53
feel adjective — no change	−.51	interview — relax	.51
		got a lift	.37
Role — 6.2%[†]		felt less depressed	.36
look adjective — role	−.86	interview — habit	−.76
time of day I usually smoke	−.62		
feel adjective — role	−.42		

[†] % of total variance.

will be discussed more fully at the end of this chapter.

The list of adjectives relating to role definition gives a clear picture of the way in which college girls wished to regard themselves and be regarded by others. The respondents wanted to feel and seem informal, frank, casual, normal, sociable, and conventional. A third of the subjects wrote that they looked poised, sophisticated, responsible, interested, and self-confident. It is likely that taking away cigarettes would rob a smoker of a great deal if it reduced her ability to portray herself in so positive a manner.

c. *Factor analysis.* The data from the diary and rating scales from the subsequent interview were subjected to factor analysis (Table 14). Sixty-five percent of the variance in the scores was accounted for by seven factors. The factor analysis coincides largely, but not completely, with the model which defines affective, social, and role-defining aspects of smoking as independent dimensions. The major factor, which accounted for 13% of the variance, relates to enjoyment and reduction of tension. It may be that since the two are associated the pleasure here is not from the smoking of a cigarette itself but from the calming effect it induces. There is a strong social factor which revolves around the use of "social" adjectives and the checking of fixed-alternative items reflecting the social context in which individual cigarettes were smoked. The tendency of respondents to feel close to others who are smoking also contributes to this factor.

d. *The relation between the context of smoking and the pattern of support.* The analysis of this relation was not sufficiently fruitful to warrant inclusion of the results. With one exception, all subjects showed a significant tendency for an idiosyncratic pattern of support for smoking to obtain over a wide variety of contexts. That is, girls who reported smoking for pleasure or tension reduction did so without regard to the situation in which smoking occurred. This was in contrast to the clear patterns of relation between pattern of support and circumstances shown by our samples of high school students and adult males cited above. We are not entirely sure why this happened; it may be that for these young women the context was not a significant factor in determining pattern of support. An alternative possibility is that our sample of their behavior was restricted to the narrow range characteristic of college life. Smokers who live at home, and go out to work or school, and to a variety of places for recreation might show a clearer tie between context and pattern of support.

e. *Comments.* Lastly, the spontaneous comments written by many respondents on the backs of the diary pages were coded for evidence of the importance of various mechanisms of support. They need little elaboration; the vivid language illustrates far better than any statistical analysis of categorized data the role played by smoking in the lives of these college students. Following are excerpts from their statements.

Habit

1. *"Once again I find myself smoking from habit, because I generally smoke when watching TV, thus I don't feel this cigarette had any effect on my mood."*

2. *"Reading for a course (still at fiance's apartment); nothing, it was automatic; [said she looked] studious, intent, sophisticated. Very often I smoke as part of an 'automatic' pattern of activities. I seldom even think about it, although I'm* conscious *of having a cigarette, i.e., with coffee, while reading, with any kind of drink, after swimming, while playing cards, and after each meal (especially supper). The activity seems incomplete without this finishing touch to the ritual. This is why I find it especially hard to describe my feelings – either I have none in particular about the cigarette or else they're interwoven into the situation."*

3. *"I got into a car for a ride to N.Y.C.: I think it's a* habit *for me to light up a cigarette whenever I get into a car. Therefore I hardly even noticed that I was smoking."*

4. *"I finished having a snack: I was annoyed (and still am) with myself when I lit this cigarette because I feel as though I've been smoking too much (can feel it in my chest) today and I know that usually a cigarette 'tastes good' after I've eaten but this one didn't."*

Pleasure

1. *"Eating breakfast: first cigarette in the morning with coffee always tastes really good and makes me feel more awake."*

2. *"I finished breakfast in the Chat (Beaver College snack bar). I was drinking tea: I always enjoy a cigarette when I drink tea – as a matter of fact I don't like to drink it unless I can smoke while drinking."*

3. *"Coffee after dinner: cigarette also tastes good after dinner and with coffee. They seem to take away the full feeling."*

Tension reduction

1. *"Talking to my parents on the phone: I had an upsetting day – with a letter from the vocations office. I told my mother of the events on the phone thus upsetting me slightly again. The cigarette helped me feel better as while smoking it I had time to just relax."*

2. *"Watching softball game: cigarette helped to ease tension as my boy friend's team was losing and I was apprehensive knowing he was going to be in a lousy mood."*

3. *"This cigarette proved very relaxing after a nerve-wracking drive."*

4. *"Playing Bridge; drinking Coke (felt aggressive, frustrated, self-pitying; looked angry, temperamental, homicidal): I keep getting these crummy cards! Always smoke more when I'm playing Bridge, but especially when I'm losing. The cigarette calmed me down a little, but I'm still mad."*

5. *"I was sitting back down in the Chat after going to the book store (felt less bored, sociable): my mouth felt terrible because I had smoked excessively last night – I was writing a term paper and always smoke heavily when I do. Therefore my mouth felt horrible this morning.*

Role

1. *"The cigarette gave me enough courage to play that outrageous bid! I've found that a cigarette often intensifies the way I feel, i.e., I felt dominant and aggressive before I lit it. (Felt dominant, aggressive, enthusiastic; like a maniac, emotional, unstable): The way I smoked it reinforced my feelings at that moment."*

2. *"Taking notes in economics (looked informal, pleasant, sociable; felt conventional, immature, frank); immature, I have hair in pigtails – sometimes people tell me I'm too young to smoke – ergo."*

The interview. In the interview the respondents were first asked in what way the diary affected their smoking. Seventeen of the 31 reported that they smoked somewhat less than usual because of the nuisance of filling out the diary.

Comparison of the respondents' estimates of their average daily consumption of cigarettes given during the senior class meeting with the count of cigarettes reported in the diary showed only a small decrease; the reported mean daily consumption for the group was 19.3 in the estimate, 16.5 in the diary count. Although the difference is significant on mean difference t test, the size of the difference is small and may partly represent the discrepancy between a generalized estimate and an actual count. Virtually all subjects tended to decrease.

The major problem subjects noted in filling out the diary was completing the section devoted to adjectives. A very large proportion of the subjects reported that it was difficult to dredge up as many as six adjectives. Most felt impelled to write that many although the instructions stated that every blank need not be filled out. Many subjects found the use of the adjectives repetitious. Several reported that "no change" was the adjective they most often wanted to use because they felt that smoking did not make them look different to other people or feel different inside.

Subjects were asked whether there was anything unusual about the day in which they filled out the diary so that any change in their normal routines could be taken into account in the interpretation of the diary material. In no instance was this considered necessary. The subjects were then asked whether there was anything more they wanted to tell us about their smoking. Many reported they smoked more than they realized although their initial estimates were actually higher than the counts in the diary period.

Next, the interviewer described six 7-point scales (see Appendix IV for the form) defining the major components of the three-dimensional model of patterns of support for smoking. These were: scales defining the degree to which the respondent believed that her smoking represented affiliative behavior, role-defining behavior, and the components of the affective dimension: habit, pleasure, tension release, and addiction. In each instance the possible responses range from "relevant" (7) to "irrelevant" (1). Each respondent was asked to rate herself on each scale.

TABLE 15
Mean Ratings[†] for Factors Supporting Smoking Given on Interview
(31 College Women)

Support	Mean	S.D.
Habit	5.2	1.3
Pleasure	5.2	1.1
Reduction of Tension	4.7	1.4
Addiction	2.8	1.7
Social	3.7	1.8
Self-image	2.1	0.9

[†]*Scale ranges from 7 for most relevant to 1 for least relevant.*

The average ratings on these six scales (Table 15) represent another self-portrait of the patterns of support for smoking among this group of young women in college. The high ratings on Pleasure and Habit and the low ratings on Psychological Addiction are compatible with the findings from other portions of the study. Despite the fact that over half of the cigarettes described on the diaries were smoked while the respondent was in the company of other smokers (see Table 12, item 10), the average score for the scale which reflects social stimulation to smoking was at the middle of the range. The rating given the use of cigarettes for definition of Self-concept was very low; this is consistent with the data from the Test of Patterns of Support but not with the relatively high frequency with which adjectives related to self-image were used in the diaries. However, the latter may be an artifact, a reflection of the demand characteristics of a task which required the subject to report "how you look." Lastly, the average score on Tension Reduction was relatively high. This is especially odd when one considers the rarity with which tension reduction was described on the diary reports for individual cigarettes. It may reflect the possibility that the relatively few cigarettes actually smoked to calm or pacify have a great emotional impact. The quantitative estimate from the diaries may, therefore, underestimate the true weight placed by the smoker on the use of cigarettes to reduce tension.

The possibility that the three affective items might form a cumulative scale, the kind originally identified by Guttman (for an elementary description of Guttman scaling see Selltiz, 1959, pp. 373 ff.) was tested by assigning a plus (+) on each item to respondents above the midpoint and a minus (−) to those below the midpoint. Table 16 provides strong evidence for the proposition that the affective factors do form a cumulative scale and are not independent. Only one of the 31 respondents failed to fit the pattern which places Pleasure at the lower end, Tension Reduction at the middle, and Psychological Addiction at the upper end of the scale. Thus, at least in the responses to relatively uncomplicated rating scales, these college women showed us that they did not view these three affective rewards of smoking as the mutually exclusive patterns described in popularized versions of Tomkins' typology (see, for example, Gross' article in *Mademoiselle*, 1969).

TABLE 16

Scalogram Analysis of Interview Questions on Affective Supports for Smoking (31 College Women)

Scale Pattern			Number of Subjects
Pleasure	Tension Reduction	Addiction	
+	−	−	7
+	+	−	14
+	+	+	9
"Errors"			
−	+	−	1

"+" indicates a rating above the midpoint of the scale, "−" indicates a rating below the midpoint of the scale.

Lastly, subjects were asked to indicate whether they planned to change their smoking behavior in the near future. Eight of the girls indicated that they hoped to stop smoking when they changed environment on graduation; four others expected to cut down.

TABLE 17

Intercorrelations of Scores on Measures of Tension Reduction as a Support for Smoking[†] (31 College Women)

Support: Tension Reduction	Test of Patterns of Support		Diary			Interview
	Pretest	Post-test	Items	Adjective "Feel"	Adjective "Look"	Rating Scale
Test of Patterns of Support						
Pretest	1.00					
Post-test	.73**	1.00				
Diary						
Items	.21	.26	1.00			
Adjective "Feel" Affective	.06	.28	.35*	1.00		
Adjective "Look" Affective	.14	.22	−.10	.05	1.00	
Post-diary Interview						
Rating Scale	.56**	.75**	.47**	.21	.10	1.00

[†]*Scores derived from Test of Patterns of Support, Diary, and Post-diary interview; none of these measures was significantly correlated with levels of smoking.*

*$p < .05$, **$p < .01$.

Interrelations among the various data of Study IV and predictions of behavior.
One of the major goals of the study was the determination of the degree of consistency among the three different kinds of data reflecting patterns of support for smoking. To search for consistency, we selected one of the components of the affective dimension, i.e., Tension Reduction, and the material relevant to each of the other two major dimensions, the social and role-defining supports. Tables 17-19 give matrices of intercorrelations among different measures of each of the three supports. These measures consist of a scale from the two administrations of the Test of Patterns of Support for Smoking and relevant material from the diary and the interview.

As shown in Table 17, there was considerable consistency among the pretest and the post-test scores (Test of Patterns of Support for Smoking) for the use of smoking as a source of tension reduction and the related rating on the interview. All three possible correlations are highly significant. In contrast, correlations between scores on the Test of Patterns of Support, the interview, and the various components of the diary were low.

As stated above, the degree to which a smoker perceives his smoking as an important source of tension reduction may not reflect the *number* of instances in which this effect has occurred so much as the intensity of the relief he has experienced on the occasions when smoking has functioned as a pacifier. Actually,

TABLE 18

Intercorrelations of Scores on Measures of Social Supports for Smoking[†]
(31 College Women)

Support: Social	Number Cigarettes	Test of Pattern of Support		Diary			Interview
		Pretest	Post-test	Items	Adjective "Feel"	Adjective "Look"	Rating Scale
Number cigarettes	1.00						
Test of Patterns of Support							
Pretest	−.48**	1.00					
Post-test	−.45**	.80**	1.00				
Diary							
Items	−.13	.52**	.54**	1.00			
Adjective "Feel" Social	−.35*	.58**	.49**	.30	1.00		
Adjective "Look" Social	−.15	.65**	.35*	.36*	.67**	1.00	
Post-diary Interview							
Rating Scale	−.30	.62	.73**	.48**	.44*	.43*	1.00

[†]*Scores derived from Test of Patterns of Support, Diary, and Post-diary Interview.*
* p < .05, ** p < .01.

although the score on the fixed-alternative Test of Patterns of Support was not significantly correlated with the frequency with which tension reduction was checked on the diary, the latter *was* correlated significantly with the rating scale completed during the interview. These data suggest that the different types of report give a relatively consistent picture of the role of tension reduction in the smoking of individual respondents.

The use of social adjectives is correlated with the Test of Patterns of Support scores on social items and is moderately close to the self-ratings on interview of the importance of social factors in supporting smoking. However, neither is correlated highly with the relevant checklist items on the diary (Table 18). The use of role-defining adjectives in the diary elicited by the request to describe how the subjects thought they *looked* is almost completely unrelated both to the scores on the relevant scale from the Test of Patterns of Support and to the self-ratings given on interview (Table 19). The adjectives describing how the subjects felt *are* modestly correlated with these scales. Thus there is some indication of consistency in the measures of the degree to which the smoking of individual subjects is social or solitary. Although the importance of role definition is not disproven, the lack of consistency among the various measures makes it difficult to choose the most appropriate technique for evaluating the importance of this factor to an individual smoker.

TABLE 19
Intercorrelations of Scores on Measures of Self-image/Role Supports for Smoking[†] (31 College Women)

Support: Self-Image	Number Cigarettes	Test of Patterns of Support		Diary		Interview
		Pretest	Post-test	Adjective "Feel"	Adjective "Look"	Rating Scale
Number cigarettes	1.00					
Test of Patterns of Support						
Pretest	.35*	1.00				
Post-test	.06	.84**	1.00			
Diary						
Adjective "Feel" Role	−.25	.34	.48**	1.00		
Adjective "Look" Role	−.22	−.04	.19	.28	1.00	
Post-diary Interview						
Rating Scale	.26	.54**	.59**	.12	−.05	1.00

[†] Scores derived from Test of Patterns of Support, Diary, and Post-diary Interview.
* $p < .05$, ** $p < .01$.

Patterns of support as predictors of academic success. The hypothesis has been advanced elsewhere that students for whom tension reduction is an important support for smoking should have poorer grades than those for whom it is not relevant. This implies that the commonly reported finding that smokers have poorer grades than non-smokers should apply only to some smokers, not to all. Data supporting this concept were reported for junior high school students by Mausner and Mischler (1967). The relation was tested with the current data by comparing the cumulative grade-point averages at the close of the senior year among groups differing in patterns of support (Table 20).

The 31 subjects in the study were classified into three groups on the basis of the affective rating scales completed during the interview. Statistically significant differences among the groups were found. Students who reported smoking primarily for pleasure had the highest grades. The lowest grades were found among the students above the midpoint of the rating scale on both Pleasure and Tension Reduction. Students who were above the midpoint on Psychological Addiction as well as Pleasure and Tension Reduction had intermediate grades.

These data appear to confirm the hypothesis that students for whom smoking is an important source of tension reduction are actually under greater academic stress than those who smoke purely for pleasure and that this stress may be inferred from the average difference of almost half of a grade category. But we have no ready explanation for the fact that those students who also reported a craving for cigarettes as well as the use of cigarettes to reduce externally caused tensions had grades intermediate between the other two groups.

Prediction of long-range change in smoking. Change in smoking at the end of a six-month period was examined in relation to the various materials of the diary project. Neither pattern of support nor the Liverant-Rotter I/E scale was predictive of change. The latter finding was surprising since this test has predicted change in smoking in other research (Platt, Krassen & Mausner, 1969; Straits & Sechrest, 1963).

The only factor which did predict change was the respondent's statement of her plans. Twelve of the 28 girls for whom we have follow-up data indicated during the interview that they hoped to cut down or stop smoking when they graduated; college life was viewed as highly conducive to smoking. As indicated in Table 21, seven of the 12 girls did fulfill their plans while only two of the remaining 16 reported that they cut down or quit.

Discussion and Summary: Study IV

The major goal of this study was the delineation of the role cigarette smoking plays in the lives of young women at college. A secondary goal was the study of interrelations among three kinds of data descriptive of patterns of support for smoking: diaries, a paper-and-pencil test, and an interview. A third goal was the test, insofar as possible with a small group of subjects, of a number of hypotheses concerning smoking behavior.

With minor differences, the diaries confirm the findings of the first two studies reported in this chapter. All three dimensions of patterns of support, affective, social, and role-defining, are identifiable in one or another portion of the data. Of course, the relative weights of the different factors among college girls differ from the mix found among high school students or middle-class Catholic men. Among the young women the various components of the affective dimension were all present and the social component was especially high. The use of smoking for role definition was clearly discernible both in the adjectives describing how the respondents looked and felt while smoking and in the spontaneous comments on the diary pages.

TABLE 20
Relation between Grades and Patterns of Smoking Derived from Interview (31 College Women)

Groups	N	Mean Cumulative Average [†]
Above midpoint on enjoyment	7	1.88
Above midpoint on enjoyment & tension release	14	1.48
Above midpoint on enjoyment, tension release, addiction	9	1.64

[†]$A=3, B=2, C=1, D=0$.

Source	SS	df	MS	F
Between groups	7226.49	2	3613.25	4.038*
Within groups	25054.71	28	894.81	

*$p < .05$.

The three kinds of data, diary, questionnaire, and interview, were generally consistent. The several areas of inconsistency occurred where it is likely that the frequency with which a theme appears in a diary does not necessarily reflect its salience to the respondent. As we pointed out, a person could obtain relief from tension from only a small fraction of the cigarettes he smokes and yet view tension reduction as a major support for his smoking because of the powerfully reinforcing effect of the few instances in which it operates. In general, we were encouraged by the levels of consistency among the three types of data to regard the easily administered Test of Patterns of Support as a useful way of asking a smoker to summarize the role played by smoking in his life. The fact that we use the test does not, however, mean that we are unaware of the degree to which cigarettes smoked at different times and in different circumstances vary in the way they reward the smoker.

Several specific findings of Study IV should be mentioned in summary. First, the Test of Patterns of Support yielded a meaningful set of scales on factor analysis, especially when the post-diary data were examined. These scales were compatible with the theoretical model for supports presented in the first chapter.

TABLE 21
Relation of Plans to Decrease Smoking Stated on Interview to Change in Smoking Levels at Six-month Follow-up Interview (28 College Women[†])

	Plans		
Follow-up Smoking Levels	Change	No Change	
Decrease of 8 or more cigarettes	7	2	
No decrease	5	14	
Total	12	16	28

$\chi^2 = 4.48$, $df = 1$, $p < .05$

[†] *Follow-up information not obtained for three respondents.*

Actually, the degree of lawfulness in the factor analysis was somewhat surprising in view of the small number of subjects. The fact that meaningful factors emerged from the analysis argues, if nothing else, that the subjects' ideas about supports for smoking coincide with those of the investigators.

Second, the respondents showed idiosyncratic patterns of support which appeared to be independent of the circumstances in which smoking took place, in contrast to the data linking external circumstances and perceived patterns of support in our high school and adult samples (cf. Studies I and II). This may be due to our inability to analyze the nature of the circumstances in great enough detail, or to the restricted range of activities in the college girl's life.

Third, patterns of support and degree of fatalism or sense of control over one's own destiny (I/E) did not predict which of the respondents would stop smoking after they graduated; only the plans expressed during the interview accurately forecast change. Perhaps a larger body of subjects and better information about attitudes towards themselves and towards the function of smoking in their lives would have enabled us to obtain lawful relations between changes in smoking and some of the components of the Patterns of Support as well as the I/E test. As we shall see later, internal/ external orientation will predict change only if a person's values and expectations concerning the outcomes of smoking or not smoking are also known (see Chapter 7).

A comprehensive discussion of all the studies presented in this chapter will be deferred until the end of Chapter 3. There we will extend our discussion of patterns of support by analyzing the interrelations of these patterns with attitudes towards smoking and with personality. Following this, we will summarize our current concepts of the natural history of smoking.

3
The Relations Among Patterns of Support
for Smoking, Values and Expectations
Concerning the Effects of Smoking,
and Measures of Personality

In the previous chapter we reported studies in which we obtained a picture of patterns of support for smoking from several groups of smokers. This picture was largely, although not entirely, derived from analysis of open-ended materials. The next step in our research was an examination of the interrelations among patterns of support, beliefs about smoking, and personality in a group of smokers large enough to permit multivariate analysis. The data were derived from pretests of subjects who participated in an experiment on the effects of role playing (see Chapters 5-7). In addition, non-smokers from the same population were tested for comparison with the smokers.

This study had several goals. The first was a delineation of the character of patterns of support for smoking in a group large enough to furnish a sound basis for the use of factor analysis. The degree of order in the factor analyses of responses on the Test of Patterns of Support from the subjects in Study IV was sufficiently great so that we were most interested in the structure which would emerge from a larger group. Secondly, on the basis of our own work (Mausner, E.P.A., 1966a) and the discussions by Straits (1965) we felt that the conceptual framework of decision theory would be a useful point of departure for studying the attitudes and beliefs of smokers. The project reported in this chapter, therefore, included the development of a psychometric instrument based on a decision-theory model, the Test of Subjective Expected Utilities (SEU). Lastly, we had been impressed by some of the findings of our earlier work which suggested that differences in average scores on tests of personality between smokers and non-smokers reported in the literature (Eysenck *et al*, 1960, Matarazzo & Saslow, 1960) should not be made the basis for conclusions about the "personality of the smoker." As Matarazzo has pointed out (Mausner & Platt, 1966b), these differences in averages are always associated with great overlap in distributions. Our suspicion was that differences between smokers as a total group and non-smokers would be far less meaningful than differences among smokers who vary in patterns of support for smoking. Thus, for example, we anticipated that smokers who were above average in generalized anxiety should rely on cigarettes for tension reduction while smokers who were not generally anxious would not. On this basis, we would predict that the reported differences in scores between smokers and non-smokers on a test like the Taylor Manifest Anxiety Scale would be maintained if non-smokers were compared to smokers who use cigarettes to reduce tension but would vanish if they were compared to smokers who do not use cigarettes for tension reduction.

The following survey, therefore, included tests selected to elucidate patterns of support for smoking, attitudinal bases for decisions about smoking, and the relation of personality characteristics to both.

Subjects and Procedures

The students at a two-year campus of Pennsylvania State University were queried about their smoking habits in January 1968 during registration. A total of 1268 replies were received, 853 from men and 415 from women, virtually the entire student body. The 238 men who reported smoking at least eight cigarettes or more per day were telephoned and asked to take part in a "study of the opinions of college students taking place on campus." Students were told that they would be paid two dollars for participation. Of the 238 smokers, 187 agreed to take part and completed the pretest materials. A random sample of the males identified at registration as non-smokers was also asked to participate; of the 62 invited, 60 actually did take part in the study.

Test Battery

The following test battery was administered to mixed groups of smokers and non-smokers: the Test of Patterns of Support for Smoking, a test of Subjective Expected Utilities for smoking and non-smoking, the Liverant-Rotter Test of Internal External Control, the Taylor Manifest Anxiety Scale, the Crowne-Marlow (1964) Test of Social Desirability, and the Kogan-Wallach (1967) "Dilemmas of Choice" test of risk-taking tendencies.

Subjective Expected Utility (SEU). The newly designed test included in the battery was based on the theoretical considerations related to decisional processes advanced by Edwards and other workers. A full discussion of these issues will be found in Chapter 4. The purpose of this test was an assessment of the subjective expected utility to the smoker of the outcomes of either of two choices, continuing to smoke or discontinuing smoking. The test listed a variety of possible outcomes. Some of the items were derived from a study of reasons given by subjects for continuing to smoke, i.e., the kind of material to be found on the Test of Patterns of Support. In this the subject is asked to describe the relevance to him of the various rewards of smoking currently and in the past. In contrast, in the Test of Subjective Expected Utilities, the subject reports on the values he places on these rewards and on his expectations concerning the degree to which smoking or not smoking would affect his ability to attain them in the future. Additional items were derived from reasons given by ex-smokers for stopping. The format of the test and the exact wording of the items are shown in Appendix VI.

For each outcome the subject was asked to make three judgments. First was the value he placed on the outcome on an 11-point scale ranging from − 5 (Don't want it to happen) through 0 (Don't care) to + 5 (Do want it to happen). The second and third judgments, listed in randomized order for the various outcomes, were the expectation that the outcome would happen to him if he *Continued to Smoke* or if he *Stopped Smoking.* These expectations were recorded on a continuous rating scale with positions marked in tens from zero chances in 100 to 100 chances in 100. Non-smokers were given a parallel form of the questionnaire in which the value items were identical to those given smokers but the expectancies asked the non-smoker to consider the chances of his experiencing the given outcome if he "began to smoke" or "continued not to smoke."

Results

The Test of Patterns of Support for Smoking. The format and items of this test may be found in Chapter 2, pages 31-32. When the protocols from the 187 male college-aged smokers in the study were subjected to factor analysis, the results were gratifyingly lawful (Tables 22 and 23). Five of the factors (1, 2, 6, 7, 8) are essentially identical to those obtained by Horn and Waingrow from their analyses of the same body of items (private communication). The only major difference between their matrix and the factors found in the current study is the placement of items relative to habit. In the current study the items which Horn and Waingrow defined as habitual smoking are tied in with some of the new items related to self-concept (factor 4). It may be recalled that Horn and Waingrow did not include material dealing with self-image in their original test of patterns of support for smoking (called by them the Test of Insight). Apparently the students who accepted the notion that they often smoke without even knowing it (Table 24) also perceived themselves as projecting the image of a "smoker."

Two factors are related to different aspects of the social character of smoking. One of these reflects the respondent's perception of the degree to which smoking is socially stimulated (factor 5). The other is related to a perception of the effect of smoking on cohesiveness of social groups (factor 3) as well as on the sense of identification that the smoker has with other smokers. If other samples show a similar tendency for items relating to social factors in smoking to fall into two independent groups, it will be necessary to recast the portion of the model for patterns of support for smoking dealing with the social dimension into two dimensions, one the simple tendency to smoke when with other smokers, the other a complex of social identification and cohesiveness.

Factor scores for each individual subject were derived by summing the ratings given by the subject on each of the relevant items (i.e., those with loadings over .50), dividing by the number of items, and multiplying by 100. Since each item is a 5-point scale, each factor goes from 100, representing total rejection of the factor, to 500, representing complete acceptance of the factor as invariably characteristic of the person's smoking.

TABLE 22
Factor Analysis of Test of Patterns of Support for Smoking (187 Male College Students)

Items	Rotated Factor Loadings – Varimax Rotation								
	Tension Reduct.	Pleas.	Social Self-image	Habit Self-image	Social Stim.	Psych. Addict.	Stim.	Sensory Motor	†
% of Variance . . .	14.084	9.384	12.628	11.456	7.337	14.706	9.793	8.862	6.541
(1) Smokers are basically different from non-smokers	0.132	0.072	-0.468	0.018	0.071	-0.037	0.045	0.031	-0.051
(2) Found cigarette in mouth—didn't remember putting there	0.133	-0.009	-0.024	0.611	0.071	-0.091	-0.024	0.009	-0.020
(3) Very aware of fact when not smoking a cigarette	0.065	0.007	0.065	0.026	-0.050	-0.191	0.179	-0.121	0.034
(4) When blue or worried, I smoke cigarettes	0.633	-0.112	-0.194	0.094	0.095	-0.126	0.211	-0.048	0.153
(5) I offer a light to someone who takes out a cigarette	0.115	-0.240	-0.027	0.106	0.116	0.009	-0.063	-0.046	0.627
(6) Smoke less when with friends who are not smoking	-0.042	0.089	-0.217	-0.063	0.614	-0.025	-0.018	0.011	0.068
(7) I find cigarettes pleasurable	0.094	-0.808	0.015	-0.067	-0.126	-0.090	0.054	0.011	0.135
(8) Smoke automatically without being aware of it	0.187	0.147	0.073	0.566	-0.028	-0.307	-0.003	-0.074	-0.082
(9) People think of me as a smoker	-0.033	0.004	-0.238	0.401	0.002	-0.135	0.152	0.017	0.159
(10) Get real gnawing hunger for a cigarette	0.123	-0.076	-0.047	0.268	-0.039	-0.705	0.058	0.001	0.075
(11) If friend recommends different brand, I would try it	0.204	0.085	-0.005	-0.165	0.166	0.003	0.244	-0.372	0.117
(12) When uncomfortable or upset, I smoke cigarettes	0.758	-0.180	-0.138	-0.002	-0.052	-0.170	0.197	-0.041	0.145
(13) Smoking cigarettes is pleasant and relaxing	0.174	-0.762	-0.016	-0.013	-0.138	-0.039	0.114	-0.024	0.081
(14) I offer cigarettes when with other people	0.056	-0.044	-0.073	0.020	-0.082	-0.104	0.078	0.003	0.584
(15) Light cigarette without realizing one still in ashtray	-0.001	-0.033	-0.027	0.474	-0.098	-0.144	0.028	-0.060	0.055
(16) Part of enjoyment is knowing I look "right" smoking	0.110	0.283	-0.112	0.316	0.078	-0.201	-0.011	-0.309	-0.100
(17) Get craving only a cigarette can satisfy	0.112	0.045	-0.081	0.195	0.033	-0.686	0.161	-0.037	-0.100
(18) If I stopped, people wouldn't recognize me without cigarette	0.004	0.073	-0.213	0.449	0.037	0.043	0.300	-0.144	0.204
(19) Light cigarette when angry	0.699	-0.053	-0.057	0.197	-0.123	-0.100	0.116	0.014	0.017
(20) I smoke to stimulate, to perk myself up	0.283	-0.135	-0.149	0.113	0.066	-0.146	0.683	-0.036	0.005
(21) Smoking helps me show what kind of person I am	0.170	0.003	-0.399	0.253	0.243	-0.022	0.258	-0.099	0.012
(22) Smoke cigarettes from habit, without really wanting one	0.096	0.384	0.023	0.340	0.032	-0.310	-0.134	-0.275	-0.182
(23) Smoke more when with friends who are smoking heavily	0.204	0.143	-0.124	0.125	0.468	-0.374	-0.079	-0.219	-0.065
(24) When out of cigarettes, it's almost unbearable	0.214	-0.104	-0.258	0.124	0.024	-0.697	0.103	-0.051	-0.036
(25) When ashamed or embarrassed, I light cigarette	0.505	0.069	-0.124	0.193	0.072	-0.247	0.010	-0.203	0.067
(26) I picture myself with a cigarette in my hand	0.100	0.141	-0.313	0.403	-0.093	-0.289	0.193	-0.196	0.133
(27) Prefer to smoke when alone rather than with other people	0.075	-0.150	0.013	0.029	0.180	0.015	0.120	-0.272	0.124
(28) I smoke to keep myself from slowing down	0.190	-0.091	-0.210	0.166	0.273	-0.163	0.477	-0.213	0.106
(29) When all in crowd smoke, they feel a little closer	0.141	-0.063	-0.465	0.044	0.071	-0.103	-0.028	-0.131	-0.012
(30) When smoking, watching smoke as exhale is part of enjoyment	-0.053	0.017	-0.184	0.043	-0.023	-0.097	-0.038	-0.503	0.048
(31) Not contented for long without smoking	0.228	-0.011	-0.151	0.170	-0.055	-0.433	0.220	-0.339	0.103
(32) When others are not smoking, I don't smoke	-0.101	0.133	-0.034	-0.063	0.473	0.161	0.141	-0.047	-0.040
(33) When upset, few things help better than cigarette	0.407	-0.056	-0.251	-0.134	0.048	-0.197	0.189	0.037	-0.124
(34) I smoke to give me a "lift"	0.324	-0.183	-0.210	0.023	0.033	-0.285	0.660	-0.075	-0.041
(35) Feel more like "myself" when smoking	0.272	-0.129	-0.449	0.173	-0.051	-0.382	0.182	-0.045	0.115
(36) Part of enjoyment comes from steps I take to light up	-0.012	-0.001	-0.454	0.113	-0.144	-0.035	0.258	-0.382	-0.045
(37) Part of enjoyment is smoking with someone I like	0.126	-0.065	-0.628	0.071	0.209	-0.120	0.064	-0.210	0.349
(38) Enjoy cigarette more when offered by someone I like	-0.000	0.061	-0.526	0.028	0.171	-0.010	0.123	-0.307	0.210
(39) Handling cigarette is part of enjoyment	0.028	0.024	-0.295	0.217	0.114	-0.071	0.128	-0.539	-0.161
(40) If I see others smoking, I want to light up too	0.293	0.036	-0.077	0.159	0.385	-0.379	0.091	-0.343	-0.097

† Unused factor.

As with the college women in Study IV, the most significant factor in the smoking of these young men was pleasure (see Table 24). This is demonstrated

TABLE 23
Summary of Factor Analysis of Test of Patterns of Support for Smoking (187 Male College Students)

Factor 1: Tension Reduction — 14% of total variance
    Feeling "blue" or wanting to take my mind off cares and worries
    Feeling uncomfortable or upset about something
    Feeling angry about something
    Feeling ashamed or embarrassed about something
    Feeling upset

Factor 2: Pleasure — 9% of total variance
    Finding cigarettes pleasurable
    Smoking cigarettes is pleasant and relaxing

Factor 3: Social Self-image — 13% of total variance
    Feeling closer in a crowd to those who smoke
    Smokers are basically different kinds of people than non-smokers
    Feeling more like "myself" when I smoke
    Enjoying the steps I take to light up
    Enjoying lighting up and smoking with someone I like
    Enjoying a cigarette more if offered by someone I like

Factor 4: Habit-Self-image — 11% of total variance
    Finding a cigarette in mouth and not remembering putting it there
    Smoking automatically without even being aware of it
    Lighting up without realizing I still have one burning in ashtray
    If I suddenly stopped smoking, people wouldn't recognize me
    When thinking of myself, picturing myself with a cigarette in hand
    When other people think of me, they think of me as a smoker

Factor 5: Social Stimulus to Smoking — 7% of total variance
    With friends who aren't smoking, tend to smoke less than usual
    With friends who are smoking, tend to smoke more than usual
    When some place others are not smoking, I don't smoke

Factor 6: Psychological Addiction — 15% of total variance
    Get a gnawing hunger for a cigarette when I haven't smoked for a while
    Between cigarettes, I get a craving only a cigarette can satisfy
    When out of cigarettes, it's unbearable until I can get them
    Not feeling content for long unless smoking a cigarette

Factor 7: Stimulation — 10% of total variance
    Smoking to stimulate me, to perk myself up
    Smoking in order to keep myself from slowing down
    Smoking to give me a "lift"

Factor 8: Sensory Motor — 9% of total variance
    Having a different brand recommended than one smoking and trying it
    Part of enjoyment of smoking is watching the smoke as I exhale it
    Part of enjoyment of smoking is handling a cigarette
    Part of enjoyment comes from the steps I take to light up

both by the mean score of 369 and by the fact that 90% of the subjects gave ratings above the midpoint of the scale. The next most important factor was social stimulation; over half (57%) of the subjects recognized that they tend to smoke more when they are with others who are smoking and less when with non-smokers. Only a third of these young men reported tension reduction as a significant support for their smoking. Psychological addiction was cited by an astonishingly large proportion of the subjects as characteristic of their smoking. The scores reflecting the stimulating and information-giving (i.e., sensory-motor) aspects of smoking are quite low. However, even here a sizable minority of the subjects gave scores above 300.

Finally, as with previous analyses based on questionnaires, there was relatively little acceptance for the items dealing with self-concept. Only 16 of the subjects gave scores above 300 for the factor which reflected a desire to identify with other smokers (Self-image, Social) and only eight responded positively to the items which dealt with self-image as a "smoker" (Self-image, Habit). However, the fact that the mean scale position for these two factors relating to self-image is approximately 200 indicates that many subjects did not totally reject the notion that they identified with other smokers or perceived themselves as smokers. As always, it is hard to know whether the tendency to check *seldom* or *never* for these items represents a feeling that agreeing with them is socially unacceptable.

TABLE 24

Means and Intercorrelation Matrix for Factor Scores: Test of Patterns of Support for Smoking (187 Male College Students)

	Tension Reduct.	Pleas.	Social Self-image	Habit-Self-image	Social Stim.	Psych. Addic.	Stim.	Sens. Motor
Average Factor Score [†]	276	369	218	190	291	253	214	214
S. D.	68	75	56	53	66	74	74	71
% of Subjects Above 300	34	90	8	4	57	43	17	28
Tension Reduction	1.00							
Pleasure	0.22	1.00						
Social Self-image	0.42	0.08	1.00					
Habit-Self-image	0.30	−0.13	0.38	1.00				
Social Stim. to Smoking	0.20	−0.19	0.33	0.20	1.00			
Psychological Addiction	0.46	0.14	0.40	0.51	0.25	1.00		
Stimulation	0.53	0.23	0.48	0.29	0.25	0.44	1.00	
Sensory Motor	0.17	−0.20	0.56	0.34	0.23	0.29	0.29	1.00

†For an explanation of the procedure for calculating these scores cf. p. 56; possible scores range from 100 (irrelevant) to 500 (most relevant).

Comparison of the population of Study V with a group of female college students. Study V was carried out with male subjects only. We were interested in knowing how the pattern of supports reported by male and female college students would compare. Therefore, in the spring of 1968 we arranged for the Test of Patterns of Support to be administered to 55 students at a small Catholic college for women. These students come from the same area as that from which many of our male subjects were drawn.

The picture of the patterns of support given by these college girls is quite similar to that given by the young men. Pleasure was almost universally cited as a major reason for smoking. Social stimulation was important for a little over half the group of women, tension reduction for about a third. In contrast to the men, however, few of the girls needed cigarettes for stimulation, relatively few enjoyed the tactual and informational properties of smoking, few acknowledged a craving for cigarettes, and virtually none recognized smoking as a source of support for the self-image.

Relations among factor scores for the male students. The lower half of Table 24 gives the intercorrelations of the factor scores. Although the factor structure derived from varimax rotation is quite orderly, with virtually no loadings above .3 on the irrelevant items for each of the factors, the final factor scales are far from independent. However, the lack of independence does not preclude the use of the scales derived from the analysis. An examination of the table shows that in no instance does any one of the scales show more than a 30% overlap in variance with any of the others.* In addition, the highly intercorrelated scales, i.e., Tension Reduction, Psychological Addiction, and Stimulation, deal with similar areas of psychological content.

A higher order factor analysis was done to look at the character of the interrelations among the scales. Table 25 shows a principal components analysis; this rather than any of the varimax rotations was the most readily interpretable. The first factor, one which includes the largest proportion of the variance, covers all of the factors in the Test of Patterns of Support except for Pleasure and Social Stimulation. Pleasure forms the center of the second factor. Social Stimulation does not appear with high loadings on any of the further factors. It may be that the content of the items on that scale represent the subjects' perception of an external force rather than the fulfillment of a need. The six scales with high loadings on the first factor *are* all related to the fulfillment of needs. The character of these higher-order factors, then, reflects the fact that some smoking is related to the existence and reduction of pressing intrinsic needs; much smoking, however, is either the effect of relatively neutral social stimulation or hedonistic gratification.

An hypothesis presented above (see Chapter 1) was that the levels of emotional support should form a cumulative scale. That is, that virtually all smokers should report that some of their smoking is purely habitual and affect free, that in addition most should report smoking for pleasure (or "positive affect" in

---

*Readers unfamiliar with correlational procedures may find this obscure. The square of a Pearsonian correlation coefficient between two measures gives the proportion of variation in one measure which can be predicted from the other, i.e., the overlap in variance.

Tomkins' terminology), that a smaller number should report tension reduction (or "negative affect smoking" in Tomkins' terms) in addition to pleasure and habit, and fewer still should report psychological addiction as an increment to the other three. If a cumulative scale could be formed, then all smokers at any given level on the scale should also report the emotional levels below it. The scalability of a series of items is tested by deriving a statistic called the index of reproducibility. If that index is above .90, the scale is considered cumulative. (For a discussion of cumulative scaling see Scott in Lindzey & Aronson, 1968, pp. 221 ff.) A computer analysis testing reproducibility indices for a variety of combinations of individual items from the Test of Patterns of Support with the 187 protocols from our sample of college males failed to give evidence of a cumulative scale; the best combination of items showed a reproducibility index of .54.

TABLE 25
Higher-order Factor Analysis of Factor Scores on Test of Patterns of Support for Smoking (187 Male College Students)

Support	Principal Components			
	1	2	3	4
	Eigenvalues			
	2.571	0.607	0.264	0.132
	Percent of Variance †			
	90.412	21.351	9.285	4.645
	Factor Loadings			
Tension Reduction	0.616	0.290	0.086	−0.103
Pleasure	0.118	0.516	−0.111	0.107
Social Self-image	0.725	−0.096	−0.243	0.017
Habit Self-image	0.564	−0.238	0.254	0.130
Social Stimulation to Smoking	0.394	−0.254	−0.011	−0.242
Psychological Addiction	0.674	0.066	0.241	0.075
Stimulation	0.661	0.238	−0.051	−0.098
Sensory Motor	0.537	−0.255	−0.245	0.139

†*Percent of variance does not add to 100 because values in diagonals of intercorrelation matrix were r^2.*

A treatment similar to that used in Studies I and II gives a picture closer to that predicted by the dimensional concept of affective supports for smoking. Each subject's score on the three most relevant scales, i.e., Pleasure, Tension Reduction, and Psychological Addiction, was categorized into two classes, above and below the midpoint of the scales (300). When the scale pattern of these dichotomized scores is tabulated (see Table 26), it is apparent that a cumulative scale does obtain, as indicated by an index of reproducibility of .94. The one source of error is the presence of a group of 25 subjects out of the 187 with scores above 300 on Psychological Addiction, whose scores on Tension Reduction are below 300. It is hard to know why these young men, who are well above average in a craving for cigarettes, do not use them for the reduction of externally caused tension.

TABLE 26
Scalability† of Major Factors in Affective Dimension from Test of Patterns of Support†† (187 Male College Students)

Scale Pattern			
Pleasure	**Tension Reduction**	**Psychological Addiction**	**Number of Subjects**
−	−	−	11
+	−	−	73
+	+	−	40
+	+	+	32
"Errors"			
−	+	+	2
−	+	−	1
−	−	+	3
+	−	+	25
			187

$^\dagger R = .94.$ †† "−" indicates score below 300; "+" indicates score 300 or higher.

The Test of Subjective Expected Utilities (SEU). There were several stages in the treatment of the data from this test. The first step was the calculation of two overall SEU (utility) scores, one for continuing to smoke, the other for stopping. For the first score, "value" for each outcome was multiplied by the "expectancy"* of the expressed likelihood of occurrence for that outcome should the subject *continue* to smoke (or begin smoking, for non-smokers). For the other, "value" for each outcome was also multiplied by the "expectancy" that the outcome would occur should the subject *stop* smoking (or continue not to smoke, for non-smokers). Both the SEU scores for continuing and for stopping were negative for undesirable outcomes and positive for desirable outcomes since the values were given either a positive or a negative sign and the expectancies were all positive, i.e., expressed as chances in 100. The utility scores were then summed for the 40 items. This resulted in two overall measures of subjective expected utility, one for continuing to smoke and one for stopping. Lastly, the difference between the utility of continuing and the utility of stopping (C − S) was computed separately for each item and the differences summed over the 40 items.

In the second step in the analysis we broke the test into its components through factor analysis. The factor analyses were carried out separately for the Values and Expectancies components. "Value" judgments on each item were treated directly. The expectancy used was the C−S score since it was the *difference* in the perceived probability of an outcome should smoking status

---

*Throughout the book the words "expectation" and "expectancy" will be used interchangeably.

TABLE 27
Factor Analysis of Expectancies (Continue-Stop Scores†) for Various Outcomes of Continuing or Ceasing to Smoke (187 Male College Students)

(If you stopped smoking) (If you continued to smoke), what are the chances that you would —

Items	Ill-Health	Tension Reduct.	††	Self-image	Hedonic-Aesthetic	Social	††	††	Mood
% of Variance	13.171	15.397	9.202	10.895	12.688	5.468	7.983	4.347	7.836
(1) be nervous?	-0.067	0.438	0.218	0.134	-0.075	0.316	-0.156	-0.178	0.296
(2) live longer than the average man?	-0.368	-0.072	0.077	0.075	0.117	0.139	-0.320	0.052	0.056
(3) enjoy your coffee?	-0.068	-0.306	0.101	-0.187	-0.023	0.008	0.069	0.383	-0.137
(4) feel depressed or blue?	-0.159	0.411	0.471	0.026	0.047	-0.039	0.043	-0.071	0.386
(5) make new friends who would be non-smokers?	-0.210	-0.079	-0.007	0.145	-0.006	-0.624	0.055	-0.008	-0.055
(6) feel proud of yourself?	-0.103	0.062	0.609	0.418	0.124	0.113	-0.078	-0.167	-0.052
(7) be energetic?	-0.290	0.009	-0.154	0.062	0.325	-0.150	-0.343	0.333	-0.171
(8) find something to calm you when tense or angry?	0.078	-0.156	0.020	0.022	-0.084	-0.190	0.130	0.099	-0.610
(9) be irritable with people?	0.023	0.631	0.075	0.289	-0.147	-0.133	-0.003	-0.006	0.204
(10) be envied by other smokers?	-0.126	-0.038	0.164	0.566	0.097	-0.046	-0.059	-0.049	0.008
(11) be able to concentrate well?	-0.115	-0.635	0.377	0.093	0.112	0.078	-0.123	-0.103	0.010
(12) be respected by non-smokers?	-0.091	-0.107	0.080	0.599	0.083	0.032	-0.016	0.133	0.180
(13) be tolerant of other peoples' smoking?	-0.040	-0.067	-0.063	-0.430	-0.103	0.019	0.132	0.197	0.030
(14) not know what to do with your hands at times?	-0.336	0.322	0.162	0.152	-0.104	-0.169	-0.005	-0.289	-0.071
(15) find it hard to get along with your friends?	0.104	0.245	0.226	-0.223	-0.030	-0.342	0.024	-0.084	0.004
(16) become short of breath after normal exercises?	0.505	0.137	-0.053	-0.013	-0.271	0.094	0.133	0.334	-0.144
(17) feel particularly close to non-smoking friends?	0.043	-0.286	-0.403	-0.533	-0.051	0.300	0.148	-0.107	-0.107
(18) get lung cancer sometime during your life?	0.826	0.080	0.048	-0.063	-0.121	0.085	-0.015	-0.034	-0.055
(19) enjoy your meals?	-0.122	-0.365	-0.018	-0.104	0.591	0.109	0.137	0.102	-0.090
(20) find something to perk you up?	-0.096	-0.275	0.090	-0.065	0.098	0.036	-0.122	-0.111	-0.582
(21) get heart disease sometime during your lifetime?	0.749	0.104	-0.043	-0.138	0.038	0.018	0.093	-0.098	-0.036
(22) have clothes which would stay in good condition?	-0.004	-0.084	0.535	0.062	0.049	-0.048	-0.048	0.053	-0.017
(23) that you would have a home with a pleasant odor?	-0.241	0.074	-0.016	0.369	0.549	0.048	0.045	0.001	-0.053
(24) that you would have stained teeth & fingers?	0.181	-0.038	0.254	-0.370	-0.263	0.246	0.055	0.017	0.023
(25) have a good appetite?	0.030	-0.136	0.371	0.097	0.442	-0.154	-0.226	0.115	0.125
(26) look "wrong" to your friends?	-0.274	0.258	-0.202	0.454	0.166	0.046	-0.298	-0.183	-0.208
(27) get bronchitis sometime during your lifetime?	0.476	-0.014	-0.077	0.035	-0.268	-0.028	0.127	-0.365	0.183
(28) cough a lot in the mornings?	0.463	-0.186	-0.066	-0.052	-0.305	0.181	-0.046	0.132	0.044
(29) have children (if you had) who would become smokers?	0.063	-0.021	-0.119	-0.115	0.042	0.159	0.361	-0.098	0.098
(30) find something to relieve short periods of boredom?	0.109	-0.087	-0.190	-0.050	0.451	0.102	0.348	0.188	-0.578
(31) have a good taste in your mouth?	-0.329	-0.108	0.037	0.116	0.452	0.096	-0.165	0.005	0.075
(32) feel really good when first arising in the morning?	-0.147	-0.252	0.302	0.185	0.077	0.194	-0.050	-0.041	-0.045
(33) be able to study well?	-0.189	-0.732	0.086	0.247	0.196	-0.095	0.284	-0.029	-0.120
(34) feel like "yourself"?	-0.053	-0.605	0.092	0.104	-0.124	0.027	0.210	0.080	-0.130
(35) become upset easily?	-0.043	0.624	0.172	0.168	0.026	0.182	-0.210	-0.093	0.145
(36) have a good sense of smell?	-0.038	-0.087	0.100	0.026	0.629	-0.178	-0.029	-0.101	0.001
(37) have enough pocket money?	-0.026	-0.146	-0.036	0.228	0.603	0.164	-0.152	0.062	0.028
(38) gain a noticeable amount of weight?	-0.054	0.106	0.296	0.082	0.118	0.055	-0.582	0.027	0.034
(39) feel yourself a slave to a habit?	0.284	0.080	-0.246	-0.184	-0.094	-0.013	0.164	-0.089	-0.177
(40) enjoy an alcholic beverage?	0.071	-0.122	0.090	-0.149	0.036	-0.110	0.615	0.125	-0.229

Rotated Factor Loadings – Varimax Rotation

† Score was difference between expectancy or perceived likelihood of event if Subject continued to smoke or stopped smoking. †† Unused factors.

change which interested us. Subjects completed the SEU test twice, once a month before and once immediately after participation in a role-playing experiment (see Chapters 5-7). The "Continue minus Stop" (C–S) and the "Values" scores were then subjected to factor analysis for both first and second administrations. All of the four analyses showed similar patterns but the most theoretically meaningful grouping of items into factors arose from the treatment of post-experimental C–S scores. An examination of trends in scores showed that even though the experimental manipulations did affect the various groups differently (see Chapter 7), the patterning of items in the various groups was essentially the same. We felt, therefore, that it was justified to use the combined post-experimental data from all subjects as a basis for factor scores.

The groupings of items resulting from these C–S factors were used to calculate factor scores for each subject on both value and expectation. Factor scores were calculated for smokers and for the random sample of non-smokers.

Table 27 gives the factor matrix and Table 28 a summary of the content of the items in each scale for the smokers. Fifty-five percent of the variance is accounted for by five factors with theoretical significance. The two most important factors are concerned with the utility of the effect on health from continuing to smoke and of the effect of stopping smoking on ability to reduce tension. The remaining three factors concern attitudes towards self and anticipation of friends' attitudes should the subject smoke or not smoke ("Self-image"), the utility of having something to affect mood ("Mood"), and the utility of greater pleasure from sensory stimulation due to the increased sensitivity experienced by the ex-smoker ("Hedonic-Aesthetic").

Separate scores for value and expectancy were calculated from the subjects' responses to the relevant items grouped under each of the factors. Each subject's SEU test yielded ten scores, five indicating the *value* he placed on each set of outcomes of smoking or not smoking (Ill-Health, Tension Reduction, etc.) and five indicating his expectation that continuing to smoke or stopping would make a difference in the *likelihood of occurrence* of these outcomes (i.e., Ill-Health, Tension Reduction, etc.), the Continue minus Stop (C–S) scores.

Factor scores were computed by summing the ratings for the individual items in each factor, and dividing by the number of items. For the value scales, in which the original scores ranged from −5 (high negative value) to +5 (high positive value), the average rating was multiplied by ten. For the expectancy scales the basic rating, chances in 100, was not modified. The Continue minus Stop scores thus range from −100 to +100. A positive C–S score means that the subject expected the outcome to be more likely should he stop smoking (or, for non-smokers, continue not to smoke) than if he should continue to smoke (or, for non-smokers, begin smoking). A negative C–S score indicates that the subject expects the outcome to be *less* likely should he stop smoking.

Table 29 gives mean factor scores on values and expectancies for smokers and non-smokers. The data on smokers will be discussed first; contrasts between smokers and non-smokers will be presented below.

It is hardly surprising that being short of breath, coughing, suffering from emphysema, lung cancer, heart disease, and "living a shorter life span than average"

TABLE 28

Summary of Factor Analysis of Expectancy for Various Outcomes of Continuing or Ceasing to Smoke (187 Male College Students)

Loadings[†]	Items with Loadings Above .35
	Factor 1: Ill Health — 13% of total variance
—	Live longer than average
+	Short of breath
+	Getting lung cancer
+	Getting heart disease
+	Getting emphysema
+	Cough in morning
	Factor 2: Tension Reduction — 15% of total variance
+	Being nervous
+	Feeling depressed
+	Being irritable
+	Being upset
—	Concentrating well
—	Studying well
—	Feeling like yourself
	Factor 3: Self-image — 11% of total variance
+	Feeling proud of yourself
+	Other smokers envious
+	Non-smokers respect
+	Looking "wrong" to friends
—	Tolerant of other people's smoking
—	Feel close to friends who smoke
	Factor 4: Mood — 8% of total variance
—	Have something to calm you
—	Something to perk you up
—	Something to relieve boredom
	Factor 5: Hedonic-Aesthetic — 13% of total variance
+	Enjoy meals
+	Home have pleasant odor
+	Have good appetite
+	Good taste in mouth
+	Feel good in morning
+	Have good sense of smell
+	Have pocket money

† "+" indicated positive, "—" negative, loadings for the scale on the individual factor.

were negatively valued by smokers. Similarly, they placed a negative value on being nervous, depressed, irritable, and unable to concentrate. In contrast they placed a positive value on having something to calm or stimulate themselves and enjoying meals, a sense of smell, an appetite, and having money. The sum total of "Self-image" items was neutral in value, but individual items showed a high value placed on "feeling proud of yourself" and "gaining the respect of non-smokers."

Smokers indicated moderate expectation that continuing to smoke would lead to illness and early death. They also expected that continuing to smoke would furnish stimulation and relief from boredom, and that stopping smoking might lead to feelings of pride as well as to greater sensitivity to the outside world.

Before any given set of values and expectancies can be used separately as predictors of behavior, the degree of independence between the two must be assessed. The pretest data from smokers showed no meaningful correlation between Value and Continue-Stop scores for each factor; thus these two components of psychological utility may be treated independently of each other.

TABLE 29
Factor Scores on the Test of SEU for Outcomes of Smoking or Not Smoking (248 Male College Students)

Factor	Value[†]					Expectancy (continue-stop)[††]				
	Smokers (N=187)		Non-smokers (N=61)			Smokers (N=187)		Non-smokers (N=61)		
	Mean	S.D.	Mean	S.D.	F	Mean	S.D.	Mean	S.D.	F
Ill-Health	−3.70	1.1	−4.00	0.8	4.38*	24.0	15	37.0	17	34.89**
Tension Reduction	−3.60	0.9	−3.60	0.9	0.01	− 7.0	14	13.0	13	93.62**
Self-image	0.04	0.8	0.06	0.7	0.05	−10.0	12	−12.0	11	0.75
Mood	2.60	1.4	1.50	1.6	24.83**	11.0	17	0.3	16	18.65**
Hedonic-Aesthetic	3.30	1.1	3.80	1.4	7.15**	−11.0	11	−27.0	16	93.06**

[†]*Values on a scale from −5 to +5,* [††]*Mean expectancy (continue-stop) on scale from −100 to +100 positions.*
$* p < .05$, $** p < .01$.

Personality and patterns of support for smoking. The term "measures of personality" describes loosely a variety of tests of consistencies of behavior. Presumably these consistencies, or traits, can be made the basis for inferences about mediating systems, the entries in the brackets in Fig. 1 (see Chapter 1), which represent our ideas about "events in the head." If the various patterns of support for smoking are also traits, it becomes theoretically interesting to see to what extent "personality" traits and "smoking" traits are associated. Our data were examined for such associations by studying the correlations among our four measures of personality and each of the scores from the Test of Patterns of Support (Table 30).

1. Risk-Taking: Correlational analysis showed no relation between scores on this test and the factor scores on the Test of Patterns of Support. However,

when three groups are created, one consisting of smokers above the mean for a given pattern of support, a second of smokers below the mean, and a third of non-smokers, a significant gradient of Kogan-Wallach scores is found for six of the eight scales (see Table 31). The nature and implications of these differences will be discussed below.

TABLE 30

Correlations between Factor Scores on Test of Patterns of Support for Smoking and Measures of Individual Characteristics (187 Male College Students)

Support	I/E	Social Desirability	MAS
Tension Reduction	.14*	−.20**	.37**
Pleasure	.09	.09	−.14*
Social Self-image	.04	−.05	.25**
Habit-Self-image	.05	−.24**	.39**
Social Stimulation to Smoking	−.03	−.20**	.24**
Psychological Addiction	.11	−.13	.26**
Stimulation	.07	−.11	.25**
Sensory Motor	.03	.04	.16*

* $p < .05$, ** $p < .01$.

2. Internal/External orientation: There was a very low, barely significant correlation between I/E scores and tendency to smoke for the reduction of tension. The relation is so tenuous that it should be replicated before being discussed. I/E scores were not related in any way to any of the other scales.

3. Social Desirability (Crowne-Marlowe test): The greater a subject's desire to present a good picture of himself, the less likely he is to report that he smokes to reduce tension, because he is with other smokers, or that his self-image is that of an habitual smoker (see Table 30). Several other scales are also negatively correlated, but not significantly. The pattern seems to indicate that the smoker with low Social Desirability scores is more likely than one whose scores are high to smoke in order to fulfill needs. For the former the particular need varies with the individual, producing three low-level but significant correlations with different scales on the Test of Patterns of Support. The smoker with high Social Desirability is likely to resemble McKennell's consonant smoker (1968), someone for whom smoking is relatively free of important motivational significance.

The negative correlations of the measure of social desirability with the scores on the Test of Patterns of Support also suggest that agreeing with the relevance of the items in the latter test to the subjects' own smoking is not a result of ingratiating tendencies, unless one interprets a rejection of the psychological significance of smoking as an attempt to "look good."

4. Manifest Anxiety Scale (MAS): Of all the measures of personality used, this scale showed the most consistent relations with the various scores on the Test of Patterns of Support. Anxiety was negatively associated with the tendency to smoke for pleasure, positively associated with all of the other scales. Two of

these associations are readily interpretable; the higher the level of anxiety among the subjects the more likely they were to report smoking to reduce tension or in response to craving. These associations could be based on nothing more than a response tendency, a generalized willingness to assent to propositions about tension and trouble. The content of the MAS and of the sections of the Test of Patterns of Support concerned with tension reduction and craving are certainly similar. However, there is evidence from the open-ended material in our other studies (see especially Study IV) that the Test of Patterns of Support really reflects the emotional rewards of smoking. If it does, then we can conclude that, while anyone might choose to use cigarettes to ease emotional stress, anxious smokers are more likely than non-anxious smokers to do so.

The remainder of the positive associations between MAS and scores on the Test of Patterns of Support may be related to the function of the MAS as a measure of general drive level, the function assigned to it in the original formulation by Taylor (1953). If the MAS is an indicator of generalized drive, then it could be predicted that subjects high in drive would tend to smoke to fulfill a variety of needs, whereas those low in drive would smoke for purely hedonic satisfactions.

The "personality of the smoker." As we indicated above, the notion that smokers have a unique combination of personality traits impressed us as specious. In an earlier study we found a significant difference in mean scores on the Taylor Manifest Anxiety Scale between smokers and non-smokers (Mausner & Platt, 1966a), but the marked overlap in the distributions made it absurd to characterize smokers as "anxious," non-smokers as "not anxious." Similarly, in the current study we also found significant differences on many of the personality tests when smokers as a group were compared with non-smokers.

Smokers were significantly higher in risk-taking tendencies, marginally higher in I/E scores, slightly lower in the Crowne-Marlowe social desirability scale, and significantly higher in the Taylor MAS. However, when the smokers were divided into groups above and below the mean for each of the scales of the Test of Patterns of Support (Table 31), the picture which emerged was quite incompatible with the concept of "the personality of the smoker."

We noted earlier that anxiety, as measured by the Taylor MAS, is correlated with almost all of the scales on the Test of Patterns of Support. Comparison of smokers above and below the mean on each of the scales with non-smokers indicated that those smokers for whom most of the Patterns of Support were relatively unimportant (i.e., who were below the mean) showed anxiety levels almost identical with those of non-smokers. Those for whom smoking was related to the reduction of tension, to the maintenance of self-concept, or to the establishment of a social identity were significantly higher in anxiety levels than non-smokers. In contrast, smokers who were *above* the mean on Pleasure resembled non-smokers, although the latter set of differences is marginal.

It is conceivable that any smoker could rely on cigarettes as an energizer, as a source of comfort during periods of stress, or as a support for his self-

TABLE 31

Individual Characteristics of Non-smokers and of Smokers Above and Below Mean on Supports for Smoking[†] (248 Male College Students)

	MAS		Risk	
	Mean	S.D.	Mean	S.D.
Tension Reduction				
Smokers below mean	15	8	47	7
Smokers above mean	22	8	45	7
Non-smokers	16	8	43	8
F[††]	16.38**		5.11**	
Social Self-image				
Smokers below mean	17	9	47	7
Smokers above mean	20	8	45	8
Non-smokers	16	8	43	8
F[††]	7.53**		5.22**	
Habit-Self-Image				
Smokers below mean	16	8	46	7
Smokers above mean	21	8	46	8
Non-smokers	16	8	43	8
F[††]	12.49**		2.89	
Social Stimulation to Smoking				
Smokers below mean	16	9	47	8
Smokers above mean	20	8	45	7
Non-smokers	16	8	43	8
F[††]	9.82**		4.32*	
Psychological Addiction				
Smokers below mean	17	8	47	7
Smokers above mean	20	8	46	8
Non-smokers	16	8	43	8
F[††]	6.65**		3.15*	
Stimulation				
Smokers below mean	17	8	47	7
Smokers above mean	20	8	45	8
Non-smokers	16	8	43	8
F[††]	6.56**		4.38*	
Sensory Motor				
Smokers below mean	18	8	47	7
Smokers above mean	19	9	46	8
Non-smokers	16	8	43	8
F[††]	3.68*		3.30*	
Pleasure				
Smokers below mean	20	8	46	7
Smokers above mean	18	9	47	8
Non-smokers	16	8	43	8
F[††]	3.70*		3.23*	

[†]*Smokers were split above and below the mean on factors derived from the Test of Patterns of Support for Smoking. Analysis of variance was based on comparison among three groups: smokers above the mean on the given pattern of support, smokers below the mean, and non-smokers,* [††] *df = 2,245. * p < .05. ** p < .01.*

concept. But people who are generally tense or hypochondriacal are more likely to see their smoking as fulfilling these functions than those who are not. This point has already been made above; the treatment reported in Table 31 adds the fact that smokers who do not use cigarettes to fulfill important psychological needs resemble non-smokers in manifest anxiety levels.

A similar analysis was carried out with the measure of risk-taking tendencies. Although the difference in risk-taking scores between the group of smokers as a whole and the non-smokers was significant, it was substantively small. When the smokers were divided into those above and below the mean on the various scales of the Test of Patterns of Support, smokers below the mean on six of the eight factor scores described themselves on the test as risk takers; subjects above the mean on these six scales resembled non-smokers in risk-taking tendencies. Apparently, people for whom powerful affective, social-affiliative, or role-defining needs are fulfilled by smoking are not necessarily risk takers. Those who continue to smoke despite the fact that it does not fill important needs *are* risk takers; the Pleasure and the Self-image-Habit factors do not generate differences among non-smokers and smokers high or low on these factors.

Although the three groups showed scattered differences in internal-external control and "social desirability," these were too small and too inconsistent to warrant interpretation.

TABLE 32

Correlation of Scores on the Test of Patterns of Support for Smoking and on Subjective Expected Utility of Smoking (187 Male College Students)

Subjective Expected Utility	Tension Reduct.	Pleas.	Social Self-image	Habit-Self-image	Social Stim.	Psych. Addic.	Stim.	Sensory Motor
Value:								
Ill-Health	−0.01	0.04	0.03	−0.03	−0.06	0.00	−0.04	0.02
Tension Reduction	0.00	−0.08	0.02	0.07	−0.08	0.08	−0.01	0.09
Self-image	0.17	0.00	−0.02	−0.03	0.05	0.00	−0.01	−0.02
Mood	0.33**	0.10	0.05	0.04	0.04	0.12	0.22*	−0.17
Hedonic-Aesthetic	0.05	0.06	0.01	−0.06	0.06	0.00	0.01	−0.04
Expectancy:								
Ill-Health	0.07	−0.11	0.04	0.22*	0.12	0.14	0.05	−0.02
Tension Reduction	−0.32**	−0.39**	−0.10	−0.06	0.07	−0.21*	−0.36**	−0.06
Self-image	−0.09	0.15	−0.10	−0.09	−0.19*	−0.20*	0.00	0.01
Mood	0.45**	0.29**	0.18	0.03	0.01	0.18	0.29**	0.01
Hedonic-Aesthetic	−0.04	0.21*	−0.04	−0.21*	−0.28**	−0.14	0.11	−0.05

*p < .05, **p < .01.

Supports for smoking and utilities. The measures of values were completely unrelated to scores on the various patterns of support for smoking; only 2 of the 40 possible correlations were significant (Table 32). For example, there was no association between the value subjects placed on the reduction of tension (SEU) and the degree to which they used cigarettes to reduce tension (patterns of support). This is understandable; after all there are other ways of reducing tension. Interestingly, the only significant correlations between values and patterns of support were for "mood." Subjects who placed a high value on being stimulated tended to report using cigarettes for this purpose. However, the correlations, although significant, were low and do not contradict the notion that valuing any given end does not necessarily commit a person to any one way of achieving it.

In contrast, there were a good many significant correlations between measures of expectancy and patterns of support. The expectancy measure, it should be remembered, indicates the degree to which the subject believes that continuing to smoke or stopping will make a difference in the probability that a given outcome will be achieved. Thus, subjects who smoke for the reduction of tension were fairly consistent in the belief that they would face difficulties in handling tension should they stop smoking, that they would find it hard to achieve the same level of enjoyment, that they would be bothered by craving, and that they would feel a need for stimulation. The associations are consonant with our ecological model. Ideas about smoking, i.e., expectations, are, at least in part, a function of the role played by the cigarette in the life of the smoker.

TABLE 33
Subjective Expected Utility (SEU) for Outcomes of Smoking or Not Smoking: Comparison of Smokers and Non-smokers (196 Male College Students)

	SEU Scores				
Scale††	Smokers (N=135†) Mean	Non-smokers (N=61) Mean	F	Smokers and Non-smokers Lowest Score	Highest Score
Continue (or Begin)					
Mean	937	433	17.5**	−1140	+4070
S.D.	705	925			
Stop (or Continue Non-smoking)					
Mean	1244	1572	7.6**	−620	+2800
S.D.	680	935			
Continue-Stop					
Mean	−306	−1138	76.4**	−3000	+2400
S.D.	572	671			

** $p < .01$. †*Includes only men who actually participated in the experiment.* ††*In all three scales Value X 10 (−50 to +50) is multiplied by Expectancy (0 to 100 for Continue and Stop; −100 to +100 for Continue-Stop.*

Comparison of smokers and non-smokers on Subjective Expected Utility (SEU).
Smokers were asked to assess the utility of continuing to smoke or stopping.
Non-smokers were asked to evaluate *starting* to smoke or continuing not to
smoke. It is possible to compare the two groups on the utility of maintaining
their current status, on the absolute utility of a new status (i.e., not smoking for
smokers and smoking for non-smokers), and on the utility of change in status.

Non-smokers and smokers differed markedly (Table 33) on all three comparisons. As compared with non-smokers, smokers valued the effects of smoking
more highly and had a greater expectation that these effects would be achieved.
Interestingly enough, and consistent with the widely held belief that smoking is
dangerous, smokers had even more positive SEU (i.e., the product of value and
expectation) for not smoking. However, the difference in SEU between not
smoking and smoking was relatively small for smokers, large for non-smokers.
The distributions of these scores showed little overlap between the two groups
(Fig. 3). Smokers clearly cared less about a change in their status than non-
smokers. If SEU is related to behavior, one would predict that very few of the
non-smokers are ever likely to smoke. And, in fact, to anticipate our long-range
follow-up (Chapter 7), none of the non-smokers began to smoke during the nine-
month interval between the pretest and follow-up surveys.

The factor scores on the test of SEU, which are based on a grouping of
items identified by means of factor analysis, provide measures of the major components of the test. These scores (see Table 29) tell something of the nature of

FIGURE 3
Comparison of Smokers and Non-smokers among Male College Students
on the Difference in Subjective Expected Utility
Between Smoking and Not Smoking

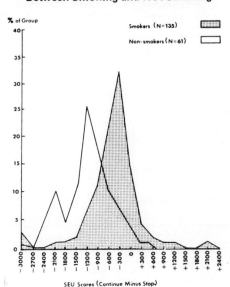

SEU Scores (Continue Minus Stop)

the differences in beliefs between smokers and non-smokers. The average scores indicate highly significant differences between smokers and non-smokers on the *expectation* that continuing to smoke will affect health. The difference in the negative value placed on being ill, although statistically significant, is negligible. Similarly, there is a highly significant difference in the *expectation* that the subject will be able to stay calm and collected (Mood) if he maintains or changes his smoking status even though the *value* placed on tension reduction is virtually identical. Smokers were more likely than non-smokers to expect that their smoking would provide stimulation and would not affect their ability to enjoy various sensual pleasures; here the values also differ, with smokers placing somewhat higher value on obtaining stimulation and slightly lower value on the hedonic-aesthetic outcomes than non-smokers.

Items not used in the factor scores show the same patterns as those manifested by the factor scores (Table 34). Of the 11 items examined, smokers differed from non-smokers in value only in three: they cared less about having new friends who might be non-smokers, about the likelihood that their children would smoke, and about being a slave to habit. But they differed significantly on 10 of the 11 items relating to expectation. In general, therefore, the marked differences between smokers and non-smokers in subjective expected utility are due primarily to differences in expectation of achieving a variety of outcomes rather than in the value placed on them.

TABLE 34

Differences between Smokers and Non-smokers on Items of Test of SEU Not Included in Factors (247 Male College Students)

Items	Value[†]			Expectancy (C-S)[††]		
	Smokers (N=187)	Non-smokers (N=60)	t	Smokers (N=187)	Non-smokers (N=60)	t
Enjoy coffee	1.80	1.81	0.03	10	−13	6.22**
New friends will be non-smokers	−0.02	0.63	3.93**	0	−2	0.89
Being energetic	3.62	3.73	0.57	−12	−20	2.53*
Getting along with your friends	4.60	4.23	0.80	0	5	3.01**
Clothes in good condition	4.02	3.97	0.26	−1	−9	5.48**
Teeth & fingers stained	−3.15	−3.65	1.78	37	47	2.04*
Care whether children smoke	−2.18	−3.08	3.09**	18	34	5.26**
Gain noticeable weight	−1.32	−0.68	1.17	−23	−12	3.19**
Being slave to habit	−2.69	−4.12	5.39**	26	43	3.66**
Enjoy alcohol	2.47	1.97	1.47	10	−9	6.39**
Something to do with your hands	2.25	1.82	1.60	−19	−7	2.83**

*p <.05, ** p <.01.[†] *Value on a scale from −5 to +5,* [††]*Expectancy on a scale from −100 to +100.*

One difference between the smokers and non-smokers is that, for the latter, values and expectancies *are* correlated; scale scores for value on each of the factors are negatively correlated with those for expectations; for smokers, value and expectation are unrelated. The correlations among non-smokers range from −.42 for Ill-Health to −.15 for Mood. Apparently for a group to whom the act of smoking itself is alien, the more negatively valued the results of smoking, the larger the expectancy scores, i.e., the greater the expectation that smoking would really make a difference to health, feeling of pride in self, etc. In contrast, for the smokers, to many of whom unresolved dissonance may be a way of life, the value placed on health, pride in oneself, etc., seems unrelated to the expectation that smoking will affect these aspects of their lives.

The differences in expectancy between smokers and non-smokers are not at all unexpected but they indicate that, whether as dissonance reduction for smokers or as self-justification for non-smokers, the two groups give appropriate patterns of replies on a measure of the utilities attached to smoking.

Summary of Study V. Each of the three goals set for this study was met to a considerable extent. The first was the delineation of the character of patterns of support for smoking. The responses of 187 male college students on the Test of Patterns of Support were subjected to factor analysis. The factors which emerged paralleled those found by Horn and Waingrow in their analysis of the affective supports for smoking. Additional items not used by Horn and Waingrow formed factors related to social supports for smoking and to the use of smoking for the definition of the smoker's self-image. The social supports turned out to be more complex than originally assumed; two factors emerged, one related to social stimulation to smoking and the other to a sense of identification with other smokers.

The second goal was the establishment of the validity of a measure of the subjective expected utility of continuing to smoke or stopping. The internal consistency of the components of the scale was established through factor analysis. The validity of the measure of SEU was demonstrated by comparison of smokers with non-smokers. As one would expect from the nature of subjective expected utility, smokers showed more positive evaluations of smoking and less positive evaluations of cessation than non-smokers. Lastly, the relations among several personality traits and patterns of support were examined through comparisons of non-smokers with smokers reporting varying levels of each of the patterns of support. The group of smokers as a whole did not show unique characteristics. Knowledge of patterns of support was found to be essential for the interpretation of differences in personality between smokers and non-smokers. Thus, subjects who used smoking for the relief of tension were generally more anxious than non-smokers. In contrast, smokers who did not use smoking for the relief of tension gave a distribution of scores on the test of generalized anxiety similar to that shown by non-smokers.

Summary and Discussion
of Part I

This volume opened with the formulation of an ecological model for the study of the natural history of smoking behavior. The formulation specifies environmental forces as physical, biological, and social. The interaction among these provides inputs to the individual, within whom a number of mediating systems, both physiological and psychological, are in operation. Behavior may be a response to intrinsic forces alone or, more usually, to these forces in interaction with external influences. Environmental factors affect behavior only when they are potentiated by appropriate mediating systems within the individual. Thus, smokers with a high need for affiliation should smoke primarily when others are smoking and would find smoking rewarding because it gives them a feeling of closeness and warmth. Similarly, smokers who are anxious should smoke when they are under stress and should report that smoking is an effective source of relief for anxiety. People who feel uncertain over identity should rely on smoking to help establish a self-concept more than those with a strong sense of identity.

This series of hypotheses does not preclude the possibility that smoking plays some role in supporting feelings of social cohesion, in reducing tension, or in rounding out a repertory of self-defining behaviors for people for whom these psychological problems are not acute. Nor does it suggest that it would *always* be possible to relate extra- and intra-individual determinants of smoking behavior. In addition, this formulation does not imply that operation of any one of these mechanisms for maintaining smoking precludes the existence of the others; they can occur side by side to different degrees within the same person. However, examination of naturalistic observations and introspective reports on smoking from groups of smokers should show trends compatible with the formulations based on the ecological model. The following discussion will examine the degree to which the data of Studies I-V may be used to support this model.

Social Factors

All of the studies confirm the well-known observation that a great deal of smoking is stimulated by the smoking of others. However, this is not the totality of our concept of the social support for smoking. Our hypothesis was that smoking would also act to increase the cohesiveness of groups and to enhance the sense of identification of individuals with fellow smokers.

We examined evidence for the thesis that smoking promotes social identification in a number of different ways. In Study IV the young women who kept diaries indicated that individual cigarettes increased their feeling of closeness to other smokers more frequently during organized social activity than in casual contacts with friends. However, the retrospective accounts of smoking in the first two studies gave relatively little evidence of an impact of smoking on the sense of group belongingness. In contrast, a high proportion of both samples of college students identified as relevant to their own smoking (Studies IV and V) items reflecting the use of smoking for social identification, although there was little relation between the tendency to report increased smoking when stimulated by groups of smokers and a sense of identification with other smokers. This lack of relation is shown both in the independence of the Social Self-image and Social Stimulation factors on factor analysis and in the protocols from the diary study.

An hypothesis linking need for affiliation with social supports for smoking was sketched above. This was not confirmed for the one sample on which the hypothesis was tested, the group of women who completed diaries. There was no correlation between a projective measure of affiliative needs and a tendency to stress social factors in the maintenance of smoking in this group. The strongest confirmation for the tie between social stimulation to smoking and social affiliation comes from the sociometric data of Study III; smokers among female college students tended to choose other smokers, and non-smokers other non-smokers, as desired partners in a variety of activities related to work and to recreation.

Lastly, the low frequency with which social stimulation to smoking was reported by the high school and adult subjects in Studies I and II seems inconsistent with the rather high level at which social stimulation to smoking was reported by college students in Studies IV and V. The inconsistency may be due to the fact that college students do much of their smoking in an intensely social atmosphere in smokers' lounges, smokers' study rooms, and snack bars.

Smoking as a Source of Emotional Rewards

Our studies do not confirm Tomkins' original concept of types of smokers having idiosyncratic patterns of habitual smoking, positive affect, negative affect reduction, or psychological addiction. Tomkins' discussion seems to imply that each type of smoker has a characteristic pattern limited to one affective support. Virtually all the smokers in our studies, adolescent as well as adult, showed mixtures of different affective supports for smoking. This is incompatible with the notion of types. The possibility that affective supports form a cumulative scale was tested in several ways. The individual items relevant to affective support in the Test of Patterns of Support were tested for unidimensionality. No combination of these items yielded an acceptable Guttman scale. However, material from the open-ended protocols given by the adolescents and adults in Studies I and II and self-ratings from the interviews in Study IV did show highly consistent scaling patterns, as did dichotomized factor scores from the young men in Study V. It remains to be seen whether properly chosen individual items can be assembled to form a cumulative scale. In any event, although we feel that our original concept of an affective dimension has some merit, we shall discuss separately our data relevant to each of the individual patterns of support.

Habit. Horn and Tomkins both describe habitual smoking as affectively neutral. This is hard to reconcile with our data. The adult men in their retrospective reports often wrote the word "habit" as a "reason for smoking" for cigarettes they "wanted most." While it is not clear precisely what they meant by "habit," it is unlikely that "wanted most" indicated affective neutrality. In both samples of college students (Studies IV and V), the items referring to habit, i.e., "smoking without realizing you have a cigarette in your mouth," were tied on factor analysis to items dealing with self-concept as a "smoker." Further, many of the adult men who labeled much of their smoking "habit," considered that "the real me" should be photographed with a cigarette. This suggests that being a smoker is an integral part of their self-image.

It is possible that there is a kind of smoking which genuinely is emotionally neutral. However, in the descriptive reports of smoking which we have gathered, the smoking which is cued off at a usual time of day by external stimuli associated with arising, eating, working, and driving largely had either affective or role-defining significance.

Smoking as a source of pleasure. Our adolescent subjects, both the high school and the college students, gave plentiful indication that a major source of support for their smoking was sheer unadulterated pleasure. While it is not clear precisely which aspects of cigarette smoking lead to this pleasurable feeling, the circumstantial descriptions of the results of smoking, as well as the answers on the Test of Patterns of Support, confirm the picture of smoking as a source of highly rewarding pharmacological and physical stimuli. Smokers describe both generalized pleasure and specific delight in the stimulating properties of cigarettes and in the "informational" character of the act of smoking. Even those smokers who gave many instances of tension reduction, or who identified themselves as being psychologically addicted, also described purely pleasurable aspects of smoking apart from the positive affect derived from tension reduction or relief from craving.

Tension reduction. The relation between ongoing anxiety, as measured by the Taylor MAS, and reports on the use of smoking for the reduction of tension provide the most striking evidence from our data for the ecological model described in the opening of Chapter 1. Smokers who use cigarettes to cut tension are significantly higher in MAS scores than those who do not. Furthermore, all of the samples in which it was possible to examine the interrelation of environmental and intrinsic factors cited tension reduction as a support for smoking more frequently in contexts which are probably tension inducing than in other contexts.

These findings confirm the fairly obvious hypothesis that external stress should lead to internal tension and thus trigger responses which have been reinforced previously because they reduced such tension. Unfortunately, the support afforded this hypothesis by retrospective accounts is weak; the association between external stress and tension reduction as a support for smoking may merely be the result of the subjects' attempts to report an internally consistent and logical picture of the universe. A more conclusive test of the hypothesis would come from careful and disinterested observation of naturally occurring smoking behavior or, even better, from experimental manipulation. If smokers placed under stress resorted to cigarettes, and the relief of tension via smoking could be demonstrated through physiological indicators, the hypothesis and the ecological model which suggested it would be solidly confirmed. The obdurate character of tension-reducing smoking and the lack of knowledge about alternate modes of easing reactions to stress among people who depend on cigarettes makes an understanding of the process of tension reduction practically as well as theoretically important.

It may be remembered that subjects in Study IV reported relatively few instances of the use of cigarettes to reduce tension, but described them very vividly; and during the interview many placed themselves above the midpoint on the scale of Tension Reduction. We explained this by positing that individual instances of tension reduction were probably rewarding to a degree out of proportion to their frequency. Had we been able to work with our subjects during periods of greater tension in their lives, the proportion of cigarettes actually used to reduce such tension probably would have been increased. The converse may also be true. The impact of such temporal variations in the use of cigarettes on responses to the relevant items of the Test of Patterns of Support remains to be assessed. Similar environmental fluctuations may affect other scales, notably those dealing with social factors.

Psychological addiction. There was relatively little evidence in the retrospective accounts from either adolescents or adults to confirm Tomkins' picture of addictive smoking. However, a fair number of the college-aged subjects accepted for themselves items in the Test of Patterns of Support which describe a craving for cigarettes not related to external sources of tension. Almost a quarter of the respondents in Study IV rated themselves above the midpoint on psychological addiction during the interview, even though there was virtually nothing in their diary protocols to support this assertion. It may be that a sense of psychological addiction, like the use of smoking to reduce externally caused tension, can be based on recollection of the rewards offered by a limited number of cigarettes. If this is true it may affect the success of attempts to change smoking behavior. Some smokers may hesitate even to attempt to abstain because they perceive themselves as dependent on cigarettes. Despite this, the actual remaking of their life patterns might not have to be as drastic as they fear. These issues will be discussed at greater length in Part II.

Smoking as Self-defining Behavior

Some of our data support the thesis that smoking is a central element in *some* smokers' repertory of role-defining behaviors. Most of the adult smokers we tested agreed that a picture of themselves *with* a cigarette showed "the real me"; a picture without a cigarette did not. A sizable minority of the college students completing the Test of Patterns of Support accepted a variety of items describing role-defining properties of cigarettes as relevant to their smoking. Somewhat more direct indication of the character of the role-defining action of smoking can be found in the adjectives cited by the respondents in Study IV in their diaries in response to the questions, "How did you look?" and "How did you feel?" In approximately one-quarter of the reports of individual instances of smoking described in the diaries, adjectives were used which were considered to indicate role definition by the social scientists who coded them. The degree to which the questions themselves may have speciously elicited role-defining content is hard to estimate.

Most investigators of smoking accept the importance to beginning smokers of the use of cigarettes to define and support the self-image. Our work indicates that it continues to be important throughout the lives of *some* smokers. Unfortunately, the techniques we have used are not ideally suited to substantiate fully this concept. Projective approaches of the kind used by Weir (1967) might elucidate further the strength of role-defining tendencies and the nature of the self-concepts for which smoking is expressive behavior.

Cognitive Supports for Smoking and the Concept of the "Personality of the Smoker"

The formulations presented above show smoking as being supported by a combination of external pressures and interior needs; these join together to create a state of affairs in which the consumption of cigarettes is highly reinforced. It is likely that a large part of this support could not readily be described in verbal terms by many smokers. However, the evidence of the Test of Subjective Expected Utility is that many smokers can state quite clearly the degree to which their smoking is supported by the confirmation of expectations that valued ends will be achieved. These ends vary from smoker to smoker. The values placed upon these ends do not differ markedly between smokers and non-smokers. What keeps the habit going is that cigarette smokers have a strong and regularly reinforced expectation that pleasure, or the reduction of tension, or the growth of good fellowship, will be derived from the use of cigarettes. Reinforcing these is the expectation on the part of smokers that continuing to smoke does not really threaten their own health, their sense of self-esteem, or their ability to lead comfortable and attractive lives.

The failure to find consistently meaningful differences in personality between smokers as a group and non-smokers confirms the notion that smokers' traits and psychological dynamics are not necessarily unique. What is unique about smokers is the *way* in which they choose to fulfill their needs, whatever they may be. For smokers with different constellations of personality, smoking fulfills particular needs consonant with their own personality characteristics.

The procedures described in Part I of this volume permit specification of the character of the interaction among three kinds of variables: patterns of support for smoking, beliefs about the consequences of smoking, and personality. They provide useful tools with which to understand the response of smokers to attempts to persuade them to give up this highly rewarding but dangerous behavior.

Part II
The Use of Role Playing to Induce Change in Smoking

4

Changes in Smoking Behavior: Reduction and Cessation

A full understanding of smoking as a behavioral complex requires that reduction and cessation as well as initiation and maintenance be studied. Undoubtedly, many smokers either cut down or stopped smoking for a variety of reasons even before the threat to health was known. However, now that cigarette smoking is recognized as a serious hazard, the study of reduction and cessation is of more than academic interest. Part II of this volume will, therefore, be devoted to these problems. First we will present a theoretical analysis of change and an examination of some of the relevant experimental literature. We will then (Chapters 5-8) describe the results of a study in which we used role playing to induce change in smoking.

The experimental approaches to be analyzed in this chapter will be limited to those in which behavioral rather than pharmacological manipulations are central. Therefore, we will not deal with the techniques of Ejrup (1965) and others for inducing cessation with the use of drugs such as the lobeline derivatives. Since we will emphasize experimental investigations we will not discuss or evaluate the many programs, sponsored by voluntary or official agencies in the field of health, designed to inform the public of the dangers of smoking or to assist smokers trying to stop.

A framework for the study of change. It became evident early in our work on change in smoking that three separate but interrelated processes would have to be analyzed before either reduction or cessation could be understood (Mausner in Mausner & Platt, 1966b). The first of these processes is change in attitudes, the development of knowledge about the ill effects of smoking and of negative feelings towards smoking. The second process is decision, a process inferred from verbal and other cues about the smoker's evaluation of alternative courses of action and consequent choices. The third is behavioral change. Here the criterion is overt behavior, reported smoking levels, rather than verbalization of intentions. An analysis of this third process, i.e., change in smoking levels, permits an assessment of the contribution to change of environmental forces, of intra-individual forces related to the processes of attitudinal change and decision, and of other factors within the individual. The remainder of this chapter is devoted to an exploration of these three processes as a prelude to the presentation of our empirical study of change.

ATTITUDINAL CHANGE

Most social psychologists would define attitudes as consisting of two components: cognitive elements, i.e., knowledge or belief, and affective elements, i.e., values or feelings. These are linked to create an attitude towards a given object. For example, the United Nations helps keep the peace (belief or opinion); keeping the peace is good (value and feeling). Together these elements form a favorable attitude. The United Nations is a source of Communist influence (belief); Communism is bad (value and feeling). A person with such beliefs and feelings obviously has an unfavorable attitude.

Attitudinal change can occur either through alteration of knowledge or opinion, or through changes in feeling. The two processes are not necessarily linked, although some research has shown an interaction between the two, with either one capable of influencing the other (Rosenberg, 1960). What frequently happens is that a person acquires new information, incorporates this into a structure of opinion, and consequently alters his feelings. Of course, these steps do not inevitably follow upon one another. New information may or may not alter opinion and feelings.

Studies of attitude change may have two goals. The first is essentially academic; experimental analyses of the determinants of attitude change provide a major test of theoretical systems in social psychology. The second goal is a determination of the degree to which changes in attitude are associated with changes in nonverbal behavior. The latter goal becomes especially important in the study of attitudes towards smoking because of the necessity for solving the problems of ill health posed by cigarettes. Our first large-scale study of cigarette smoking was primarily devoted to the first goal but included data relevant to the second. It consisted of an investigation of attitudinal change as a function of variation in the character of an informational message and of the relation between attitudinal and behavioral change. Since the study has been reported in detail elsewhere (Mausner & Platt, 1966a), it will only be summarized here.

Information and Attitudinal Change: Study VI

We have already referred in Chapter 1 to the change in attitudes towards smoking from the high point of acceptance following World War II to its current disrepute. In 1964 a national sample which included smokers and non-smokers showed an almost universal awareness of the impact of smoking on health (Horn & Waingrow, 1966b). Nearly 70% of the smokers and 85% of the non-smokers agreed with the statement, "Smoking cigarettes is harmful to health." But only half the smokers were concerned about the effect of smoking on their *own* health.

It is likely that knowledge about the effects of smoking on health is even more widespread now than it was in 1964. The information about the threat to health from smoking has been disseminated by the mass media as well as by individual physicians, teachers, and other prestigious sources. The methods of spreading information have been chosen essentially by intuition; relatively little systematic inquiry has been directed towards identifying optimal ways of informing people of the threat or insuring that the information will lead to maximal change in attitudes and behavior.

One of the classical studies of this issue, i.e., the nature of the persuasive message which would most effectively sway attitudes towards smoking, was carried out by Horn in a number of high schools in Portland, Oregon (Horn, 1960). Horn conducted a controlled study in which the effect of smoking on health was presented in a variety of ways. These included messages emphasizing the meaning of smoking to the smoker's current health and to his long-range chances for survival. Other messages included statements by authoritative sources, a two-sided communication, and an attempt to induce students to persuade their parents not to smoke. The "remote" approach, which stressed the long-range dangers of smoking, had the greatest effect both on attitudes and on the rate of recruitment of new smokers. However, Cresswell et al. (1967) in a replication of the Portland study, found that a "contemporary" approach which focused on the immediate impact of smoking on the health of high school students, was more effective than the "remote" approach. As usual, it is hard to know whether the difference in findings is due to changes in values or in knowledge over the passage of time, to differences in the populations studied, or to subtle differences in the experimental procedures.

Background for a study on the use of programmed learning to change attitudes. As Leventhal has pointed out in his survey of the use of mass communication to change attitudes towards smoking (Leventhal, 1968), most of the attempts to saturate either communities or schools with information using conventional techniques of health education have had little impact on smoking. In Study VI we dealt with two possible reasons for these failures. The first was that people do not really attend carefully to mass communications. The second was that the information presented in mass campaigns is too general to be convincing. Most mass communications depend on slogans; they are perforce unable to present the chain of evidence leading to the conclusion that smoking is harmful.

To force subjects to attend carefully to a message about smoking, we used a Skinnerian linear program as the vehicle for information (Skinner, 1962). In Skinnerian programs, subjects are given a series of incomplete sentences, i.e., frames. The completion of the sentence should be fairly obvious (e.g., the opposite of black is_____). The subject is led to learn by making his own spontaneous reactions to the cues presented by the incomplete sentences. Since completing the sentences requires intellectual activity, the subject must attend to the content of the material with which he is working.

A limited test of an hypothesis concerning the effect of variation in the character of informational messages was carried out by contrasting two programmed messages with differing content. One program attempted to teach some basic ideas about drawing inferences from epidemiological evidence and then presented the evidence linking smoking with lung cancer. The other program sought to teach some rules for identifying trustworthy authorities and then cited a series of authoritative figures who have supported the cigarette smoking–lung cancer link. According to our hypothesis, the first of the programs should have greater long-range effect than the second.

Subjects and procedure. In order to test the hypotheses on groups other than the usual college students, subjects were drawn from three different populations: parents from the PTA of a local private school (120 in number), high school students attending the summer session of a suburban high school (63), and unemployed working-class adults with less than twelfth grade education making application for work at a state employment office (138). Both smokers and non-smokers were included. The study was presented to the subjects as a project in which new techniques in health education were being tested. At the outset the subjects were unaware that the issue was cigarette smoking. Although they had the option of not participating, the subjects were not volunteers in the usual sense; in all instances the contact was initiated by the research staff. Unemployed and high school subjects were paid; the middle-class group of adults worked in exchange for a donation to their PTA.

Immediately after they were recruited, subjects took the Holtzman Inkblot Test, the Taylor Manifest Anxiety Test, and a questionnaire on their smoking habits. On the following day, approximately 20 subjects at a time were brought together for the first experimental session. They were divided by random assignment into three groups, two experimental and one control, and the following tests were administered: (1) a 5-item Guttman scale measuring feelings about smoking (Horn, 1960), (2) a test of information about lung cancer and its relation to smoking, (3) a semantic differential on the concept "smoking cigarettes," (4) a questionnaire measuring opinions about the cause of lung cancer, (5) a programmed booklet containing the experimental message. One experimental group received a programmed message presenting the major *evidence* linking smoking and lung cancer. The second received a message identifying various scientific *authorities* who were convinced of the link. The control group received a program on procedures for the classification of animals. Subjects who reported unqualified acceptance of a causal relation between smoking and lung cancer on the questionnaire were eliminated from the sample. The measures of feelings, information, and opinion were repeated immediately after the completion of the teaching program.

In an effort to test the stability of change, subjects were recalled to receive one of two counterarguments which claimed that a causal link between smoking and lung cancer has not yet been established. One counterargument dealt with the evidence; it presented the notion that correlational findings cannot be used to prove causal relations. The other program presented the opinions of a number of presumably bona fide authorities who had expressed doubt about the link between smoking and lung cancer. The interval between the original learning and the counterargument was two weeks for the two adult groups. The high school sample returned for the retest after a longer interval, six weeks, because the end of the initial experiment coincided with the end of summer session and the group could not be reassembled until the start of the fall term.

Results. Among all three populations the initial level of information about the effects of smoking was low. Although virtually all subjects had a vague idea that smoking is related to lung cancer, few had any specific information about either the relation of the incidence of lung cancer to smoking levels (taught in the *Evidence* program) or the wide range of authorities in medicine and public health who accept the causal nature of the relation (taught in the *Authority* program).

The programs were technically adequate. Linear programs should be constructed so that the reader makes virtually no errors. In this we were successful; the average proportion of incorrect responses in the 140-frame programs ranged from 7% among the unemployed subjects to 4% in the high school and PTA groups. The material taught by the programs was retained, as indicated by a highly significant increase in correct responses on a 15-item test of information administered before and immediately after the programs. There was relatively little decrement in information during the period between the initial session and the return for the counterarguments. As expected, the control group in each population showed no changes.

In each of the three groups of subjects a large majority shifted towards acceptance not only of the thesis that smoking *is* implicated in lung cancer, but also that social action should be taken to discourage smoking. This change occurred after completion of either program. The change in opinion was greatest among those subjects who initially knew the least, the unemployed group. These alterations in opinion did not revert over the passage of time between the taking of the first program and the counterarguments. The major effect of the counterarguments was to lead subjects to say that "more research is needed."

In general, newly acquired information about both evidence and authority had less effect on feelings about smoking, as measured by Horn's 5-item cumulative scale, than on intellectual acceptance of the thesis that smoking is related to lung cancer. In each of the three groups, among those subjects who changed, significantly more shifted towards anti-smoking than towards pro-smoking positions on the scale measuring feelings. However, about one-third of the unemployed group and half of the other two groups showed no change. Neither of the counterarguments had much impact on feelings.

We compared the effects on attitudes of the two programs and of the subject's smoking status by means of a two-way analysis of covariance. The criterion measure was the subject's score on Horn's measure of feelings about smoking obtained *after* he had worked through the programmed material. The covariate was his score on this test *before* the exposure to the program. This analysis permits the assessment of relative change due to an experimental manipulation. Subjects were split into four groups (smokers vs. non-smokers, subjects taking the *Evidence* program vs. those taking the *Authority* program) to determine to what extent each of the variables, i.e., smoking status and program, affects change in feelings. In all three samples the two programs induced the same increase of negative feelings towards smoking. The changes were significantly greater among non-smokers than among smokers.

We included a second measure of attitudes to make sure that the effects noted in this experiment were not dependent on the peculiar characteristics of either of the measuring instruments. The semantic differential showed similar trends to those from the more conventional attitude test devised by Horn. Three kinds of scales were used on the semantic differential; the concept rated was "Smoking Cigarettes" and the scales included a series of pairs of adjectives related to evaluation (i.e., Good-Bad), to activity (i.e., Fast-Slow), and to potency (i.e., Strong-Weak). After the subjects had completed either program, they showed a significant, but slight, tendency to rate "Smoking Cigarettes" closer to *Bad* than *Good,* closer to *Fast* than *Slow,* and closer to *Strong* than *Weak* as compared with the first administration. This change makes sense; an activity which is believed to cause lung cancer is more likely to be perceived as bad, strong, and quick than one which is seen as a harmless diversion.

Finally, we examined the effect of programmed learning on smoking levels, as reported by the subjects on their return to receive the counterargument. There was virtually no change. Approximately the same number of subjects increased and decreased; most did not change at all. This happened despite the fact that most subjects indicated increased acceptance of the association between cigarette smoking and lung cancer and *of the necessity for generalized anti-smoking activity* and that a sizable proportion showed more negative feelings about smoking than before they had acquired their new knowledge. And there was no relation between change in any of the measures of attitude and changes in smoking behavior.*

Discussion of Study VI. The results of this study seem to support Festinger's thesis (1964) that attitudinal change rarely *leads* directly to action. There is no question that a wide variety of subjects did learn and that the cognitive component of their attitudes did change. But their behavior, i.e., the number of cigarettes they smoked, did not. However, on the basis of this study one should not conclude that learning would never lead to changes in behavior. Perhaps with different kinds of information or with different populations informative messages which were well learned would affect behavior.

The reports in the literature about the effect of information on behavior are inconsistent. Briney (1966) found that girls who had information about the effects of smoking on health were less likely to smoke than those who did not; there was no such link among boys. And in both Horn's original Portland study (1960) and Creswell's replication (Creswell *et al.,* 1967) a reduction in rate of

---

*Detailed presentation of the data from this study was not included in this volume. The programmed materials, tests, and tables with the findings are available in our report to the Public Health Service (Mausner & Platt, 1966a).

recruitment of new smokers *was* found to result from some of the informational campaigns, although, as has been noted, the particular message which worked was not the same in the two studies. However, there is no way of knowing whether reduction in recruitment was due to the informational content of the campaigns or the very existence of anti-smoking programs and the social pressures they generated. The only possible verdict about the effectiveness of information is the Scottish "not proven."

Insights from Dissonance Theory

One of the most important influences in experimental social psychology in the past decade and a half has been the assumption of a basic human drive towards "cognitive balance." Simply put, the drive towards cognitive balance is based on a supposed abhorrence of inconsistency, a tendency on the part of all human beings to want to maintain consonance among their various systems of belief. Presumably, if a person is exposed to new information which is not consonant (i.e., is dissonant) with what he already knows, he is put into a state of tension which can be reduced by changing his previous pattern of beliefs or by rejecting the new ideas. This set of assumptions about cognitive balance was first stated by Heider (1958) and developed into formal theories of attitude change by Osgood and Tannenbaum (1955), Rosenberg and Abelson (in Rosenberg *et al.,* 1960), and others. The most influential formulation was that of Festinger (1957), whose theory of cognitive dissonance has been the starting point for a tremendous amount of research.

Cigarette smoking would seem to be a natural behavior for investigation designed to test the implications of dissonance theory. The smoker is almost a perfect illustration of a man in a state of cognitive dissonance; if he has the usual belief in the desirability of remaining alive and healthy, and if he values the rewards of smoking, then the widely circulated information about the impact of smoking on health must produce dissonance. And, indeed, Festinger aptly described the dilemma of the smoker in his first book on cognitive dissonance (1957, pp. 5-6):

> . . . let us now examine how dissonance may be reduced, using as an illustration the example of the habitual cigarette smoker who has learned that smoking is bad for his health. He may have acquired this information from a newspaper or magazine, from friends, or even from some physician. This knowledge is certainly dissonant with cognition that he continues to smoke. If the hypothesis that there will be pressures to reduce this dissonance is correct, what would the person involved be expected to do?
>
> 1. He might simply change his cognition about his behavior by changing his actions; that is, he might stop smoking. If he no longer smokes, then his cognition of what he does will be consonant with the knowledge that smoking is bad for his health.
>
> 2. He might change his 'knowledge' about the effects of smoking. This sounds like a peculiar way to put it, but it expresses well what must happen. He might simply end up believing that smoking does not have any deleterious effects, or he might acquire so much 'knowledge' pointing to the good effects it has that the harmful aspects become negligible. If he can manage to change his knowledge in either of these ways, he will have reduced, or even eliminated, the dissonance between what he does and what he knows.
>
> But in the above illustration it seems clear that the person may encounter difficulties in trying to change either his behavior or his knowledge. And this, of course, is pre-

cisely the reason that dissonance, once created, may persist. There is no guarantee that the person will be able to reduce or remove the dissonance. The hypothetical smoker may find that the process of giving up smoking is too painful for him to endure. He might try to find facts and opinions of others to support the view that smoking is not harmful, but these attempts might fail. He might then remain in the situation where he continues to smoke and continues to know that smoking is harmful. If this turns out to be the case, however, his efforts to reduce the dissonance will not cease.

The empirical studies which have been done to test Festinger's concepts have consisted of a search for evidence that smokers do, in fact, engage in a variety of attempts to reduce dissonance. Presumably dissonance between the idea that smoking is harmful and the idea that continued smoking is tolerable could be reduced if the smoker were to avoid contact with information about the effects of smoking on health or, in the event that he could not evade the issue, if he were to be skeptical of the evidence. The propaganda of the tobacco industry is readily available to any smoker who wishes to reduce dissonance by means of skepticism. Doubts about the effects of smoking on health are expressed in the press, in Congressional hearings, and in publications of the Tobacco Industry Research Committee, which is headed by a noted biologist, Dr. Clarence Cook Little. In addition, Sir Ronald Fisher, a famous statistician, and Dr. H. J. Eysenck, a well-known personality theorist, have discussed their reservations about the link between smoking and lung cancer. These reservations are based on the notion that correlation between smoking and illness does not necessarily imply causality, but rather that an underlying factor, presumably genetic, might predispose to smoking and, in some smokers, to disease. Furthermore, the cigarette industry has stressed the fact that there has been relatively little direct laboratory evidence about the effects of smoking on health, a point which is increasingly inaccurate (see especially the work by Auerbach cited in U.S. Public Health Service, 1968).

Of course, there are some ways of smoking which lower the level of risk. Many smokers reduce dissonance by translating diminution of risk into an illusion of total immunity from harm if they smoke lightly, do not inhale, or use low-tar and nicotine cigarettes or filters. Lastly, the low *absolute* risk of dying from lung cancer, even for heavy smokers, is always a comforting thought to those who are too knowledgeable to accept other forms of dissonance reduction but cannot or will not stop smoking.

There is very little systematic evidence concerning the relative frequency with which the dissonance-reducing maneuvers described above are actually used by smokers. However, there have been some limited investigations into the presence among smokers of several individual forms of dissonance reduction. One thesis is that smokers would avoid information about the smoking-lung cancer link ("I was so bothered by reading that smoking caused cancer that I gave up reading"). In a test of this thesis Feather (1962) gave both the smokers and the non-smokers among a group of college students a list of five magazine titles and asked the subjects to rank the articles in the order in which they would prefer to read them. There were four titles unrelated to smoking and two forms of a critical article. One form of the critical title stated that smoking is definitely a cause of lung cancer; the other form indicated that smoking may not lead to lung cancer. Smokers were more interested in the critical article than in those unrelated to smoking regardless of which form of the title was presented. In fact, smokers tended to be most interested if the article *opposed* their own point of view. That is, if they believed that smoking causes lung cancer their rankings showed interest in the title which expressed doubt about the relation; if they were not convinced that smoking causes lung cancer, they chose the title which upheld the relation. This experiment was replicated by Brock (1965) but with an added manipulation. Some subjects were given the titles in vacuo; others were faced by a pile of magazines and expected actually to read the articles they chose. Even under the latter circumstance there was no tendency for smokers to avoid material describing the hazard to health from smoking. As Brock points out, this result is consistent with a variety of studies showing that people do *not* usually avoid dissonant information.

In contrast, in a very ingenious experiment, Brock and Balloun (1967) discovered that smokers would work harder to eliminate static from a tape-recorded message opposing the smoking-cancer link than from a message supporting the relation. Non-smokers, in contrast, more frequently eliminated static from the message supporting the smoking-cancer relation. Thus smokers, at least in this group of college student subjects, did show selective attention to dissonance-reducing information.

As Festinger pointed out, another way for the cigarette smoker to reduce dissonance is to disbelieve the information that smoking is harmful. In our own work, reported earlier in this chapter, we failed to find a lower level of initial belief in the smoking-cancer link among smokers than non-smokers, although we did find consistently that smokers learned our programmed material less well than non-smokers and fewer of the smokers came back to our second experimental session. Lichtenstein's data (1967) support dissonance theory; in his work smokers among college students minimized the dangers of smoking and denied the scientific evidence relating smoking to lung cancer. In addition, they tended to reduce dissonance further by believing almost universally that they could stop smoking if they wanted to.

Denial of the validity of the evidence linking smoking to cancer probably requires a remarkable ability to filter out unwanted information. In a very interesting study Wolitzky (1967) shed some light on this process. He exposed a group of male college students, which included both smokers and non-smokers, to the Stroop experiment. In this, subjects are required to read aloud color names printed in a variety of colored inks. The experiment measures the degree of cognitive "restriction" or "flexibility" by noting the ease with which subjects can pronounce color names printed in differently colored inks. For example, a relative inability to read the word "red" printed in blue ink shows "cognitive restriction." Cognitively restricted subjects tended *not* to deny the cigarette-cancer link. Subjects who were able to resist the Stroop effect, i.e., who were "cognitively flexible," tended to deny the evidence linking smoking to lung cancer. This relation occurred among smokers at all levels of smoking; it did not occur among non-smokers. Wolitzky concludes that the tendency to reduce dissonance by denial seems to relate to a general ability to handle information about the outside world selectively.

There are two studies which did not find differences between smokers and non-smokers in formally stated beliefs about the harmfulness of smoking, but nonetheless show subtle evidences of dissonance reduction among smokers. Pervin and Yatko (1965) worked with smokers and non-smokers randomly drawn from the undergraduate student body at Princeton. The smokers and non-smokers did not differ in knowledge about the relationship between smoking and lung cancer, in attempts to minimize the dangers of smoking, in estimations of danger from cancer in the general population, or in tendencies to seek out relevant information about the dangers of smoking. However, the smokers, although admitting on an abstract level the serious danger from smoking, minimized the danger to themselves, reporting that they assumed their cigarette consumption was below the dangerous level or that a cure for lung cancer would be found before they became victims.

Similarly, in a survey of volunteers for a "health study" in England, Spelman and Levy (1966) reported that 92% of the smokers among their subjects did not differ significantly from non-smokers in ability to report the cause, symptoms, and treatment of lung cancer. However, when the subjects estimated the prognosis of 10 common diseases, including lung cancer, the dissonance-reducing behavior of heavy smokers emerged. Their judgments of prognosis for the nine other conditions were as accurate as those of non-smokers, but they *underestimated* the poor prognosis of lung cancer.

In general, the formulations of dissonance theory have not led to precise and testable hypotheses. As was evident from the very first statement by Festinger, almost any reaction by smokers which accompanied their continuing to smoke could be construed as leading to reduced dissonance. However, the focus on ways in which smokers try to achieve emotional comfort without giving up the rewards of smoking has certainly stimulated important investigations into the psychological aspects of smoking. In the section which follows we will explore the use of a decisional model which does not make assumptions about a universal human tendency to reduce cognitive unbalance.

DECISION

In the introduction to this chapter three processes were defined as relevant to change in cigarette smoking: attitudinal change, decision, and behavioral change. The word "decision" is used to refer to the assessment by an individual of the relative merits of one or another behavioral choice. This may mean a single set of events; upon exposure to new information an individual may react internally to make a choice which can be fixed in time and reported. Alternatively it may be a long drawn out process. For the smoker, a decision to change could be a quick reaction to a communication from a doctor or a long battle in which each cigarette represents a briefly fought and unhappily lost skirmish between knowledge and desire. For a smoker who is trying to stop, each moment of the day's routine in which he had previously smoked could require a brief replaying of the agonizing which preceded the original decision to quit.

Decision, attitudinal change, and behavioral change. The three processes seem to be relatively independent. As we found above, attitudinal change was possible without concomitant behavioral change. It is possible that decision to change could also occur in the absence of attitudinal change, i.e., after orders from a doctor. Or decision and attitudinal change may be inextricably related. Even if decision can occur without preceding or concomitant attitudinal change, it is possible that attitudinal change must inevitably *follow* upon the making of a decision. In fact, the newer version of dissonance theory (Brehm & Cohen, 1962; Festinger, 1964b) predicts that commitment will be followed by attitudinal change which creates a structure of beliefs consonant with the changed behavior.

Decision is not inevitably followed by *successful* modification of behavior; in fact, as the history of New Year's resolutions would suggest, it may not be followed by any implementation at all. Therefore, we shall treat decision as an inferred event, one of the elements inside the brackets in Fig. 1, independent of attitude *or* behavior. In so doing we shall specify observable behavior from which decision may be inferred in the hope of describing lawful interrelations of attitude, decision, and behavior.

A model for the study of decision. It has always been a part of folk wisdom that people will act to increase pleasure and diminish the likelihood of pain. A formal statement of this notion emerges with great clarity in the work of nineteenth-century utilitarian philosophers such as John Stuart Mill or economists such as Ricardo. The "economic man" they picture is fully knowledgeable about all possible outcomes of various courses of action, and able to choose in a rational way the outcome leading to the most desirable consequences. The naive notion implicit in this formulation was that the desirability of consequences was objectively determinable, and that it is the *objectively* most desirable outcome which is always chosen. As insights into human behavior developed through the growth of the social sciences, the unreal picture of economic man gave way to a more nearly recognizable human being, one who chooses among possibilities whose outcomes cannot always be forecast exactly, and whose choices are based on limited knowledge and, sometimes, on a somewhat less than rational weighing of alternatives.

Nevertheless, if one wants to predict decision, it should be possible to obtain from people some clue about the way in which they perceive the outcomes of alternative choices. It is not the objective likelihood of occurrence of various outcomes which matters; it is the way in which people perceive these outcomes. As indicated in our discussion of the test of Subjective Expected Utility (see Chapter 3), two kinds of variables are needed as a basis for inferences about that perception. The first of these is the subjective *value* placed on each of the consequences of any given choice. The second is the *expectation* of the likelihood of occurrence of each outcome. These two variables determine Subjective Expected Utility (SEU) much as objective value (i.e., dollars) and objective probability of occurrence (the frequency with which red comes up on a roulette wheel) determine the utility discussed by economists.

The measure of utility, whether objective or subjective, is the product of value and probability of occurrence. For subjective expected utility, a zero value indicates that an outcome has no attractions; no matter how likely it is to occur it will not be chosen. But even where value is positive, if expectation of occurrence is zero, the product of expectation with value will still be zero and this outcome also will be totally unattractive. There are outcomes with negative value, of course, such as ill health. These will lead to negative utilities and reactions of avoidance.

In mathematical decision theory, a payoff matrix is formed in which choices are ranged on one axis and all possible outcomes on the other. A precise prediction of economic attractiveness can be made by adding the product of value and probability of occurrence, i.e., objective utility, for each choice. According to the model, people should select the choice whose overall utilities are maximal. For example, a person may be faced by a choice of either of two combinations of cards. One occurs once in 100 times and carries a payoff of ten dollars; the other occurs 50% of the time but carries a payoff of only one dollar. The model indicates that the latter choice has greater utility. (The product of value and probability of occurrence is 0.5 vs. 0.1 for the former choice.) On a purely economic basis, therefore, it should be preferred.

Subjective expected utility deals with psychological rather than economic data. Here the *subjective* value of an outcome must be determined, and the *perceived* probability of its occurrence estimated. A man might have to choose between taking a train and driving. Even if he hates trains and loves to drive, his choice will still be affected by expectation of comfort or discomfort on the trip; he might very well take the train in winter if the roads are glazed by a freezing rain. The choice is based on the difference in SEU between driving and taking the train in those particular circumstances.

The illustrations in the preceding paragraphs use a "static" utility model. That is, they deal with a single decision in which a person faces a choice among immediate outcomes with relatively easily measured utilities, objective or subjective. Such a model has limited application to many areas of human affairs. Decisions must often be made about complex and continuing problems in which any one choice is a part of a chain of decisions in which the choice made at any point affects all succeeding elements of the chain. Unfortunately, a quantitative model for chains of decisions is extremely difficult to create. We shall, therefore, limit ourselves to the basic notion that an estimate of value and expectancy, i.e., perceived probability of occurrence, makes it possible to assess the likelihood that a person will make one or another choice. Such measures will be used as general predictors of behavior in what one might call an informal decisional model. We have already used this model to differentiate the perceptions of smokers and non-smokers. The fact that the measure of SEU did differentiate smokers and non-smokers is an indication of the validity of the measure and the usefulness of the model. The list of outcomes which was the basis for the Test of Subjective Expected Utility (see Chapter 3) should also define the payoff matrix for smokers faced by pressures to change. Thus, even without a formal mathematical approach, we can use estimates of SEU as predictors of behavior.*

The use of a decisional model, even if informal, could provide a subtle measure of the impact on the smoker of environmental forces which inhibit or support smoking. In a practical sense, if one could discover the factors which affect the SEU values of various outcomes of the decision to continue smoking or to attempt to stop, it might be possible to identify the elements in a persuasive message which lead to change or which fail to create change. One could determine the degree to which such a message added newly perceived outcomes to the elements of a decisional matrix or affected the values or the expectations of already known outcomes in individuals who maintain or change their smoking behavior.

BEHAVIORAL CHANGE

The previous sections of this chapter dealt with actual change in smoking behavior only peripherally. The emphasis was on "interior" processes, attitude and decision, as inferred from verbalizations. In the present section the emphasis shifts to the determinants of change in smoking behavior.

A number of problems in the study of change in smoking are inescapable. The first is the necessity for dealing with a smoker's *reports* of his level of smoking as if these were direct observations. In virtually all of the research in this area the experimenter has assumed that his subjects have not lied when they reported changed (or unchanged) levels of smoking. The difficulties of obtaining direct observation of a behavior which occurs episodically throughout the day are too obvious to need discussion. Certainly, the burden of proof is on the investigator to demonstrate that his data are both reliable and valid, that reports of change are not due to attempts on the part of the subject to be ingratiating, or, indeed, that they are not the product of experimenter bias. Without a reliable and inexpensive

---

*For a good introduction to the ideas of quantitative decision theory see the article by Ward Edwards *et al.*, in *New Directions in Psychology II*, 1965. A theoretical model derived from the study of decisional processes was applied to the prediction of attitudinal change and subsequent behavioral change by Janis and Mann (1968). One of their illustrations of the factors leading to decision was based on inferences about the thought processes of a smoker attempting to weigh the consequences of continuing to smoke or of stopping. A similar formulation is found in an unpublished manuscript of Straits (1965). Janis did not use Edwards' terminology (1961) for a mathematical decisional model whereas Straits did.

biochemical indicator of smoking levels, however, research on smoking behavior must continue to rely on the reports of subjects, buttressed as far as possible by internal checks of their accuracy.

There are several quantitative aspects of cigarette smoking which could be used as indicators of change. Apart from changes in the actual number of cigarettes consumed, these include changes in the proportion of each cigarette smoked, in the amount of inhalation, and in the brand, length, and variety of cigarette (i.e., from plain to filter-tipped). Discussions of "success" or "failure" of techniques for inducing change are hard to compare since there are no generally accepted criteria. Some writers prefer to deal only with complete cessation (Horn, 1968b), while others use percentage reduction (Schwartz & Dubitzky, 1968c) or contrast those changing by some absolute amount with those changing by less than that amount (Platt, Krassen & Mausner, 1969). Lastly, time periods over which changes have been evaluated have varied from a few days to three weeks for "short-term success," and from several months to a year or more for "long-term success." Where possible, we will define the criterion of change used in each study cited in the following discussion; the reader will have to consult the original sources for the details.

In the last two years three intensive discussions of the literature on attempts to induce change in smoking have been published (Bernstein, 1969; Keutzer, Lichtenstein & Mees, 1968; and Leventhal, 1968). In view of this we will not attempt an exhaustive account of previous work, but rather will present some ideas about change, supporting these by citation of relevant studies and theoretical analyses. The discussion will deal with three issues. The first is the relation between decision and change. The second is the prediction of change from measures of individual differences. The third is an evaluation of some specific techniques for inducing change.

Decision and behavioral change. This section will contrast the determinants of verbal statements of intention to reduce or eliminate smoking with those of actual change. One of the most serious problems in interpreting reports of experiments on decision and change is the evaluation of the degree to which change in smoking is due to the experimental manipulation, is spontaneous, or is due to extraneous variables. Even though the changes in experimental groups can always be compared to those in control groups, it would still be important to know how much spontaneous reduction in smoking might be expected in any population and to have information about factors favoring such reduction. Most of the experimental studies are carried out with relatively small groups of subjects selected from restricted populations. For all of these reasons baseline data would be highly valuable. Fortunately, Horn and Waingrow (Horn, 1968b; National Clearinghouse for Smoking and Health, 1969) have twice gathered baseline data on reduction and cessation on a national basis.

In a paper given in 1968, Horn described the results of two 90-minute interviews carried out at a 20-month interval with a national sample of over 1500 smokers. During the 20 months between interviews, over half of the respondents *considered* giving up smoking; about a third actually tried. Fifteen percent of the 1500 achieved short-term success, i.e., three weeks of abstinence, but only half that number was able to refrain from smoking for as long as three months.

As compared to respondents who had not made the decision to attempt a change in smoking (i.e., had not *considered* change, in Horn and Waingrow's terms), those who did decide to change were younger, had higher incomes, were better educated, and more likely to be married. Their smoking levels were lower, they were more likely to smoke filter-tipped cigarettes or low-tar and nicotine brands, and a higher proportion reported having talked with a doctor about smoking.

Actual cessation occurred primarily among subjects who smoked lightly and used filter-tipped cigarettes. The chief predictor of both short-range and long-range success was the statement in the initial interview that the respondent did not think that he would be smoking five years hence. Interestingly, those respondents who tried to stop, but whose short-term success was not maintained, were the ones for whom the personal relevance of the threat to health was highest, as indicated by responses on the initial interview.

Although Horn's data are extremely detailed and provide information based on a sample of the entire population, their usefulness is limited by the weaknesses of all retrospectively gathered information. In many ways, the most valuable insights into the dynamics of change come from experimental manipulations, even if these are carried out with limited populations.

Leventhal and his colleagues have carried out an important series of laboratory experiments and field studies of the effects of the induction of fear on smoking and other health-related behavior. In many of their studies they have investigated the interaction of two manipulated variables, the level of emotionality aroused by messages and the presentation to subjects of specific instructions for taking action in response to persuasive messages. They were also interested in several individual characteristics of the subjects, notably degree of self-esteem and feelings of vulnerability to the threat described in the messages.

The findings of this series of studies are complex. Niles (1964) reported that subjects who felt themselves vulnerable to cancer were not more likely to take an X-ray after a highly threatening message than after a milder message; subjects who felt relatively less vulnerable did tend to take X-rays as the level of threat increased. In contrast, Leventhal and Watts (1966) did not find a positive relation between level of threat and tendency to follow the recommendation to take an X-ray among "non-vulnerable" subjects, but reproduced Niles' finding that increasing threat increased tendency towards action among subjects who felt relatively invulnerable. Watts (1966) actually manipulated feelings of vulnerability. He reported that subjects who were given a feeling of personal danger and also subjected to to a highly threatening message (a film showing surgery for lung cancer) did not materially reduce their smoking levels, although each manipulation by itself did tend to depress the level of smoking. Lastly, in experiments which did not involve smoking, increasing the level of fear arousal led to increased acceptance of a message urging subjects to take tetanus shots (Dabbs & Leventhal, 1966) and to take precautions to avoid automotive accidents (Leventhal & Trembly, 1968). However, this effect was obtained only among subjects high in self-esteem; it did not emerge among subjects whose self-esteem was low. Apparently there is a strong interaction among self-esteem, feelings of vulnerability, and willingness to act on recommendations given in an anxiety-arousing message; the arousal of anxiety works only for people who regard themselves favorably and who feel relatively invulnerable to the threat embodied in the message.

This seems to argue that the arousal of anxiety is not a universally effective way of inducing action. Indeed, Leventhal and Niles (1964) found that arousing anxiety led more often to a statement of *intention* to act than to action. However, in a later series of studies, Leventhal and his colleagues discovered that the arousal of anxiety can be an effective force leading to action if the subject is provided with clear and detailed instructions. For example, Leventhal, Singer, and Jones (1965) found that Yale students were more likely to take tetanus shots if they were given *both* a fear-inducing film and a map of the campus showing the health center than if they had either alone or neither. The presence or absence of specific instructions had no effect on verbally expressed decision, but did affect behavior no matter what the level of fear induced. In a carefully designed study Leventhal, Watts, and Pagano (1965) examined these issues by varying the level of fear induction and specificity of instructions in messages given smokers. Initially, subjects exposed to a fear-arousing movie expressed significantly stronger intention to stop smoking than those who viewed a less powerful film. However, the short-term follow-up revealed no differences in actual smoking levels among the various groups who had seen either film. As time went on, however, those subjects who had been exposed to a fear-inspiring film and had also received specific instructions cut down their smoking levels by a far greater margin than the subjects who had seen the film but had not been given instructions. Our own first study of role playing, which will be described below (Platt, Krassen & Mausner, 1969), yielded results compatible with those of Leventhal and his colleagues. That is, subjects for whom the experimental procedure led to high levels of anxiety tended to report verbal intentions to change but did not change in their actual smoking behavior.

Leventhal (1970) summarizes the results of his research by arguing that the arousal of anxiety in itself leads only to verbalizations about change. A person must not only fear the consequences of not changing, but must believe in his capacity to change, must be able to imagine the steps which lead to change, and must have a repertory of techniques available, before he can embark on the road to change. In the next section we shall review the data which suggest that there are individual differences in temperament which make it more likely that this combination of factors will exist in some people than in others.

Individual differences as predictors of change. We have already noted from Horn's national sample of smokers that the respondents who stopped smoking were younger, better educated, and lighter smokers than those who continued to smoke. Of course, this general description, based on averages, hides the group of smokers who stop because they have become seriously ill. The existence of this group is evidenced by the high death rates of people who have stopped smoking for less than one year (Surgeon General's Report, 1964). This phenomenon complicates the analysis of psychological data on ex-smokers unless those who stop because of serious illness are treated separately.

The psychological characteristics which common sense dictates *should* characterize smokers who are successful in changing are easy enough to describe. The changer should be a calm, effective, well-organized person who has a high level of achievement orientation and a strong belief in his ability to control his own destiny. And, indeed, the data bear out the prediction.

Weatherly (1965) gave the Edwards Personal Preference Schedule to a population which included persons who had never smoked and ex-smokers as well as smokers. While there were no overall differences on the various scales of the Edwards PPS between smokers and non-smokers, those repondents who had successfully stopped smoking were characterized as low in deference, high in aggression, and high in achievement needs. Schwartz and Dubitsky (1968c), whose study of intervention in smoking has been mentioned previously, carried out an intensive analysis of personality characteristics of their subjects. They report that their "successes," i.e., subjects whose smoking had decreased by at least 85% after various treatments, were less anxious than unsuccessful subjects, more self-confident, and generally showed a higher level of personal adjustment. They were contented with work, with their levels of achievement, and with their sexual and social interactions. Like Straits, Schwartz and Dubitsky also found that a social environment which did not encourage smoking was associated with success.

A psychological test which taps the beliefs we have indicated as important for success in cessation of smoking is the Liverant-Rotter Test of Internal/External Control, the I/E test, (James *et al.*, 1965, and Rotter, 1966). This measures the subject's belief in his ability to control his own destiny (internal control) as opposed to a sense of fatalism (external control).

The data relating I/E scores to change are contradictory. James, Woodruff, and Werner (1965) had the foresight to plan a study of the immediate effects of the Surgeon General's Report. They obtained scores on the I/E test from a group of college students and found that the smokers who stopped smoking during the period immediately after the release of the report were more internally oriented than those whose smoking did not change. Straits (1965) noted that those of his respondents who attempted to stop smoking, whether successfully or not, were internally oriented; there was no relation between I/E score and success in stopping. Similar results were reported by Straits and Sechrest (1963). Keutzer (1968) also reported a failure to find differences between successful and unsuccessful participants among volunteers for a smoking clinic. However, all of her subjects had a strong internal orientation, and their attendance at the clinic indicated that they *were* making an attempt to change.

In our own pilot study of role-playing behavior, to be described in the next chapter (Platt, Krassen & Mausner, 1969), all of the subjects who decreased smoking immediately after participation in the experiment were internally oriented. In most of the studies relating I/E to change in smoking, the criterion was short-range change; the degree to which this measure predicts long-range change is as yet undetermined. Our own study did include a long-range follow-up. I/E *was* predictive of long-range change for the very small sample we studied, but the effect was not as dramatic as for the immediate changes following role playing.

The pattern which emerges from these studies is not entirely clear. But, in general, internal orientation appears to be characteristic of smokers who make an attempt to change. These people apparently have not only a general belief in their ability to control their own destinies but also a specific belief in their ability to stop smoking. However, the success of attempts to stop smoking is probably due to a multitude of factors within the smoker and in his environment; among these internal orientation may play only a minor role.

An evaluation of techniques for intervention in smoking. Not the least of the problems in encouraging change is the need for procedures to assist the smoker who *is* attempting to stop or cut down. In the following section we will discuss various approaches to the engineering of change, with special emphasis on aids to the new ex-smoker. Although none of the research reported in this volume is directly concerned with mass applications, for the sake of completeness we will comment briefly on this problem.

As noted in Chapter 1, there have been changes in the absolute level of smoking in the population, in the relative prevalence of smoking as compared with levels predicted from pre-1955 rates of increase, and in the nature of the cigarette, i.e., the shift to filters. These changes occurred during a period in which public and private agencies have mounted vigorous educational campaigns on the dangers of smoking, most recently by means of ingenious and highly professional TV spot commercials. Unfortunately, there is no way of knowing whether the changes would have occurred in the absence of the formal programs, merely from normal dissemination of the news about the scientific discoveries concerning smoking. As Wiebe pointed out during the discussion of this issue in the Beaver College conference (Mausner & Platt, 1966b), it is extremely hard to evaluate the effect of specific campaigns carried on through the mass media. Certainly evaluations of anti-smoking programs in limited populations have shown little or no impact on smoking. (For a summary of this literature see Wakefield, ed., 1969, pp. 46-50.) It is only with special groups such as students in the health professions (Watne *et al.,* 1964) or with the additon of participation by prestigious individuals (Morison *et al.,* 1964) that noticeable changes in smoking levels have been achieved.

The most frequently used technique for assisting smokers who want to stop is the so-called "smoking clinic." One prototype is the widely publicized Five Day Plan conducted by members of the Seventh Day Adventist Church. This is a combination of intensive education, fear arousal, and indoctrination in techniques of stopping which rely heavily on healthful living and exercise as substitutes for smoking. An evaluation of one Five Day Plan was carried out by Thompson and Wilson (1966). Their report notes that at the end of a year only 16% of the participants were not smoking. A much more comprehensive evaluation of 13 tobacco-withdrawal clinics in Norway modeled after the Five Day Plan yielded similar results (Berglund, 1969). While the immediate impact of the clinics was great, the rate of recidivism was high, and after six months fewer than 20% of the participants reported that they were non-smokers. A significantly higher proportion of non-smokers was found among participants whose families did not include a smoker compared with those who did have a smoker in their households.

Probably the most carefully designed study of procedures for intervention was carried out under the aegis of the Kaiser-Permanente Health Plan in the Bay area of California (Schwartz & Dubitzky, 1968c). In this study smokers were asked to volunteer for a smoking-control program. The volunteers were assigned to one of seven treatment or two control groups. Among the treatment variables studied were the use of tranquilizers or prescription of a placebo, alone or in combination with individual or group counseling. Control groups did not participate in any treatment.

The results are devastating for proponents of the specific kinds of interventions studied. Although individual counseling and participation in clinics (i.e., group counseling) had modest success on short-range follow-up, subjects who were given a prescription for a placebo and whose sole activity was to go to a pharmacy to have the prescription filled showed about as great a rate of success on one-year follow-up as any other treatment group. In all of the treatment groups about 20% of the subjects were not smoking at the time of the long-range follow-up; in the control groups 11% were not smoking (Schwartz & Dubitzky, 1968b). These results are comparable with those of Thompson and Wilson and of Berglund. Apparently knowing that they were part of an organized research and taking a pill were sufficient to produce change among subjects who were predisposed to change.

In the data cited above, clinics were evaluated in terms of rates of change among participants. Two reports tell something of the return from clinic procedures when the baseline used is the number of smokers *invited* to join. Rosenblatt and Allen (1968) distributed questionnaires to 3000 college students. Half answered the questionnaire, but only 54 individuals expressed interest in attending a clinic, and only 9 actually came to meetings. Similarly, in a massive project originating in the school system of Philadelphia, Allen and Fackler (1967) sent home with school children over 30,000 questionnaires inquiring into the parents' smoking status. Of the 11,000 smokers, almost half indicated interest in a smoking clinic, 257 attended a mass meeting, and 150 came to a series of smoking clinics. It is true that the results among those attending the clinic were fairly promising. At the end of six months 56 of the 150 had stopped smoking, and at the end of the year 35 still abstained. But neither report encourages the belief that massive attempts to bring people into smoking clinics are worth the effort.

If the "talking therapies" characteristic of individual counseling and smoking clinics do not seem to work, perhaps the miracle could be found in an application of the new techniques of behavior modification which use operant conditioning (Krasner & Ullman, 1965; Wolpe, 1964). Keutzer, Lichtenstein, and Mees (1968) reviewed a variety of projects in which operant techniques were employed. These include the application of punishing electrical shocks in conjunction with smoking, or the blowing of hot smoky air at the subject while he smokes. Rewards such as blowing cool mentholated air at subjects when they stop smoking also have been used. In addition, several projects have employed various desensitization procedures. Keutzer and her colleagues noted that the reports vary in quality; few of the studies had adequate controls. In a controlled study (Keutzer, 1968), behavior modification was not found to be superior to use of a placebo. On the basis of the literature survey and of Keutzer's empirical work, they concluded that while behavior modification is generally superior to no treatment, it rarely yields better results than those obtained from more conventional techniques.

Anecdotal reports of the success of hypnosis in the treatment of smokers have received wide circulation. Despite the dramatic effects which have been described in the press and popular magazines, it is hard to evaluate the usefulness of this technique in the virtual absence of systematic controlled investigation. One very limited controlled study by Graff, Hammett, and others (Graff *et al.*, 1966) indicated that hypnotherapy carried on by a competent psychiatrist was superior to other forms of intervention. The psychiatrist developed a close personal relation with the patient before hypnosis was attempted. An unpublished paper by Kline describes a marathon session in which hard-core smokers who had tried unsuccessfully to stop many times spent 12 consecutive hours together under the direction of a therapist. Hypnosis was used as a relaxing and sensitizing measure along with the usual procedures carried on in sensitivity training. Of the 60 patients involved in this program, 53 (88%) were still not smoking at the end of a year. The unusual nature of the procedure and the striking results are certainly impressive.

One aspect of the control of smoking which has not received adequate attention is the need for differentiated procedures to meet the requirements of smokers with varying patterns of support for smoking. Although both Tomkins and Horn have suggested specific approaches for smokers showing one or another "type" of smoking (Horn, 1969), so far as we can determine there is no empirical evidence supporting their recommendations. The final conclusion to which we must come is that, as of now, the art of assisting smokers who wish to stop is in a most primitive state.

Summary

There seems to be little evidence that the learning of new information about the relation between smoking and illness leads directly to changes in attitude towards smoking or that attitude change induces behavioral change. Educational campaigns and other programs designed to increase information have been only moderately successful in reducing cigarette smoking. And although smoking clinics and other forms of intervention may lead to more negative attitudes, there has been no relation between success in stopping and degree of attitude change.

This finding, however, does not eliminate attitude change as a possible precursor to behavioral change. It may be that unless people are convinced that smoking is dangerous, they will continue to smoke. Negative attitudes may be a necessary, although far from sufficient, cause for giving up cigarettes. Inducing negative attitudes may be important in another sense, not as a method for inducing change in individuals, but for creating a climate of opinion where smoking and smokers are the objects of ridicule and distaste. If it were possible to create in a large proportion of the population even so minimal a change in feelings as that obtained in the experiments cited in this chapter, the social impact might be considerable. A change in emotional climate might have an effect on public sanctions applied to smoking and decrease the extent of economic assistance given to the tobacco industry. This in turn might lead to increased social pressures on smokers to stop.

The chief conclusion from our consideration of processes of decision was that the insights of mathematical decision theory should be used to deal with the impact of persuasive appeals on smokers, but that a formal application of that theory is impracticable. We developed an informal scheme for the assessment of the values and expectations which smokers might attach to the results of choosing to continue to smoke or of attempting to stop. In the remainder of this volume we shall present an investigation in which the concepts presented in Part I are applied. We shall use a combination of the ecological model for the analysis of the natural history of smoking and the decisional model for the analysis of change to predict the behavior of smokers in an experiment in which role playing is used to induce change in smoking.

5
Background for a Study of the Effects
of Role Playing

STUDY VII

Two lines of evidence suggested the desirability of investigating the impact on a smoker of playing the role of a participant in an interaction between a physician and a patient. The first was the success of Janis and his colleagues in inducing attitudinal change (Janis & King, 1954; King & Janis, 1956) and behavioral change (Janis & Mann, 1965; Mann & Janis, 1968) by persuading subjects to act in a manner contrary to their usual beliefs. The second line of evidence was that showing the influence of physicians on their patients. Horn reported that many of the respondents in his national sample who stopped smoking "spontaneously" had talked with a doctor about their smoking. In two experimental studies, one by Poussaint, Bergman, and Lichtenstein (1966) and one by Mausner, Mausner, and Rial (1968), a significant proportion of patients who were given a brief anti-smoking message by a doctor, or even (in the former study) by a medical student posing as a doctor, reduced their levels of smoking. In both studies the changes persisted after six months (Lichtenstein, Poussaint & Bergman, 1967).

We had three overall goals for this study of role playing. The first was to determine whether role playing would prove effective in inducing smokers to decrease or stop. The second was to investigate sources of individual variation in behavior following role playing. This goal was set primarily to test the usefulness of both the ecological model of smoking and the decisional model for predicting change. The third was to determine, insofar as possible, the long-range effect of role playing and the long-range validity of prediction from measures of individual differences in patterns of support for smoking, in personality, and in subjective expected utility.

Some characteristics of role-playing studies. There have been two major characteristics of experiments on role playing; first, the subject is required to be active to some extent in creating a role or determining the precise nature of a message. Second, the role he is asked to take demands the expression of beliefs different from those he holds privately.

With a consistency rare in the experimental social sciences, investigators have found that subjects who participate in role playing shift in attitude towards the position they presented during their essay in make-believe. Why this takes place has been the subject of intense controversy. Advocates of cognitive dissonance theory (e.g., Zimbardo, 1965) maintain that the effort involved in expressing counter-attitudinal beliefs generates dissonance which can be reduced only via change in attitude. The position of Janis and his colleagues (expressed in Elms, 1967 and Janis & Gilmore, 1965) is that the person engaged in role playing is forced to re-examine the arguments for the position he is presenting. This forced attention leads to attitudinal and, sometimes, to behavioral change.

Janis and Mann (1965) were the first to explore the effects of role playing on cigarette smokers. Their subjects, female college students, took part in an interaction with a "doctor" (played by one of the investigators) in which the subject, acting the role of "patient," was told that she had lung cancer. The subjects engaged in an hour-long ordeal in which they performed a soliloquy in the "doctor's" waiting room, received the news of their illness, ruminated about it, arranged for an operation, and then discussed the causes of lung cancer with the "doctor." A control group heard a tape-recorded interaction covering the same material. The subjects who participated in role playing not only reported significantly greater immediate reductions in cigarette consumption than the control group, but maintained this decrease on 18-month follow-up (Mann & Janis, 1968).

A pilot study of role playing. Our decision to use role playing in our own research was first implemented in a pilot study (Platt, Krassen & Mausner, 1969) which will be summarized here.

Janis had asked subjects to play only the role of patient. In view of Janis' theoretical discussions it seemed reasonable that a "doctor" should have an even better opportunity to rehearse the arguments against smoking than a "patient." He should also, presumably, be able to remain sufficiently disinterested so that defensive avoidance would inhibit change even less than for a person playing the role of "patient" (see discussions of Janis' position on anxiety and attitudinal change in Janis and Mann, 1968, and the comments on his model in the latter part of this chapter). One aspect of the Janis and Mann 1965 study, reported to us informally, supported our hunch. The experimenter-confederate who played the doctor's role (Leon Mann) had been so moved by the necessity for telling people, even in play, that they had a fatal disease, and so impressed by the dangers of smoking, that he became an anti-smoking crusader.

We decided, therefore, to investigate the consequences of playing both the doctor's and the patient's role. Our subjects were 44 of the middle-class, Catholic men described in Study II. They were assigned to play either the doctor or the patient in a conference following a physical check-up. The alternate role was played by a student of acting in his early twenties. The "patient" was informed by the "doctor" that he had lung cancer and would have to undergo a pneumonectomy. The hazards of the operation were discussed, and the patient was told that even if the operation were successful, he would have to give up smoking to save the good lung.

In a follow-up telephone interview five days after the role playing, half of the 44 experimental subjects reported no change in the number of cigarettes smoked, 16 subjects reported a decrease in smoking, and 6 an increase. The excess of subjects who decreased their smoking is significant by sign test. The mean daily consumption of cigarettes following the role playing decreased significantly, if minimally, for the entire experimental group. In contrast, of 17 subjects in a control group whose smoking status was measured at points separated by a five-day interval, only one decreased and one increased in smoking between the pre-test and the five-day follow-up. No subject, experimental or control, stopped smoking between the pre- and post-tests. Since small changes in reported numbers of cigarettes smoked may be due to error in reporting, it was decided to divide the experimental group into "changers" and "non-changers" at the level of the median reduction in smoking, i.e., eight cigarettes per day. The nine subjects who decreased by this amount or more were designated as changers in further analyses. There were no significant differences in proportion of changers between subjects who played the role of doctor and those who played the role of patient, although there was a tendency for the "doctors" to show a greater average decrease; there were indications from the post-experimental interview that the "patients" felt more defensive about their role and about their own smoking.

As indicated earlier (see Chapter 4), subjects who reported a decision to stop smoking, but whose reported smoking levels were not reduced, had given evidence of higher levels of situational anxiety than those whose verbal expressions of decision were consistent with the changes in their smoking. As also noted in Chapter 4, the changers were all internally oriented (i.e., had low I/E scores).

THE DESIGN OF THE ROLE–PLAYING STUDY

Character of the Role Playing

The considerations which led to our use of the role of "doctor" as well as "patient" in the pilot study still impressed us even though that study showed only minimal differences in effect between the two roles. We decided, therefore, to continue using both roles, but made a number of changes in procedure between the pilot study and the succeeding investigation.

We have been impressed that young people seem to find a discussion of the dangers of lung cancer rather remote. And, in fact, lung cancer is extremely unusual among people of college age. Therefore, we decided to shift to a scenario which would force the subject to pay attention to current dangers to his health derived from the continued smoking of cigarettes. The evidence has been increasing that cigarette smoking has a marked effect on morbidity (1968 Supplement to the Surgeon General's report). Thus, it is a valid reflection of current research to inform subjects, via the content of role playing, that even apparently healthy smokers are suffering damage to their bodies from smoking, damage which gives warning of possible future illness.

Three themes were chosen for the content of the interaction between "doctor" and "patient." They were the tendency of smoking to affect adversely the cellular morphology of the lungs, the elasticity of lung tissue, and cardiovascular function. Even among college students abnormal cells have been found upon cytological examination of sputum in a fairly high proportion of smokers (Robbins & Lichlyter, 1968). Many studies have demonstrated that smokers suffer a diminution of forced expiratory volume, i.e., the ability to exhale air from the lungs. Lastly, there is mounting evidence that smokers have an increased risk of arteriosclerotic cardiovascular disease. In the scenario of the role playing each of the themes was presented by means of a clinical test which the "doctor" used to demonstrate to the "patient" that he was damaging himself by continuing to smoke. The details of the tests are given in Chapter 6.

In our pilot study there was no control group among the subjects who came to the laboratory. The only control group was a randomly selected sample of smokers who participated neither in the pretest nor in the laboratory experience but whose smoking histories were taken five days apart. For the present study two control groups were deemed to be desirable. Both were to complete all the pretests and post-tests. In an analogy to Janis and Mann's design, one group of control subjects would be exposed to the content of the interaction but would not themselves play the roles. While it was possible that some internal role playing would take place as a result of empathy between observers and subjects, it was felt that the most significant impact on the observers should be from the information exchanged during the interaction between role players. The other group of controls would have no contact at all with the role-playing experience.

Previous work suggested that merely being asked about smoking (Mausner, Mausner & Rial, 1968) and taking tests about attitudes towards smoking, might have some effect on smoking behavior, especially if the interview occurred in a context likely to remind the respondent about the impact of smoking on health. Thus, it would have been most desirable to have an "after-only" control group whose smoking status and beliefs, tested only once, would provide a baseline against which the bahavior of all other groups could be studied. Unfortunately, since the pool from which we planned to draw our subjects was not large enough to permit an after-only control group, we were limited to four groups: Controls, Observers, "Doctors," and "Patients."

Predictors of Change

One of our major goals was the determination of factors which would predict a smoker's behavior after the experience of playing the role of "doctor" or "patient." We used two kinds of predictors. One consisted of responses from the subject to questions about his subjective expected utilities concerning smoking and his reactions during the experiment. From these responses we hoped to be able to make inferences about mediating systems, or "events in the head," which might influence the subject's later behavior. The second kind of predictor consisted of measures of ongoing, presumably stable, characteristics of the subject, tests of personality and patterns of support for smoking.

Subjective Expected Utility (SEU) as a predictor of change. We have already noted (see Chapter 3) that smokers and non-smokers differ somewhat in the *values* they place on the results of smoking or not smoking, and much more in the *expectation* of occurrence of these results. Our hunch was that the experience of role playing would make smokers change their subjective expected utilities in the direction of non-smokers. The notion that change in SEU would be the critical factor in inducing changed behavior was derived partly from our previous contact with smokers and partly from Hochbaum's model (1958, 1960) for behavioral change in reaction to threats to health. Hochbaum proposed that volunteering to take an X-ray in a public health screening program would result from the combined effect of at least four sequential factors. These were: (1) recognition by the subject of the threat to health, (2) perception of this threat as a serious rather than a trivial danger, (3) perception by the subject that his own health is actually threatened, and (4) acceptance of the notion that taking an X-ray is a relevant action which would reduce the likelihood of occurrence of danger to health. Each of Hochbaum's factors involves values, i.e., the desirability of good health. Each also involves expectations, e.g., perception of the probability of occurrence of disease, or the probability that taking an X-ray would permit protective measures and so help the subject guard against disease.

Our specific prediction, then, was that after role playing, those subjects whose SEU for smoking became more negative and whose SEU for not smoking became more positive would decide to attempt to change their smoking behavior. Further, we expected that once a decision based on changed SEU were made, those subjects who enjoyed the appropriate combination of circumstances and individual characteristics would succeed in cutting down or quitting.

The arousal of anxiety. Participating in a charade in which one discusses danger to health should arouse some anxiety even in the most equable of subjects. Thus the role-playing experiment permits an examination of the relation between the level of anxiety aroused and subsequent changes in both attitude and behavior. We have already discussed the research of two men who have contributed greatly to the literature about the effects of anxiety on health-related behavior. Both Janis (1967) and Leventhal (1970) have recently written theoretical analyses of the general issues raised by the relation of anxiety to attitudinal and behavioral change.

Janis has proposed a three-dimensional model to handle the effects of the arousal of fear on attitudes and behavior. Using his terminology, the three dimensions are the level of fear itself, the level of defensive avoidance generated by fear-inspiring events, and the level of vigilance, or cognitive efficiency. The first of these dimensions includes "reflective fear," which is a consequence of the rational examination of personally relevant threat (e.g., the reaction to drinking from a bottle labeled "poison") and "neurotic fear," which is a purely visceral kind of panic usually based on past anxieties. The second dimension, defensive avoidance, is familiar to anyone who has ever succeeded in not thinking about an approaching menace; it is the equivalent of the Freudian mechanism of denial.

The third dimension, vigilance, relates to a person's ability to utilize information about the outside world; a low level of vigilance implies inadequate processing of incoming cues.

Janis' system deals with the conflict between vigilance and fear-based avoidance. He presents this conflict as a phenomenon which functions differently at different levels of fear. At any given level of fear, the interaction of vigilance and defensive avoidance determines the degree of attitude change in the following manner: at very low levels of fear there is little motivation for change, but also no inhibition of change by defensive avoidance. At moderate levels of fear, change is maximal since inhibition from defensive avoidance grows more slowly than the stimulation of change by the arousal of vigilance. However, at high levels of fear, defensive avoidance is sufficiently great so that change *is* inhibited. The result is an inverted U-shaped curve.

Janis has a special prediction for the results of role playing. He feels that role playing is effective in inducing change because it somehow aborts the growth of defensive avoidance. Therefore, among subjects engaging in role playing, change should increase proportionately with the degree to which fear is aroused. Although Janis cites data in which something very much like "neurotic fear" is measured to support his assertion, his theoretical model stresses the importance of "reflective fear," the anticipation of undesirable results from a given action.

Our concept of subjective expected utility does not require a direct measure of level of emotionality; yet in dealing with "value" the subjects do, in a way, report on their feelings. Presumably the more they *fear* illness, the lower the negative value they assign to it on the appropriate scale on our test. And the greater their *anticipation* of illness, the higher the score on the measure of expectation. Thus, our measure of SEU taps content similar to Janis' reflective fear. The difference is that our measure indicates a balance between positive and negative anticipations and values, and that it is primarily cognitive, while Janis' concept seems to imply variation in the level of drive as a function of fear. Whether the difference between a "cognitive" and a "motivational" concept is meaningful is, of course, moot. The important question in deciding on their identity is whether the two sets of concepts are anchored in the same data and may be used to generate the same predictions.

Although we did not derive our design from Janis' model, it may be possible to test some of its assumptions by relating his theoretical terms to our measurements. The model is, admittedly, hard to translate into specific predictions. But, so far as we can tell, if a subject's "reflective fear" is aroused by role playing, this should be shown by our measure of SEU. Then, from the model, one would predict a curvilinear relation between SEU and change in behavior subsequent to role playing. This prediction assumes that level of vigilance or attention is relatively constant among our subjects. If it is not, then the curves predicted by Janis at any given level of vigilance would not be expected to appear. Janis feels (personal communication) that no such curvilinear relations would occur with "neurotic fear."

Leventhal, after a careful analysis of the available data, rejects the notion that emotional reactions themselves would be related to change in either attitude or behavior. To him, change is always consequent on cognitive rather than affective variables. Fear-arousing circumstances are important because they furnish cues to adaptive responses. If the subject *has* a repertory of such responses, then he can cope with the causes of fear even if his emotion is very intense.

Thus, Leventhal would probably predict that neither changes in SEU alone nor the arousal of anxiety would lead to modification of behavior. These changes would lead to appropriate behavior only if the subject knew precisely what to do to face the threat embodied in the role playing. The current study was not designed to test Leventhal's concepts, but we were sufficiently impressed by the results of his investigations (see Chapter 4) so that detailed instructions on how to stop smoking were given to all experimental groups.

While we did not expect that the level of anxiety shown by our subjects would predict behavioral change, we were interested in noting whether we would replicate the finding of our pilot study that increased anxiety led to verbal commitment. Thus, we included measures of both chronic or ongoing anxiety, i.e., the MAS, and acute or situational anxiety.

INDIVIDUAL CHARACTERISTICS OF SUBJECTS AS PREDICTORS OF CHANGE IN BEHAVIOR

Patterns of smoking. In a previous section (see Chapter 3) we presented our theoretical notions about the varieties of supports for smoking and an instrument for measuring them, the Test of Patterns of Support. Common sense suggests that the role played by this behavior in the smoker's life should determine, in large part, the likelihood that he can give it up. Thus, knowledge of the patterns of support should help to predict change.

As pointed out in Chapter 1, there was some indication from previous work that subjects with a high level of social support to smoking would be less likely to change than those subjects for whom smoking was primarily an individual matter (Mausner, Mausner & Rial, 1968; Schwartz & Dubitzky, 1968a). Subjects for whom smoking represents a "psychological addiction" would probably be unlikely to alter their behavior as a result of one brief experience in a psychological laboratory. Tomkins (1968) has suggested that subjects for whom the primary support for smoking is pleasure should find it easy to give up smoking and develop alternate forms of hedonic reward. We had no way of knowing whether this would happen or whether the impact of role playing would be greater on those for whom smoking was also necessary to reduce tension. We did suspect that the use of smoking as a support for the self-image would probably create patterns of response more resistant to change than patterns of smoking based purely on hedonic factors.

In general, we expected that smokers for whom smoking effectively fulfills needs of any kind might find it hard to change, whereas those for whom it is primarily a source of mild gratification would find it relatively easy to change once the character of their values and expectations, i.e., SEU, was altered. This prediction is based, in part, on the work of McKennell (1968) who describes the former group as "dissonant," the latter as "consonant" smokers. In an extensive survey of British smokers he discovered that the smokers whose *habit* was deeply rooted often deplored their smoking and had made unsuccessful attempts to change; the "consonant" smokers rarely had attempted to change because they really did not disapprove of smoking. Once they did make an attempt, however, it was usually successful.

Self-reports on the likelihood of change. Horn (1968) has reported that the best predictor of long-range success in stopping smoking is an expressed belief that one could stop in the future. Subjects in our diary study (see Chapter 2) were also able to predict whether they would succeed in stopping after they graduated from college. It is far from clear whether this is because most people are trapped by their predictions through the necessity for reducing dissonance, or whether it is because people genuinely do have insights into their own behavior or into their ability to control their destinies. Whether predictions of one's own behavior are self-fulfilling prophecies or reasoned end products of decisional processes is moot. The fact remains that they have worked. In the current study, therefore, we invited the subject to predict the likelihood that he would be smoking in the future. We thus built in the possibility that the subject himself would tell us directly about the impact of our manipulations on his plans and about his perception of the likelihood that these plans could be implemented.

Personality as a Predictor of Reactions to Role Playing

Personality tests were included in a study of role playing and smoking for two reasons. The first was to determine in general whether the thesis of the "conforming personality" drawn by such writers as Crutchfield (1955) and Janis and Hovland (1959) would be confirmed. That is, would role playing have a greater impact on smoking behavior among subjects whose pattern of traits corresponded with the picture of conformists than among nonconformists? The second reason for including measures of personality was to explore certain specific issues (see Chapter 4) about the relation of personality to change in smoking behavior.

The concept of a "conforming personality" implies a consistent tendency to yield to persuasive appeals. Contrariwise, a "nonconformist" refuses to yield no matter how persuasive the appeal. Neither of these notions has been supported by recent research. It is more likely that personality tests reflect some of the "events in the head" which determine how a person selects the persuasive appeals to which he will respond positively. Thus, one would predict that there would be no *universal* and unequivocal relation between measures of personality and tendencies to change following the receipt of a persuasive appeal. Rather, personality tests should differentiate the kind of person for whom different appeals will be effective. The relation among level of induction of fear, self-confidence, and response described in Leventhal's work (see Chapter 4) illustrates this use of personality tests.

In the current study we used personality tests, but did not believe that they would directly predict the effects of role playing. However, we did expect that, taken in conjunction with our measures of patterns of support, and with changes in SEU, personality tests would increase the ability to make sense of individual differences in reaction to the experimental manipulation. Following is a discussion of each of the measures included in the pretest battery.

Internal/External control. As indicated in Chapter 4, there is some evidence that a belief in the ability to control one's own destiny may be a necessary concomitant of attempts to modify *any* behavior; this has been found to predict the tendency of smokers to try to stop. Actually, the relation is complex. In our pilot study of role playing (Platt, Krassen & Mausner, 1969), while all of the subjects who changed their smoking levels were internally oriented, not all internally oriented subjects changed. It is likely that only those subjects who were convinced of the necessity for change, and who also were not fatalistic, went on to modify their behavior. The prediction tested in the current study, therefore, was that those subjects who were internally oriented *and* who changed their subjective expected utilities for smoking would be likely to respond to the role-playing experience by altering their smoking behavior.

Risk-taking tendencies. For someone who accepts the data linking smoking with increased likelihood of disease, smoking certainly should be perceived as a risky behavior. Presumably, then, if one could measure the degree to which people are willing to take chances, a test of such a trait, in combination with a measure of SEU, should predict the likelihood that people will continue to smoke.

The work of Kogan and Wallach (1964) has provided a paper-and-pencil test which affords the psychologist some insights into a subject's risk-taking tendencies. The test, entitled the "Dilemmas of Choice," presents a series of dilemmas faced by fictional characters. In each the protagonist must decide whether to undertake a highly attractive risky venture or one which is relatively safe but less attractive. The subject selects the level of certainty of success at which he would be willing to choose the attractive but risky alternative. Kogan and Wallach found that scores on their test predicted risk-taking tendencies in a laboratory experiment only under rather special circumstances. They gave subjects a test of situational anxiety and one of "defensiveness," i.e., the desire to seem consistent and to show socially approved behavior (the Crowne-Marlowe test described below). Subjects whose scores on the two tests indicated a high level of both anxiety and defensiveness consistently made only risky or non-risky choices in the laboratory experiment no matter what the circumstances. These choices were predicted by scores on the Dilemmas of Choice. Subjects who were not anxious and also not defensive varied their choices in the laboratory experiment on the basis of the particular circumstances of the choice. Their scores on the Dilemmas of

Choice, therefore, did not furnish good predictions of behavior in the experiment.

In view of Kogan and Wallach's reports we did not anticipate that scores on the Dilemmas of Choice would predict directly whether subjects would or would not yield to the pressures presumably generated by the experience of role playing. However, we did expect that risk taking would contribute to the prediction of behavior following role playing along with the character of supports for smoking, perception of the dangers of smoking, and generalized tendencies towards action. It would be difficult to spell out beforehand the nature of all possible predictions for such a complex matrix of determinants. One could sketch a few possible combinations. For example, subjects who are not consistent risk takers, who perceive the dangers in smoking, and for whom smoking does not fulfill important needs, are most likely to change following role playing. Subjects who *are* risk takers might very well continue to smoke even if they perceive the dangers, and even if smoking does not fulfill important psychological requirements.

Social desirability. The test devised by Crowne and Marlowe (1964) measures the tendency of subjects to portray themselves as impossibly good. A high score means that the subject has identified himself as someone who never gossips, never rebels, always goes out of his way to help people in trouble, is never annoyed, has no anti-social impulses. We felt that if an association between scores on the Crowne-Marlowe test and *reports* of change were not found, this would provide indirect validation for the use of verbal reports of smoking levels. Presumably, if change in smoking were predicted directly by the Crowne-Marlowe test, that would suggest that reports of change could be a reflection of nothing more than ingratiation. Furthermore, we planned to test some of Kogan and Wallach's hypotheses concerning the interrelation of "social desirability," anxiety, and risk-taking tendencies.

General level of anxiety as a trait. The Taylor Manifest Anxiety Scale includes a variety of items tapping a subject's tendency towards hypochondria, towards psychosomatic symptoms such as diarrhea or sleeplessness, towards tension, anger and nervousness. It is one of the most widely used measures of a personality trait in American psychology. There have been reports that subjects high on the MAS are more likely to "conform" than subjects with low scores (for example, Crutchfield, 1955). Thus, one could predict that this test might be positively related to change following role playing. However, we were extremely skeptical of the likelihood of such a finding. Subjects who are anxious are likely to use smoking for tension reduction (see Chapter 3). These smokers would probably be *more* resistant to change than less anxious subjects. Here, as elsewhere, the expectation was that scores on the Manifest Anxiety Scale would assist in predicting change if they were used in conjunction with other measures, notably those of patterns of support for smoking.

EVALUATION OF THE RESULTS OF THE EXPERIMENT

The complex problems posed by a choice of criteria of change in studies of smoking have already been outlined in Chapter 4. In the present study, the ideal criterion would have been a count of the actual numbers of cigarettes the subjects smoked during a period of days prior to and subsequent to role playing. This was, of course, completely impossible. However, ashtrays were made available to subjects and the number of cigarettes they smoked during a post-experimental session were counted as an "unobtrusive measure" (Webb *et al.,* 1966) of the impact of role playing. For the most part evaluation of levels of smoking was dependent on the subjects' verbal reports. A number of internal checks were applied to test the likelihood that these reports were accurate.

We planned to maintain contact with our subjects and carry out a long-range follow-up of the results of role playing. Therefore we sent the subjects materials from the study several times during the course of the months following their visit to the laboratory. The final contact was a telephone interview six months after the experiment. In this interview we asked about levels of smoking, experiences with smoking during the period since the post-experimental tests, and reactions to the experiment.

Summary of Hypotheses

In summary, the following hypotheses were proposed for test in the study to be reported in the next two chapters.

1. Subjects playing the role of a "patient" or a "doctor" discussing the deleterious consequences of smoking to the health of the patient will reduce or eliminate their cigarette smoking.

2. The proportion of subjects changing their smoking will be highest among smokers playing the role of "doctor," moderate among those playing the role of "patient," lower among a group observing the interaction, and least among controls not exposed to the content of the role playing.

3. Reduction in smoking following role playing will be positively related to changes in the subjective expected utility of smoking. Subjects for whom the negative utilities of continuing, or the positive utilities of stopping, are increased, will be most likely to reduce or eliminate smoking.

4. Measures of personality will not directly predict tendencies to change level of smoking following role playing. However, these measures will be predictive if used in conjunction with tests of patterns of support for smoking or of subjective expected utility. For example, subjects who are internally controlled (low I/E scores), and whose SEU for smoking has become negative, will be likely to reduce their smoking or stop following role playing; subjects who are externally oriented (high I/E) are unlikely to change their smoking behavior, especially if SEU has not been affected by role playing.

5. Smokers for whom the use of cigarettes fulfills important needs, as indicated by their responses on the Test of Patterns of Support, will be less likely to be affected by role playing than those for whom smoking does not fulfill such needs.

6. A subject's own perception of the likelihood that he can change will be predictive of change in smoking.

6
Procedure of the Role-Playing Study

SUBJECTS AND RECRUITMENT PROCEDURES

The subjects in the experiment were male college students attending a two-year campus of the Pennsylvania State University in suburban Philadelphia. The character of this group has been defined in Chapter 3, in which we presented an analysis of the results of the test battery used as pretests for the experiment. During the course of the pretests, subjects were not informed that they would be asked to participate in further experimentation. However, all of the smokers who took the pretests were called by telephone during the following week and asked to take part in another study. They were informed that two projects were being run at Beaver College. One was said to be on visual perception, the other on "ways in which people can give ideas and opinions with which they may not agree." The subjects were told that they would be assigned randomly to one or the other of these projects.

Of the 187 smokers who completed the pretests, 135 agreed to come to the laboratory at Beaver College for the experiment. They (i.e., the 187 smokers) were randomly assigned to one of four experimental groups before they were called. These were: (1) a control group who were asked to participate in an experiment on the psychophysics of the perception of the rate of alternation of a flickering light, (2) observers of the role playing, (3) subjects asked to play the role of "doctor," and (4) subjects asked to play the role of "patient." Our aim was to have equal numbers of "doctors," "patients," and control subjects, and half that number of observers. The subjects came one at a time except that where an observer was to be included in the experimental run two subjects were asked to come at the same time. Subjects in the control group had participated in the same pretests as those in the experimental groups. At the end of the psychophysical experiment they completed the same post-tests as all other subjects.

Procedure of the Role-playing Experiment

Role players. The subjects who were assigned to one of the two role-playing groups were briefed by a member of the experimental staff upon arrival in the laboratory. Subjects assigned to the "doctor's" role were given the following instructions:

> You are seeing a patient for a conference after a routine check-up. You have known him and his family for many years. You should tell him that he is fundamentally in good health but that you are concerned about his smoking. Several tests indicate that his smoking is damaging him. You will show him a breathing record, a sputum cytology report, and an electrocardiagram, all indicating abnormalities. Urge him to make the decision to give up smoking or at least cut down. The patient will ask you whether you plan to continue to smoke. Make it clear that stopping will be very hard for you but that you are planning to stop smoking.

Subjects assigned to the role of "patient" were given the following instructions:

> You are seeing your family doctor for a conference after a routine check-up. He has known you and your family for many years. He is going to talk with you about your health and ask you to make some decisions. You will discuss these decisions with him. At some time during the discussion you should ask him what he would do if he were faced by the same decision. If he is evasive, you should press him for an answer. When he answers, agree to do what he says he will do.

The subjects were then given a cue sheet to aid them in the role playing and led to an experimental cubicle furnished to simulate a doctor's office. The "doctors" were given a white lab coat to wear and were instructed to sit behind a desk. On the desk prominently displayed was an ashtray with several stubbed-out cigarette butts. Also prominently displayed was an X-ray viewing box with a film of a diseased lung clearly visible. The member of the experimental team who played "patient" was led in and introduced. For role-playing sessions in which the subject was a "patient" the office was similarly arranged, but the member of the experimental team who played "doctor" was sitting at the desk prior to the arrival of the "patient." In all instances the experimenter who interacted with the subjects was one of the writers (Mausner), a bald, bespectacled, middle-aged psychologist.

All of the role-playing interactions followed the same scenario. The "doctor," either subject or experimenter, gave the "patient" a brief analysis of his clinical tests. One prop used in the role playing was an actual spirometer record showing the tracing of a patient with severe emphysema. A plastic overlay showed a normal tracing for contrast. The "doctor" also demonstrated to the "patient" his purported electrocardiogram and sputum cytology report, the latter indicating the presence of Stage III, i.e., "suspicious," cells. Two of the props are reproduced in Appendices VII-A (spirometer record) and VII-B (cytology report).

After demonstrating the physiological impairments presented as related to smoking the "doctor" urged the "patient" to stop smoking. At this point in the interaction there were a number of minor variations in the conduct of the role playing, depending on the reaction of the subject. Some subjects initiated a discussion of their own actual health. This was especially true of subjects playing the role of "patient." A number of the subjects who played "doctor" engaged in rather strenuous badgering of the "patient." In any event, shortly after a discussion of the "patient's" decision, the "patient" was supposed to press the "doctor" to indicate whether he himself would stop smoking; it was apparent from the ashtray with stubbed-out butts that the "doctor" was himself a smoker. The "doctor" indicated that he had decided to stop smoking in the very near future although he recognized that this would be a very difficult decision. Sometime during the course of this discussion the X-ray with the diseased lung was mentioned. It was presented as the film of a patient who had died of lung cancer. It was clearly indicated, however, that this was not the "patient's" own X-ray.

The observers. Subjects playing the role of observer were told, "This study has to do with how well people can take the part of another person and give their thoughts and ideas in an unrehearsed skit. You will watch two people in a skit. One will play the role of a doctor, the other of a patient. You are to rate each of them on how well they play the role they are taking."

Observers were taken to a room behind a one-way screen. They were able to watch the role playing and listen to the interaction through the use of a pair of headphones. Immediately after the role playing each observer rated both performers on their degree of emotionality and on their overall involvement in the role playing. The rating sheets used by the observers are found in Appendix VIII. The experimenter who played the second role also rated each subject on these characteristics.

Post-tests. Immediately after the experimental session, all subjects (including control subjects) were asked to fill out a Sarason-Mandler (1952) Test of Situational Anxiety (see Appendix IX) and to repeat the Test of Subjective Expected Utility concerning outcomes related to smoking (Appendix VI). "Doctors," "patients," and observers were also given a questionnaire about their feelings during the experiment (see Appendix X). The subjects who had participated in or observed the role playing were given a booklet* describing some aids to people who want to stop smoking. The subjects were told that they could use the hints in the booklet if they were interested in stopping smoking or cutting down. At no time were these subjects urged to stop smoking by the experimenter. The booklet did not include any persuasive material or any discussion of the dangers of smoking. It provided information presumably helpful to smokers who wished to change.

An ashtray with several stubbed-out butts was placed on each desk where subjects completed their post-tests. A count was made of the cigarettes smoked

---

*This booklet, furnished by Dr. Howard Leventhal of the University of Wisconsin, was an elaboration of a booklet originally prepared for a smoking control program in the New York City Department of Health (for text of the booklet see Appendix XI).

by the subjects during the half-hour period in which they completed the post-tests.

Initial follow-up. Five days after the session at Beaver all subjects, including control subjects, were called by telephone and questioned about their level of smoking at that point and about any recent changes in smoking. We had previously found that asking subjects how much they smoked on the previous day sometimes produced replies unrepresentative of typical smoking levels since the day prior to the interview may have been unusual because of illness or some other event. Therefore, we included among our questions concerning smoking an inquiry about "the number of cigarettes smoked yesterday" and "the number of cigarettes usually smoked." For the form of this questionnaire see Appendix XII. The telephone interviewers did not know the group to which the respondents had been assigned.

Further contacts with subjects. Approximately two months after the role-playing session each subject in the experimental groups was sent a copy of a profile showing his own scores on the Test of Patterns of Support. For a sample profile see Appendix XIII. Accompanying this profile was a pamphlet written by the investigators giving a differentiated set of hints to individual smokers based on our own previous studies and on work done by Fredrickson (1967), Horn (1968 a), Pumroy and March (1966), Tomkins (1968), and others. For the text of this pamphlet see Appendix XIV.

Approximately six months after the role playing all but seven of the original subjects, including the non-smokers, were reached by telephone and interviewed about their smoking. For the form of the interview see Appendix XV. Subjects were queried about their current level of smoking; the smokers were also asked for their recollections of the experiment, and any experiences they might have had if they had attempted to change their smoking behavior during the interim.

Treatment of the Data

Scoring procedures. Scores for the major psychological instruments used in the current study were obtained by standard procedures. Thus, the tests of risk taking, Internal/External Control, social desirability, and manifest anxiety were scored according to the directions given in the literature. Factor scores for the test of supports for smoking and Subjective Expected Utility were obtained following the procedures described in Chapter 3.

Additional scores were obtained for a section of the test of SEU which was not cited in Chapter 3. Subjects had been asked what value they placed on staying away from smoking for a week, a month, and a year. They indicated this value on a scale ranging from -5 to $+5$. They were also asked to indicate their expectation of the likelihood that they *could* stay away from smoking for a week, a month, and a year. These expectancies were recorded on scales going from zero to 100 chances in 100. Scores for both the value and the expectancy of refraining from smoking were obtained directly from the subjects' pretest and post-test protocols.

Measures of change. The number of subjects was too small to permit matching of individuals in different groups on the basis of pretest levels of smoking. Therefore change in smoking was analyzed by means of a covariance approach. For convenience in treating individual differences in degree of change, regressed scores were computed for our criterion measures. These were obtained by determining the line of best fit for the regression of pretest on post-test measures, and then calculating the residual, i.e., differences between the actual post-test score and that predicted by the regression line for each subject's pretest score. Regressed scores were computed for smoking levels and for the measures of subjective expected utility. For the latter, regressed scores were calculated not only for the overall measures of SEU but also for each of the factor scores (see Chapter 3). The regressed scores for the latter were obtained separately for value and expectancy. The particular expectancy used was the difference between the expectation of occurrence of each outcome if the subject continued to smoke and if he stopped (C-S). C-S was then used to obtain a regressed score indicating the shift in expectancy from pretest to post-test.

In analyzing the data on change in smoking, four criteria were used. These were: (1) an absolute measure of the change from pretest level to the "number of cigarettes smoked yesterday" reported on the post-test interview, (2) an absolute measure of change from pretest levels in the number of cigarettes "smoked usually," (3) regressed scores using pretest and post-test estimates of number of cigarettes smoked yesterday, and (4) regressed scores using pretest and post-test estimates of number of cigarettes smoked usually. In the following chapter the criterion used in each analysis will be identified.

Statistical analyses. Our basic technique was to prepare a record for machine tratment of all scores from each individual subject. Subjects were characterized as changers or non-changers in two ways. The first separated out those smokers who had reduced their smoking levels by half a pack or more a day or had stopped entirely. The considerations which led to adoption of this splitting point will be discussed in the following chapter. The second division used the regressed scores. All subjects with regressed scores below zero were put into one group. These subjects had smoking levels at the post-test *lower* than those predicted by the regression line relating pretest and post-test scores. Subjects whose regressed scores were zero or were positive, i.e., those with smoking levels at or greater than those predicted by the regression line, were put into the other group. The second split included among the changers all those identified in the first split as changers, and, in addition, subjects whose decrease was less than half a pack but still great enough to place them below the regression line. In essence, the first split contrasted subjects whose decrease was substantive with all other subjects; the second split contrasted subjects whose relative smoking level had decreased by any amount with those whose relative level had remained constant or increased. A computer program was used which furnished frequency distributions for the contrasting groups on every variable in the subject's record, and carried out an analysis of variance which tested the likelihood that differences in the means of changers and non-changers on each variable were due to chance (Dixon, 1965).

Similar analyses of variance were run contrasting scores on our variables for the four experimental groups, and for changers and non-changers within each of the experimental groups. Next, we used the MANOVA program of the University of Miami Computer Center (Clyde *et al.*, 1966) to do two-way analyses of variance. One of the two classifications consisted of a split of subjects into those above and below the mean for each of the factor scores on the Test of Patterns of Support. The other classification was based on various measures of individual differences. Similar two-way analyses of variance were carried on for a variety of other double classifications which we expected might lead to interesting interaction effects.

Lastly, we determined which variables in our battery of predictors were significantly correlated with the criteria of change. We then used a program for multiple correlation to determine the degree of independence of the predictors.

Since we were interested in studying overall prediction of change as well as the impact of the experimental procedure, all of our analyses of change were run separately for the entire group of subjects and for the three experimental groups without the controls.

7
Results of an Experiment in Role Playing

The data of this study will be presented in four major sections. The first will be concerned with an analysis of the effects of the experimental manipulation; it will contrast the four treatment groups. The second section will take an overall look at the determinants of change in smoking by comparing subjects who changed with those who did not; in this section the analyses will be restricted to the impact of individual variables. In the third section the interaction of variables predicting change will be studied through the use of multiple regression and of two-way analyses of variance. Lastly, a brief account will be given of the results of the long-range follow up.

THE EFFECTS OF THE EXPERIMENTAL MANIPULATION

Initial Character of the Groups

There were no significant differences among the subjects assigned to the four treatment groups in levels of smoking, in distributions of scores on the personality tests, or the subscales of the Test of Patterns of Support. Nor did the four groups differ in scores on the overall measure of Subjective Expected Utilities. When they were compared on the 10 subscales, five for values and five for expectancies, there was no significant variation among them on nine of the 10 scales. On the tenth, the expectation that change in smoking behavior would affect ability to reduce tension, the "patients" were slightly but significantly higher than the other three groups. Thus the random assignment of subjects did yield essentially equivalent treatment groups.

Change in Reported Levels of Smoking

Comparison of group means. In all four groups, some decrease in smoking occurred between the first and the second reports (Table 35). The groups differ in extent of the decrease (F=3.05, df 3/132, $p < .05$). The drop in average smoking levels is significant only for the three groups exposed to the role playing as indicated by mean difference "t" tests. The reason is evident in Table 36, which shows that almost a fifth of the control subjects reported increased levels of smoking. Only 6% of the subjects in the other groups reported increases.

An alternate, and somewhat more sensitive way, of looking at change is to examine relative rather than absolute change. This is done in two ways in Table 35; values are given for mean percent decrease and for the mean regressed smoking score (for a discussion of regressed scores see Chapter 6). Percentage decrease was relatively high among the "doctors" and observers, low among the "patients" and controls. The regressed scores give the most dramatic indication of the variation in the effect of the different experiences. The mean regressed score was almost zero for the observers, positive for the controls and "patients," and highly negative for the "doctors." That is, when the entire group of subjects was used to define the regression of post-experimental on initial levels of smoking, the "doctors" fell well below that line. Regressed smoking scores did not differ significantly among "patients," controls, and observers. The "doctors" and observers also did not differ significantly from each other ($t = 1.12, n = 61$). However the "doctors" did differ significantly in regressed smoking scores from both the "patients" ($t = 2.02, n = 79, p < .02$) and the controls ($t = 1.74, n = 61, p < .05$, one-tailed test). Since it was predicted that experimental subjects would change more than controls, the one-tailed test is appropriate for the latter comparison.

TABLE 35
Levels of Smoking Before and Five Days After Role-playing Experiment
(135 Male College Students)

| | N | Mean Number of Cigarettes per Day | | | Mean Difference t | % Decrease | Mean Regressed Smoking Score |
		Pre-experiment	Post-experiment	Decrease			
Controls	32	17.20	15.20	2.00	1.59	10	11.19
Observers	23	21.20	16.22	4.98	4.10**	23	.29
Doctors	39	20.33	13.67	6.67	3.72**	24	−20.67
Patients	41	17.34	15.23	2.11	2.56*	14	10.75

*$p < .05$, **$p < .01$.

Subject's perception of change related to "actual" change. In the five-day follow-up interview, the subjects were asked to report on the number of cigarettes they smoked and also whether there had been any recent changes in their smoking habits. The responses were used to classify the subjects along two axes: one was the difference in the number of cigarettes reported before and after the experiment, the other whether the subject *said* he had changed his level of smoking. The four groups differed in the proportions who said they changed, ranging from 25% among the controls to 46% among the "doctors" (Table 37). But even more striking is the fact that virtually all of the "doctors," observers, and controls who said they changed were found to have reported a smaller number of cigarettes after the experiment than before. Even those "doctors" who did not decrease by half a pack, our criterion for changers, gave reports which showed that their levels of smoking had dropped. In contrast, among the "patients" who said they changed, almost half (7 out of 15) did not report decreased levels of smoking on the post-experimental interview. The lower half of Table 37 indicates that most of the subjects who did not think they had changed their levels of smoking reported the same number of cigarettes on both interviews. However, there was a fair proportion (30%) who, if we are to believe both reports of the number of cigarettes usually smoked, decreased their consumption without being aware of it.

TABLE 36
Changes in Levels of Smoking Following the Role-playing Experiment
(135 Male College Students)

| | N | Increased[†] | | No Change | Decreased[†] | | |
		10 or more	1-9		1-9	10 or more	Stopped
Controls	32	2	4	15	5	4	2
Observers	23	0	1	8	7	7	0
Doctors	39	1	2	11	1	8	4
Patients	41	1	1	27	7	3	2

[†]*Cigarettes per day.*

Effect of the Experimental Manipulation on Psychological Measures

Behavior observed during the experiment. Immediately after the role playing the experimenter who played the role opposite each subject rated the subject on two 7-point scales. The first dealt with the subject's level of emotionality, the second with the degree to which the subject entered into the role, i.e., his involvement in the acting. The two groups, "doctors" and "patients," differed significantly on both scales. The "patients" were rated as more emotional, the "doctors" as more clearly engaged in the creation of the role. The findings, of course, may be contaminated by the investigator's preconceptions about the behavior of subjects in the two roles. It was one of the initial hypotheses that "patients" would be more self-referred and "doctors" more disinterested.

Situational anxiety. The role playing was followed by higher levels of reported anxiety among "doctors" and "patients" than among the observers; the control experiment led to the lowest levels of anxiety (Table 38). The overall differences among the groups are significant. But "doctors" and "patients" did not differ in mean levels of situational anxiety. Thus, the subjects' own reports on their levels of anxiety did not confirm the experimenter's ratings of emotionality. Perhaps these ratings reflect in part the success with which subjects entered the role. If the subjects' reports are to be believed, some subjects who played "doctor" must have felt less calm, and some "patients" less upset, than they appeared to the experimenter. We should note that there was no relation between computed change in smoking levels and situational anxiety within any of the experimental groups. However, subjects who *said* they changed, but did not, reported relatively high levels of situational anxiety. A high proportion of these subjects were "patients."

The post-experimental interview gives some insight into the source of situational anxiety. Subjects were asked what they were thinking about during the experiment and were classified into two categories on the basis of their replies. The first consisted of subjects who reported that they had been thinking about the task of role playing or other impersonal concerns (task-oriented). The second consisted of subjects who indicated that they had been thinking about themselves and their own smoking in relation to the experience of pretending to be a doctor or a patient or of observing the charade (self-referred). Following are some of the comments which formed the basis for the classification:

TABLE 37

Relationship between Global Statement about Decrease and Change in Number Reported as "Usually Smoked"

(135 Male College Students)

Subjects Who Said They Decreased

Group	N	Number of Subjects			
		Increase †	No Change †	Decrease 1-9 †	Stopped or Decreased 1/2 Pack or More †
Controls	8(25%)	0	2	3	3
Observers	7(30%)	0	2	2	3
Doctors	18(46%)	1	0	6	11
Patients	15(36%)	0	7	4	4
	48	1	11	15	21

Subjects Who Said They Had Not Changed

Group	N	Increase	No Change	Decrease 1-9	Stopped or Decreased 1/2 Pack or More
Controls	24(75%)	6	13	2	3
Observers	16(70%)	1	6	5	4
Doctors	21(54%)	2	11	6	2
Patients	26(63%)	2	20	3	1
	87	11	50	16	10

†*Computed changes in number of cigarettes per day.*

Task-oriented

"I was thinking of ways that I could convince a person to stop smoking. I was also trying to get myself mentally organized for the part."

"Wondering what the questions would be and what I would be told."

"I'm afraid I felt like a guinea pig, and concentrated more on the actual mechanics than any intended message."

"The only thing I was thinking of was what I was going to say."
"I was thinking of playing my part effectively."

Self-referred

"I was thinking that if I continue to smoke, this situation, instead of just acting out a part, could really come true."

"The case history in the role sounds like my real life."

"That I was smoking for a reason that didn't make much sense to me."

"That eventually, I might be the patient 20-30 years from now!"

"That if I was faced with the same situation, I would at least cut down on, if not stop completely, my smoking."

"I began to take the whole situation more seriously. I guess I could actually picture this happening to myself."

TABLE 38
Levels of Situational Anxiety During the Role-playing Experiment
(135 Male College Students)

| Group | N | Situational Anxiety | |
		Mean	S.D.
Controls[†]	32	10.6	4.3
Observers	23	12.5	5.3
Doctors	39	14.9	5.8
Patients	41	14.3	5.9

$F = 4.41$, $df = 3,131$, $p < .01$. [†]Participated in a perceptual experiment.

Among all three experimental groups, but especially among the "patients," the subjects who were self-referred had the highest levels of anxiety (Table 39). As the numbers of subjects in each cell indicate, the proportion of subjects who identified with the role rather than dealing with the content in a disinterested manner was highest among the "patients," 63%, as compared with 54% and 52% for the "doctors" and observers, respectively.

TABLE 39
Situational Anxiety and Categorization of "Thoughts during the Experiment"
(103 Male College Students)

| | Task-oriented | | | Self-referred | | | |
| | Situational Anxiety | | | Situational Anxiety | | | |
	N	Mean	S.D.	N	Mean	S.D.	t
Observers	11	10.3	4.7	12	14.5	5.2	1.94*
Doctors	18	13.0	4.7	21	16.7	6.3	1.98*
Patients	15	10.2	6.0	26	16.6	4.1	3.79**
Total	44			59			

*$p < .10 > .05$, **$p < .01$.

Change in subjective expected utility. * One of our major hypotheses (see Chapter 5) was that role playing should have a marked effect on attitudes. Attitudes towards smoking were measured in the current experiment mainly through the various components of the Test of Subjective Expected Utility. Our prediction was confirmed only for the measure of SEU for *stopping* smoking, and only for one group. The "doctors" changed towards a higher utility for stopping than did the controls, as indicated by the regressed total SEU for stopping ($t = 1.88$, $n = 70$, $p < .05$, one-tailed test). The difference between the observers and the controls approached significance; the average scores for patients and controls were almost identical. The four groups did not differ significantly in regressed overall SEU for *continuing* or in the average of the C–S scores calculated for each subject. The tenuous nature of these findings suggests that the effect of the role playing on attitudes was minimal. However, later on we will present a second-order analysis relating experimental manipulation, change in SEU, and change in smoking which will show more clearly the impact of the experimental manipulation.

The factor scores derived from the SEU test for the experimental groups were analyzed to determine which aspects of utility were affected by the experimental manipulation. Only one of the five, that of self-image, showed clear differentiation among the groups. "Doctors" believed that they would feel proud of themselves if they stopped smoking; "patients" showed this belief to a lesser extent. ($F = 2.91$, df 3,131, $p < .05$).

Subjective expected utility of not smoking. As a final part of the Test of Subjective Expected Utility, in both the pre-experimental and post-experimental session, subjects were asked to rate the value of not smoking for a week, a month, and a year. The rating was given on the same scale (-5 to $+5$) as that used for the outcomes of smoking or not smoking. They also rated their expecta-

---

*For the reader who is having trouble keeping track of the interrelations among the various SEU scales, the following summary may be helpful. The subject made three judgments on each of 40 items, each describing an outcome of smoking or not smoking: (1) value of the outcome, (2) expectation of probability of occurrence of the outcome should he *continue* to smoke, (3) expectation of occurrence should he *stop* smoking. The following scales were generated:

    a.   Overall SEU for Continuing: 40 items—Value X Expectation (Continue)
    b.   Overall SEU for Stopping: 40 items—Value X Expectation (Stop)
    c.   Overall SEU for Change: 40 items—Value X (Expectation Continue minus Expectation Stop)
    d.   *Five* factor analyzed scales on each of which groups of items describing related outcomes (Self-Image, Ill-Health, etc.) are scored separately. There were two scores on each factor scale. The first was the average of the *Values* placed on the outcome described in the items, the second was the average of the *Expectations* of change in the outcome should the subject stop smoking (Continue minus Stop).

On each of these scales (a-d) three scores were obtained: *Pretest, Post-test* (immediately after the experiment), and the *Regressed* score which indicates the relative impact of the experimental experience.

tion of success in staying off cigarettes for a week, a month, a year, again on a scale measuring "chances in 100" from zero to 100.

For each subject we calculated the difference between pre-and post-experimental values for not smoking and expectations of the likelihood of success. Mean difference *ts* were computed separately for the experimental and control groups. There was a significant tendency for subjects in the experimental groups to increase the value placed on stopping and the expectation of success in stopping; no such change occurred in the control group (Table 40). This is the most straightforward indication we have of the impact of role playing on attitudes.

Summary of Effects of Manipulation

The four experimental groups did not differ among themselves on the pre-tests in virtually any of the measures used in the study. Role playing led to more immediate reduction in smoking levels among "doctors" than "patients"; observers changed almost as much as "doctors." Most subjects who reported lower levels of smoking on the post-experimental interview than on the pretest indicated an awareness of change; only among the "patients" was there a sizable group whose global reports of change were not substantiated by their counts of number of cigarettes smoked. The experimenter noted higher levels of anxiety among "patients" than "doctors," but greater involvement in the role among the latter. The subjects' own reports of situational anxiety indicate that both roles led to higher anxiety levels than the experience of being an observer or a control subject. There was a marginal tendency for "doctors" to change their utilities for stopping smoking. This was probably due to an increase in the value placed on the self-mastery implied by success in eliminating smoking. The experimental subjects ("doctors," "patients," and observers) changed their responses on the items dealing with the value of stopping and the expectation of being able to refrain from smoking. After the experiment they reported increased value for re-fraining from smoking and greater expectation of success. No such change oc-curred among the controls.

FACTORS PREDICTING CHANGE

In the next series of analyses the four study groups were combined and the total body of subjects then split on the basis of reported reductions in levels of smoking. The rationale for combining the groups was that subjects who changed should show similar characteristics no matter what the source of the change. For example, if pattern of support for smoking predicts the likelihood of change, subjects who do not crave cigarettes (i.e., those low on the scale of Psychological Addiction) should be over-represented among changers whether the experience that led to change was playing "doctor" or "patient," observing, or reacting to whatever forces in the outside world affected those few of the control subjects who cut down on smoking. As will be seen below, when we carried out two-way analyses of variance with the study groups on one axis and the various pre-dictors of change on the other, we did not discover any important interaction effects. On this basis we felt that it is valid to discuss the predictive effects of such variables as SEU, patterns of support, and personality, apart from the nature of the experimental manipulation.

TABLE 40
Mean Differences in Value and Expectancy of Success In Stopping Smoking (Pre- and Post-test)

	Mean Difference	S.D.	t
Experimental Subjects[†] (N=103)			
Value[††]: Week	−.56	1.76	3.25**
Value: Month	−.66	1.97	3.40**
Value: Year	−.38	2.37	1.62
Expectancy of Success:[‡] Week	−4.17	24.48	1.73*
Expectancy of Success: Month	−6.02	24.83	2.46**
Expectancy of Success: Year	3.59	21.04	1.73*
Control Subjects (N=32)			
Value: Week	.06	2.09	.17
Value: Month	−.03	2.36	.07
Value: Year	−.56	2.55	1.25
Expectancy of Success: Week	−1.56	18.16	.49
Expectancy of Success: Month	−1.87	21.17	.50
Expectancy of Success: Year	−1.56	16.87	.52

[†] *Observers, "Doctors," and "Patients."* [††] *"How much do you care about staying away from cigarettes for a week . . . a month . . . a year?" (−5 to +5).* [‡] *"What are the chances that you could be successful in staying away from cigarettes for at least a week . . . a month . . . a year?" (0 to 100).*
*p < .05 (one-tailed), **p < .01 (one-tailed).

As noted in Chapter 6, changers were identified in two ways. The first used absolute reduction and set the division at a reduction of one-half pack of cigarettes a day. This was chosen as a "natural" division point; of the subjects who decreased, all but one cut down by either one-half pack or more or by seven cigarettes or less. The one exception was a subject who had initially given eight cigarettes a day as his average daily consumption but had been included in the study population because he had smoked half a pack on the day before the pretest. He stopped entirely, giving a reduction of eight cigarettes a day. Thus, in the following analyses, where changers are identified through absolute reduction, the group refers to subjects who either reduced by ten cigarettes or more or stopped smoking entirely. In the second procedure regressed smoking scores were used as a criterion; changers are defined as those below the regression line of post-test on pretest smoking levels (see Chapter 6).

With absolute reduction as a criterion, the changers were slightly but significantly higher in initial smoking levels than the non-changers (Table 41). They reduced their smoking levels after the experiment by approximately three-quarters of a pack per day. The average reduction among the non-changers in the number of cigarettes usually smoked was about one-quarter of a pack.

Subjective Expected Utility (SEU) as a Predictor of Change

Initial differences between changers and non-changers. The two groups did not differ initially in the absolute levels of overall SEU for continuing or stopping. But the prospect of changing was relatively more appealing to those subjects who later changed, even before the exposure to role playing. This is indicated by the significant difference in initial C–S scores (Table 42).

TABLE 41
Smoking Levels of Subjects Categorized as Changers and Non-changers (135 Male College Students)

Variable	Changers (N=31)		Non-changers (N=104)		
	Mean	S.D.	Mean	S.D.	F
Initial Level[†]	20.9	11.6	17.4	7.4	4.00*
Post-experimental Level[†]	8.8	8.2	16.4	7.6	
Average Change per Subject[††]	−14.8	8.5	−6.1	40.7	

*$p < .05$, [†]*Number of cigarettes smoked the day before questionnaire*, [††]*Number of cigarettes usually smoked.*

The major impact of role playing was on the utilities for *stopping*. The post-experimental SEU scores for stopping, both absolute and regressed, clearly differentiated subjects who reduced or eliminated smoking from those who did not (Table 42). There was a small, statistically significant but substantively slight, difference between changers and non-changers in regressed SEU scores for continuing to smoke. The C–S scores are, of necessity, much larger among the changers than the non-changers, and the sign of the difference is reversed. For the changers, stopping had by far the higher utility than continuing, hence the negative C–S scores; for the non-changers continuing had higher utility and the C–S scores were positive.

In order to determine whether the difference between changers and non-changers would hold even when the criteria for change were less vigorous than in the previous treatment, the group was split at the mean (i.e., zero) of the regressed smoking score (Table 43). All of the subjects classified as changers in the previous treatment fall below the regression line, i.e., have negative regressed scores. The group with negative regressed scores also includes subjects who reduced their smoking levels by amounts less than half a pack, but more than would be expected from the slight downward drift in smoking in the entire population. The differences in SEU between changers and non-changers seen with absolute change (Table 42) were also found when regressed smoking scores were used as the criterion of change. (Table 43).

Components of the Test of Subjective Expected Utility. Changers and non-changers were contrasted for each of the component factor scores of the SEU test (for a description of the items contained in each subscale see Table 28). These included pretest and post-test measures of both value and expectancy, regressed scores of value and expectancy, and the product of value and expectancy for the post-experimental test on each of the groups of outcomes (Table 44).

There are two differences on the pretest between those subjects who later changed and those who did not. The changers were less worried than the non-changers that giving up smoking would reduce their ability to find sources of stimulation and pleasure (Mood). The non-changers had a somewhat more pronounced expectation that reducing tension without smoking would be difficult. The latter finding may be confounded because of the over-representation of

TABLE 42
Overall Subjective Expected Utility Scores for Changers and Non-Changers Criterion: Absolute Change in Levels of Smoking
(135 Male College Students: All Treatment Groups Combined)

Variable	Changers (N=31) Mean	S.D.	Non-changers (N=104) Mean	S.D.	F
Pre-experimental[†]:					
Continue	800	654	979	718	1.52
Stop	1298	598	1228	704	0.25
Continue-Stop	−498	494	−250	584	4.6*
Post-experimental:					
Absolute[††] Continue	812	618	796	687	0.01
Absolute Stop	1565	676	1199	675	7.01**
Absolute C-S	−753	643	−403	430	12.37**
Regressed[‡] Continue	106	362	−31	485	2.13*
Regressed Stop	244	495	−72	485	10.09**
Regressed C - S	−184	531	54	391	7.49**

[†]*For ranges on pre-experimental SEU, see Table 33 (Chap. 3).* [††]*Range on absolute post-experimental SEU: Continue −350 to 2,450; Stop −20 to 2,870; C-S −2,370 to 680.* [‡]*Range on regressed SEU: Continue −1,282 to 1,059; Stop −1,244 to 1,357; C-S −1,938 to 1,269.*
*p < .05, **p < .01.

"patients" among the group of subjects who did not change. The failure of some of these subjects to change may be due to an expectation that tension reduction would be difficult without cigarettes. On the other hand, the major cause may be an inhibiting effect of the role of "patient." The fact that regressed SEU scores also predict change, however, suggests that the key factor was the impact of the experiment rather than pre-existing differences in expectations.

The impact of the experiment on attitudes is most clearly shown by the *regressed* scores for the sub-scales of the SEU test, i.e., the factor scores. Change is predicted by two of the five factors. Changers increased the value they placed on being envied by other smokers and on being proud of themselves should they stop smoking (Self-image). They also changed in the *expectation* that smoking or not smoking would have an effect on their health (Ill-Health). When the absolute post-test SEU scores were examined, changers and non-changers differed on three of the factor scores: Self-image, Ill-Health, and Tension Reduction. Value was important for the first of these, expectation for the latter two. The fact that regressed scores on Tension Reduction were not related to change in smoking may be due to the pretest difference in these scores between those subjects who changed and those who did not.

TABLE 43
Overall Subjective Expected Utility Scores† for Subjects *Below* (Changers) and *Above* (Non-changers) Mean. Criterion: Regressed Smoking Scores
(135 Male College Students. All Treatment Groups Combined)

Variable	Changers (N=67)		Non-changers (N=68)		F
	Mean	S.D.	Mean	S.D.	
Pre-experimental:					
Continue-Stop (C-S)	−415	534	−200	592	4.93*
Post-experimental:					
Absolute Continue	804	633	795	708	0.01
Absolute Stop	1415	655	1152	704	5.02*
Absolute C-S	−611	513	−357	471	8.95**
Regressed Continue	41	395	−40	520	1.06
Regressed Stop	94	473	−92	519	4.76*
Regressed C-S	−79	427	78	435	4.47*

†*For ranges on pre-experimental SEU, see Table 33 (Chap. 3), on post-experimental SEU see Table 42. *p $<$.05, **p $<$.01.*

TABLE 44
Differences between Changers and Non-changers on Factor Scores from Test of Subjective Expected Utility†
(135 Male College Students: All Treatment Groups Combined)

Variable	Changers (N=31)		Non-changers (N=104)		F
	Mean	S.D.	Mean	S.D.	
Pre-experimental:					
Expectancy: Mood	6.1	14.7	13.0	18.5	3.71*
Expectancy: Tension Reduction	−0.6	10.7	−8.3	14.5	7.60***
Post-experimental:					
Regressed Value: Self-image	2.3	4.4	−0.7	5.1	8.34***
Regressed Expectancy: Ill-Health	4.7	9.6	−1.4	11.9	6.70**
Absolute Value: Self-image	2.5	4.7	−0.8	5.2	9.84***
Absolute Expectancy: Ill-Health	31.1	14.3	24.3	14.2	5.50**
Absolute Expectancy: Tens. Red.	1.1	12.3	−6.0	12.0	8.09***
Absolute SEU: Ill-Health	−1,294.5	765.4	−962.7	645.2	5.70**
Absolute SEU: Tension Reduction	−85.7	451.8	229.3	475.6	10.71***
Absolute SEU: Self-image	−37.7	85.7	3.4	61.7	8.78***

†*For ranges on pre-experimental SEU, see Table 33 (Chap. 3), on post-experimental SEU see Table 42. *p $<$.10 $>$.05, **p $<$.05, ***p $<$.01.*

Intra-individual Variables as Predictors of Change

Levels of smoking. When changers were identified on the basis of absolute changes in smoking, they were found to be somewhat higher in initial smoking levels than non-changers. There is a significant correlation between the amount of change and the initial level of smoking ($r = .41$, $n = 134$, $p < .01$). However, this finding was not maintained when regressed smoking scores were used ($r = .10$, $n = 134$). Apparently those changers who smoked heavily cut down by larger absolute amounts than the changers who smoked lightly. However, relative change was constant over the entire range of smoking levels.

Patterns of support for smoking. The men who reduced or eliminated their smoking differed from those who did not change in three of the factor scores on the Test of Patterns of Support (Table 45). These relations were examined by using change as a continuous variable and noting the correlation of scores on the Test of Patterns of Support with the amount of reduction in smoking. The subjects were then, as usual, dichotomized on the basis of both absolute change (at one-half pack per day reduction) and regressed levels of smoking (at a regressed score of zero). Changers and non-changers were then contrasted.

TABLE 45
Relation of Reduction in Levels of Smoking to Scores on Test of Patterns of Support (135 Male College Students: All Treatment Groups Combined)

Support	Correlation with Reduction in Smoking	Correlation with Regressed Smoking Score
Pleasure	.15	.23**
Tension Reduction	.24**	.34**
Psychological Addiction	.19*	.32**

	Criterion: Absolute Change				Criterion: Regressed Smoking Score			
	Changers (N=31)		Non-changers (N=104)			Changers (N=67)		Non-changers (N=68)	
	Mean	S.D.	Mean	S.D.	F	Mean	S.D.	Mean	S.D.	F
Pleasure	345	95	373	72	3.18	347	85	386	66	8.46**
Tension Reduction	268	66	283	67	1.19	266	64	293	67	5.70*
Psychological Addiction	248	78	264	74	1.11	242	72	279	74	8.67**

$*p < .05$, $**p < .01$.

The changers used cigarettes to a lesser degree for the reduction of tension, they reported craving for cigarettes at a lower level, and they indicated a lesser degree of pleasure from smoking than the non-changers. The differences are modest when absolute change is used as a criterion; differences in mean scores are not significant and the correlations, although significant, are low. The relation of pattern of support to change is more evident with regressed smoking scores as the criterion; reassignment of the moderate changers increased sharply the separation between changers and non-changers. Apparently even slight changes in smoking levels are unlikely to occur among people who are aware of "craving" for cigarettes or who rely on smoking to reduce tension. The fact that subjects who changed also reported lower levels of pleasure in smoking will require comment below (see Chapter 8). These findings are not related to the level of smoking; the amount subjects smoked is independent of scores on the components of the Test of Patterns of Support (see Chapter 3).

It should be noted that the absolute level of the "pleasure" scores for the entire group of subjects was quite high. Changers did not find cigarettes *unpleasant;* they merely accepted the items describing cigarette smoking as pleasurable somewhat less enthusiastically than their fellows. Similarly, the level of psychological addiction in the entire group was fairly low, as would be expected from their age. Subjects who changed, however, rejected more vigorously than non-changers the proposition that they "craved" cigarettes.

SEU for not smoking as a predictor of change. One overall measure of attitudes which differentiated experimental from control subjects was the answer to the questions, "How much do you care about staying away from cigarettes for a week . . . for a month . . . for a year?" and "What are the chances that you could be successful in staying away from cigarettes for at least a week . . . a month . . . a year?" These answers provide some valuable insight into the determinants of change following exposure to role playing (see Table 46). Changers indicated on the pretest that they valued not smoking somewhat more than non-changers. The contrast is more marked when the comparison used is that between subjects above and below the mean regressed smoking score than when changers are rigorously defined as those who cut down by half a pack per day or more or stopped. In the former split, men whose attitudes made them susceptible to influence but whose behavioral change was minimal were included in the group of changers. The differences in value are small, about one unit on an 11-unit scale (−5 to +5). In contrast, the differences in expectation of success in stopping are highly significant and, in terms of proportion of the scale, larger than for value. The differences in expectation of success between changers and non-changers average 20 units on a 100-unit scale (zero to 100 chances in 100).

The impact of the experiment on the utility of stopping smoking was not very different for the changers and non-changers (Table 47). Both groups developed an increase in the value placed on not smoking. On the whole, neither group showed significant changes in the expectation of being able to abstain. The point is important. Even with an experimentally induced change in value, many of the subjects did not change their smoking behavior. What mattered was the initial expectation of success (see Table 46). That was, apparently, sufficiently high among the changers so that an increase in the *value* placed on not smoking could lead to action. For the non-changers, who initially cared little about stopping, pessimism about the possibility of change may have been enough to inhibit action even with a change in values.

TABLE 46

Comparison of Changers and Non-changers on Pre-experimental Value of Stopping Smoking and Expectancy of Success†

(135 Male College Students: All Treatment Groups Combined)

Time Interval	Value			Expectancy		
	Changers Mean	Non-changers Mean	F	Changers Mean	Non-Changers Mean	F
	Criterion: Absolute Change in Levels of Smoking					
	(N=31)	(N=104)		(N=31)	(N=104)	
Week	1.42	.29	4.55*	64.84	56.35	1.49
Month	1.10	.10	2.48	50.97	36.92	4.55*
Year	.87	.17	.93	35.81	24.23	3.64
	Criterion: Regressed Smoking Score					
	(N=67)	(N=68)		(N=67)	(N=68)	
Week	1.19	−.09	8.50**	67.76	48.97	11.02**
Month	1.02	−.35	6.76**	51.34	29.12	17.66**
Year	.87	−.19	3.07	35.08	18.82	10.66**

†See Footnote to Table 40 for precise wording of items and character of scales.
*$p < .05$, **$p < .01$.

Summary. Before we move on to the discussion of personality, a brief summary of the main findings concerning SEU and patterns of support for smoking may be helpful. The subjects who changed demonstrated on the pretest that they had a slight preference for the status of non-smoker and also were reasonably confident of their ability to maintain that status. On the pretest of Subjective Expected Utility, the changers as a group showed higher utilities for the consequences of not smoking than for continued smoking. Changers differed from non-changers in pattern of support for smoking. Non-changers were more likely to view their smoking as a source of pleasure and of relief from tension, and to report a craving for cigarettes. The result of role playing was to increase the value placed on *not* smoking for those subjects who later decreased or eliminated their smoking. The big change was not an increase in fear of the consequences of continued smoking but rather an increase in the desirability of the positive effects on health and pride in self. Unfortunately, these changes occurred primarily among subjects whose *need* for cigarettes was relatively low.

TABLE 47

Comparison of Changers and Non-changers on Mean Differences from Pre- to Post-test in Value and Expectancy of Success in Stopping Smoking (103 Male College Students: Experimental Subjects Only[†])

	Mean Difference	S.D.	t
Changers (N=25):			
Value[††]: Week	−.76	1.74	2.19*
Value: Month	−.84	1.82	2.31*
Value: Year	−.72	2.07	1.74***
Expectancy of Success[‡]: Week	−4.80	24.17	.99
Expectancy of Success: Month	−5.20	27.86	.93
Expectancy of Success: Year	7.20	23.90	.15
Non-changers (N=78):			
Value: Week	−.50	1.77	2.49**
Value: Month	−.60	2.02	2.63**
Value: Year	−.27	2.46	.97
Expectancy of Success: Week	−3.97	24.72	1.42
Expectancy of Success: Month	−6.28	23.96	2.32*
Expectancy of Success: Year	−2.44	20.08	1.07

*$p < .05$, **$p < .01$, ***$p < .05$ (one-tailed).

† Control subjects showed no significant difference before and after the experiment.

†† Negative sign indicates higher value placed on not smoking at post-test.

‡ Negative sign indicates greater expectation of success at post-test.

Measures of personality as predictors of change. One of our hypotheses (see Chapter 5) was that tests of personality would not directly predict the impact of role playing. This was confirmed for all but one of the tests we used, i.e., three of the four showed no correlation with any of the measures of change. However, these tests were indirectly associated with change. The exception was that the Taylor MAS scores *were* directly related to regressed smoking score; more anxious subjects were less likely to change than those low in anxiety. However, the negative association of anxiety with change was accompanied by interaction effects to be discussed below.

Unobtrusive measures of behavior during and after the experiment. During the role playing the "doctors" were instructed to say, after they were queried by the "patient," that they planned either to stop or to cut down their smoking. "Patients" were instructed to agree to follow the "doctor's" directions. Virtually all of the subjects followed these instructions, although several found it very difficult to say something as part of the role playing which they did not really feel to be true. The responses of the subjects during the role playing were recorded and classified into three categories: (1) A definite statement of "intention" to quit smoking, (2) A statement of "intention" to cut down, (3) No mention of cutting down or quitting. For the purpose of analysis the latter two categories were combined leaving one group whose members said they would stop smoking (approximately 40%) and another group whose members said they would cut down or evaded the issue.

There was a significant tendency for subjects who said they would quit during the role playing to report lower levels of smoking in the five-day follow-up interview than they had given initially (see Table 48). Apparently the mediating processes which differentiated subjects who later changed began to affect the behavior of most of them during the role playing. However, there was no association between the expression of commitment to change during the role playing and global statements about change on the post-experimental interview (see Table 49).

TABLE 48

Response during Role Playing Related to Change in Smoking on Five-day Post-experimental Interview ("Doctors" and "Patients")

Response During Role Playing	Post-experimental Interview		
	Reduced by 1/2 Pack of Cigarettes per Day or Stopped	Other	Total
Said would quit	11	20	31
Said would cut down or didn't know	6	42	48
	17	62	79†

χ^2 = 5.89, df = 1, p < .01. †Data from one subject could not be coded.

At the start of the post-experimental testing session an ashtray with stubbed-out cigarette butts was placed before each subject as silent indication that smoking would be permitted. Virtually none of the subjects who reported lower levels of smoking on the follow-up than on the initial questionnaire smoked during this post-experimental session (Table 50). The proportion of smokers during the session was highest among the controls and observers, lower among the "patients," and lowest among the "doctors." The difference in proportion of subjects smoking between "doctors" and controls is significant. This adds another piece of evidence for the greater impact of role playing on "doctors" than on "patients," and for the relation between the events during role playing and later behavior.

Independence of the Predictors of Change: Multiple Regression

The previous sections have examined a series of predictors of change individually and indicated the degree to which each was related to the measures of decrease in levels of smoking. Since some of these predictors were interrelated, it was essential to assess their independent contribution to the variation in

change in smoking. This was done through multiple regression, with both absolute and regressed change as criteria. Variables significantly related to the regressed smoking score were selected for entry into the multiple regression analysis. Fourteen of them account for a multiple correlation of .68 (Table 51). Not
all of these variables yield significant F values for entry (Guilford, 1956), but the
entire array is included in the table as it was generated by the computer.

TABLE 49
Response during Role Playing Related to Global Statements about Change on
Five-day Post-experimental Interview ("Doctors" and "Patients")

Response During Role Playing	Post-experimental Interview		
	Said They Changed	Other	Total
Said would quit	16	15	31
Said would cut down or didn't know	17	31	48
	33	46	79†

$\chi^2 = 2.03$, N.S. †Data from one subject could not be coded.

The reader may note that a number of variables which have been described
as strongly predictive of change on the basis of analyses which treat one variable
at a time do not appear in the multiple regression analysis. For example, one
variable which does not appear is the regressed total SEU for stopping, which
demonstrated the impact of the experiment on the subjects' attitudes towards
the results of not smoking. This variable does not appear on the multiple regression because it is highly correlated with the post-test SEU for stopping. Since
the correlation of regressed smoking score, our criterion measure, is slightly higher for the latter than for the former, the multiple regression shows the post-test
SEU for stopping rather than the theoretically more interesting regressed score.

TABLE 50
Smoking during Post-experimental Tests Related to Change in Smoking at Five-
day Follow-up (135 Male College Students)

Group	Total Number of Subjects	Number of Subjects Who Smoked		
		Changers	Non-changers	Total
Controls	32	1	8	9 (28%) †
Observers	23	1	5	6 (26%)
Doctors	39	0	3	3 (8%) †
Patients	41	1	7	8 (17%)

†Difference in proportion between Controls and "Doctors": $t = 2.2$, $p < .05$.

The degree to which the correlations of these various predictors with the measure of change in smoking is dependent on differences among the various experimental groups is not indicated by the multiple regression analysis. Assignment to the groups, as a non-continuous variable, could not be included here. It would have been desirable to run multiple regressions on each of the four study groups separately, but the number of subjects in each was far too small. Again, as previously, we must note that there were no interaction effects with two-way analyses of variance contrasting the various predictors against the study groups. This supports the notion that it was justified to combine the groups, and that the character of the multiple regression is probably independent of the treatment effects.

TABLE 51

Summary of Multiple Regression Analysis of Predictors of Change Following Role Playing (103 Male College Students: Experimental Subjects Only) Criterion: Regressed Smoking Scores

Variable	Correlation with Criterion	Multiple R	F
Value: Stopping Week, Pre-exp.	−.35	.35	14.12**
Psychological Addiction	.30	.45	9.48**
Value: Self-image, Post-exp.	−.27	.51	7.73**
Initial Smoking Level	.07	.54	4.41*
SEU: Stopping, Post-exp.	−.23	.57	4.68*
Stimulation	.03	.59	3.22
Expectancy: Mood, Post-exp.	.23	.60	3.10
SEU: Ill-Health, Post-exp.	.18	.61	2.09
Tension Reduction	.23	.62	1.81
Value: Mood, Pre-exp.	−.07	.63	1.91
Value: Aesthetic, Post-exp.	−.14	.65	2.23
Value: Ill-Health, Pre-exp.	.26	.67	5.00*
Value: Stopping Month, Pre-exp.	−.35	.67	1.20
SEU: Tension Reduction, Post-exp.	.27	.68	1.07

$*p < .05, **p < .01.$

In summary, the multiple regression shows (see Table 51) that subjects who decreased their smoking valued being able to stop smoking, did not smoke for tension release, did not crave cigarettes, had smoking levels initially somewhat higher than average for the group, and developed increasingly positive subjective expected utility for stopping after the experiment.

INTERACTIONS AMONG PREDICTORS

The major predictors described in the previous section hold when the *group* of changers is compared with the *group* of non-changers. Within each of these groups, however, there are exceptions to the general trends. For example, four of the 31 changers were more than one standard deviation *above* the mean for the entire population in Psychological Addiction; 10 were *below* the mean in regressed SEU for stopping, two of them by more than one standard deviation; some of the changers were relatively high in situational anxiety. Thus, it is important to examine the interaction among predictors to learn something of the effect of combinations of variables. This may be done in a number of ways. In most instances we chose to use two-way analysis of variance. The criteria used were various measures of change. Four groups were set up by dividing the entire body of subjects above and below the mean for two predictors at a time. Thus, we could compare levels of change among subjects high and low on regressed SEU for stopping and, simultaneously, high and low on MAS. Since the number of possible combinations is large, we chose those which promised results of theoretical interest. The MANOVA program of the University of Florida Computer Center was ideal for this analysis since it adjusts for groups of unequal sizes. The trends resulting from these analyses will be described verbally and values of F given where appropriate. However, to conserve space, the means of various subgroups will not be given, except for one series of analyses (Appendix XVI).

Obviously, many theoretically useful questions could have been answered by higher-order analysis. We could have looked at change among subjects high and low in regressed SEU for stopping, high and low in MAS, and high and low in the use of cigarettes for the reduction of tension. However, to divide our subjects into eight groups would have reduced the number in each to such an extent that interpretation would be impossible. Therefore, no such procedures were carried out.

Interactions with Subjective Expected Utility

Total SEU scores and patterns of support for smoking. The influence of a pattern of craving or of the use of smoking to reduce tension was so strong that most subjects with high scores on these factors did not change even if the role playing affected their subjective expected utilities. Only one of the subscales of the Test of Patterns of Support showed an interaction with utility. The degree to which subjects described themselves as stimulated to smoke by social situations did interact with SEU. The men who considered themselves solitary smokers, and for whom the difference in SEU between continuing to smoke and stopping (C–S) became greater after the experiment, reported the highest absolute level of reduction in smoking (interaction $F = 4.4$, df 1,124, $p < .05$).

Regressed total SEU for stopping smoking and other predictors: A multiple regression analysis. As has been indicated, one of the theoretically most interesting predictors of change was the regressed SEU score for stopping smoking. Rather than examine each of the interactions of this factor with other predictors, especially since the independence of the findings would not be evident through such an analysis, we split the group of subjects into those above and those below the mean on the regressed SEU for stopping. Multiple regressions were then run for the two groups: those subjects whose SEU for stopping *was* affected by the experiment and those whose SEU was *not* affected. Tables 52 and 54 show the multiple regressions with regressed smoking scores as criteria; Tables 53 and 55 show the regressions with absolute change in smoking. Since we were interested in the impact of the role playing, this analysis was carried out only for the three groups of subjects who were exposed to the interaction between "doctor" and "patient."

TABLE 52
Summary of Multiple Regression for Subjects with High Utility for Stopping Smoking (50 Male College Students: Experimental Subjects Only)
Criterion: Regressed Smoking Score

Variable	Correlation with Criterion	Multiple R	F
Initial Smoking Level	.41	.41	9.58**
Value: Stopping Week [†]	−.40	.52	6.60*
Grade-point Average	.19	.63	9.53**
Psychological Addiction	.33	.68	5.23*
Age	.16	.71	3.45
Expectancy: Stopping Month [†]	−.40	.75	5.92*
Stimulation	−.11	.77	3.08
Tension Reduction	.25	.78	2.43
Regressed Grades (College Boards)	−.25	.79	2.25
Expectancy: Stopping Year [†]	−.20	.81	2.76

*$p < .05$, **$p < .01$. [†]*Pre-experimental data.*

TABLE 53
Summary of Multiple Regression for Subjects with High Utility for Stopping Smoking (50 Male College Students: Experimental Subjects Only)
Criterion: Absolute Change in Number of Cigarettes Smoked

Variable	Correlation with Criterion	Multiple R	F
Psychological Addiction	.32	.32	5.45*
Value: Stopping Week [†]	−.30	.42	4.25*
Grade-point Average	.27	.54	7.67*
Age	.19	.58	2.50
Expectancy: Stopping Month [†]	−.31	.63	4.52*
Initial Smoking Level	−.05	.66	3.47
Stimulation	−.04	.69	2.46
Expectancy: Stopping Year [†]	−.14	.71	2.47
Tension Reduction	.22	.73	2.68
Regressed Grades (College Boards)	−.23	.75	3.47

*$p < .05$, **$p < .01$, [†]*Pre-experimental data.*

There are several differences between the two sets of multiple regressions, as well as several common elements. For the first time in these analyses, information about the subjects' academic situation emerges as a significant predictor. As noted in Chapter 6, the record for each subject included his scores on both verbal and mathematical Scholastic Aptitude Tests and his cumulative grade-point average through the end of the previous semester. A regressed score for grades was calculated on the basis of the difference between the subject's absolute grade-point average and that which would be predicted from his SAT scores. Thus, students with positive regressed scores are "over-achievers," those with negative regressed scores are "under-achievers."

TABLE 54
Summary of Multiple Regression for Subjects with Low Utility for Stopping Smoking (53 Male College Students: Experimental Subjects Only)
Criterion: Regressed Smoking Scores

Variable	Correlation with Criterion	Multiple R	F
Pleasure	.35	.35	7.29**
Initial Smoking Level	−.31	.46	5.44*
Value: Stopping Month[†]	−.30	.52	4.16*
Psychological Addiction	.26	.57	3.89
Situational Anxiety	−.16	.62	4.46*
Age	−.22	.66	4.38*

*$p < .05$, **$p < .01$. [†]Pre-experimental data.

Situational anxiety, which had shown no direct relation with change in other analyses, emerged as a significant and independent predictor, but only for subjects whose utilities were not affected by the experiment. In this group there was a slight but statistically significant tendency for subjects who were upset by the experiment to reduce their smoking more than those who were not. Grades were related to change in smoking for both groups, but in different directions. For the subjects whose SEU *was* affected by the experiment, both absolute and regressed grades were significant predictors. Subjects in this group who changed their smoking had somewhat higher absolute grades than those who did not change. They also had grades *higher* than would be predicted from their college board scores. In contrast, among subjects whose utilities were *not* affected, the changers had *lower* grades than predicted from their board scores. To summarize, for the subjects whose utilities were changed by the experiment, reduction in smoking occurred among students who were fulfilling their academic promise by obtaining high grades. Among subjects whose utilities did not change, reduction in smoking occurred among students who were doing poorly in school compared to expectation, and who reacted to the experiment by becoming anxious.

This finding suggests that two mechanisms led to short-range change. The cognitive mechanism, indicated by change in subjective expected utilities, operated for bright, academically effective, tension-free students. The arousal of anxiety was not necessary for change among these subjects. However, as indicated by lack of *negative* correlation with situational anxiety scores, anxiety-arousal need not inhibit change. For those subjects whose SEU was *not* affected, change could occur if they perceived the role-playing experience as a source of anxiety; the fact that these students also tended to be "under-achievers" may indicate a general lack of cognitive control in their lives.

TABLE 55
Summary of Multiple Regression for Subjects with Low Utility for Stopping Smoking (53 Male College Students: Experimental Subjects Only)
Criterion: Absolute Change in Number of Cigarettes Smoked

Variable	Correlation with Criterion	Multiple R	F
Initial Smoking Level	−.74	.74	60.14**
Value: Stopping Month †	−.08	.79	10.32**
Psychological Addiction	.11	.81	4.89*
Grade-point Average	−.24	.83	4.71*
Situational Anxiety	.01	.84	2.86
Pleasure	.30	.85	1.76
Age	−.26	.85	1.70
I/E	−.22	.86	1.34
Risk	−.24	.86	1.36
Tension Reduction	.13	.86	1.01

*$p < .05$, **$p < .01$. † *Pre-experimental data.*

Subjective expected utility and personality. The following analyses are based on four-way splits in which the entire group of subjects was divided simultaneously at the mean on a measure of personality and on either the overall scales or on a subscale of the Test of Subjective Expected Utility. The means for subgroups and the relevant significance tests on two-way analysis of variance may be found in Appendix XVI. For each significant interaction, identification of the two variables will be followed by a description of any subgroups which deviate noticeably on one of the measures of change in smoking.

a. Internal/External orientation. Scores on the test of internal/external orientation reflect the degree to which subjects are fatalistic (external orientation) or believe that they can exercise control over their destinies (internal orientation). Our prediction (see Chapter 5) was that change would be maximal among subjects who were internally oriented and whose utilities shifted by the role-playing experiment in a direction favoring not smoking. This was not confirmed for the overall SEU measures. However, when the data from the factor scores in the test of SEU were examined, the subscale concerned with Ill-Health furnished meaningful findings. A marked reduction in smoking was found among subjects who were internally oriented and whose SEU for Ill-Health following the experiment was most negative (Appendix XVI-1).

This seemed to confirm our initial hypothesis, but when the factor score for Ill-Health was broken down into its components of value and expectancy, the pattern changed. As with SEU as a whole, change was maximal among subjects who were internally oriented and for whom the value placed on ill-health became more negative following the experiment (Appendix XVI-2). But with expectancy, greatest change occurred among subjects who were *externally* oriented and whose expectations that continued smoking would lead to ill-health were increased by the experiment. As our hypothesis predicted, the least change occurred among externally oriented subjects whose expectations of ill-health from smoking were *not* affected by the experiment (Appendix XVI-3, 4). These findings occurred with either absolute change or regressed scores used to differentiate changers from non-changers.

These interactions account for the failure of I/E scores to be directly related to the impact of role playing on smoking in our experiment. The initial hypotheses were obviously inadequate. We had not expected externally oriented subjects to change at all, and had expected internally oriented subjects to change only if their utilities were affected by the experiment. The latter did happen. But, apparently, externally oriented subjects also acted to reduce their levels of smoking if their expectations were altered. This fits the general formulation of an internally oriented person as one who responds to his values, of a fatalistic person as one who reacts primarily to outside threat, if he reacts at all.

b. Crowne–Marlowe Test of Social Desirability. It may be remembered that subjects with high scores on this test accept as true of themselves a series of "good," socially sanctioned behaviors and reject identification with others which are almost universal but mildly censurable.

Social Desirability vs. Regressed Expectation: Tension Reduction (C-S) (Appendix XVI-5). Change occurred among subjects with high Social Desirability scores who developed a *high* degree of expectation that they would have difficulty in reducing tension if they stopped smoking and also among nonconformists who anticipated little difficulty in coping with tension if they stopped smoking.

Social Desirability vs. Value X Expectancy: Tension Reduction (Appendix XVI-6). This treatment shows maximal change among the persons with high Social Desirability scores and low utilities for reduction of tension by smoking. By a wide margin, the least change occurred among persons with high Social Desirability scores but a strong positive utility for the reduction of tension by smoking. The finding seems contradictory to that described in the previous paragraph. The apparent contradiction is due to the difference in meaning of absolute and regressed scores, and to the fact that significant differences in average reductions may hide individual variation. The latter would be exposed only with higher-order interactions. In the present instance one could suspect that some subjects with high Crowne-Marlowe scores entered the experiment with relatively little expectation that not smoking would pose problems of tension reduction. One result of the experiment may have been that their anticipation of such problems was heightened (i.e., their regressed scores were high) but that, nevertheless, for other reasons they made an effort to limit their smoking. Other subjects with high Crowne-Marlowe scores had high initial SEU for the use of cigarettes as tension reducers. The fact that their anticipation was not diminished by the experiment may have been a major factor in inhibiting change. These subjects all had high regressed smoking scores (Appendix XVI-6). They probably include the few subjects whose smoking actually increased.

Social Desirablility vs. Regressed Value: Mood (Appendix XVI-7, 8). The highest degree of change occurred among subjects with high Crowne-Marlowe scores who cared less after the experiment than before about smoking as a source of stimulation and pleasant feelings.

In summary, change seems to be favored by a combination of a tendency to present oneself in a favorable light and a low utility for smoking in the hedonic-affective area. However, some subjects with low Crowne-Marlowe scores also changed, especially those for whom the experiment decreased anticipation of problems in coping with tension.

c. Taylor Manifest Anxiety Scale. This widely used test asks subjects to report on a variety of behavioral tendencies loosely grouped under the rubric "anxiety." These include the tendency to psychosomatic symptoms, restlessness and sleeplessness, feelings of being ill at ease and upset. It may be remembered that MAS score and change in smoking were found to be inversely related (main effect, two-way analysis of variance).

MAS vs. Regressed SEU for Stopping (Appendix XVI–9). The subjects who reduced their smoking most were those with low MAS scores and *positive* utilities for stopping; those who reduced smoking the least had high MAS scores as well as *positive* utilities for stopping. We noted previously that not all of the subjects whose SEU for stopping was affected by role playing changed their smoking behavior. This interaction indicates that behavioral change may have been inhibited among anxious subjects. The significant interaction effect ($p <$ .03) is accompanied by a main effect for MAS significant at the .06 level. In this discussion the criterion measure has been the regressed score based on the number of cigarettes reported to have been smoked the day before the interview; there was a trend in the same direction, although it was not statistically significant, for absolute change and for the regressed number of cigarettes "usually smoked."

MAS vs. Regressed Expectancy: Self-image (Appendix XVI-10, 11, 12). The items from the Test of Subjective Expected Utility which make up the scale of Self-image focus on feeling proud of oneself at stopping smoking or being envied by other smokers. It may be recalled that change in *value* on these items clearly predicted a subject's success in changing his smoking levels. The fact that expectation for these items was not also related to change is clarified by the interaction with anxiety. Anxious subjects whose expectation of feeling proud was not affected by the experiment changed least among the four groups in the analysis. In contrast, subjects who were low in anxiety reduced their smoking even if they did not increase in their expectation that this would make them feel proud of themselves. One can assume, because of the strong relation of scores on the "value" scales for this factor to change in smoking, that many of these non-anxious subjects did develop an increased sense of the value of feeling proud over quitting.

d. Risk-taking tendencies. The Kogan-Wallach Test differentiates subjects who urge a fictional character to chance failure in order to reach a desired goal from those who require relative certainty of success.

Risk vs. SEU for stopping (Appendix XVI-13, 14). Three of the four subgroups showed essentially the same level of change. One subgroup stands out; change was minimal among conservative subjects whose utilities for stopping were low. This finding is not entirely unexpected. A major cognitive predictor, SEU for stopping, was important in differentiating changers from non-changers among the conservative subjects, but not among the risk-takers.

Patterns of Support for Smoking and Personality.

Another series of two-way analyses of variance was run by dividing the subjects at the mean according to their scores on the subscales of the Test of Patterns of Support and also on each of the measures of personality. Since situational anxiety related to role playing was one of the factors investigated here, the treatment was confined to the three experimental groups, i.e., observers, "patients," and "doctors." The following interaction effects emerged:

Psychological Addiction vs. Risk-taking tendencies (Appendix XVI-15). As we have noted previously, there was a strong tendency for subjects who changed to report lower-than-average scores indicating a craving for cigarettes, i.e., there was a main effect for this factor. And, as was pointed out earlier, this did not interact with changes in utility. However, there was an interaction with risk-taking tendencies. The combination of low scores on Psychological Addiction and *low* risk-taking tendencies led to the greatest reductions in smoking among the groups in the four-way division, i.e., to a significant interaction effect. This contrasts with the interaction of risk taking and SEU; there it was the *risk-takers* with positive utility for stopping induced by the role-playing experiment who changed. Thus, some subjects who changed were characterized by a combination of low risk-taking tendencies and low scores on Addiction, others by high risk-taking tendencies and the development of positive utilities for stopping.

Tension reduction vs. Situational anxiety (Appendix XV1-16). Those subjects who changed most were characterized by little tendency to use smoking for tension reduction and by low levels of situational anxiety. In other words, change occurred among subjects who were not upset by the role-playing experience and for whom cigarettes do not act as a pacifier. However, we have already noted (see p. 143) that this generalization holds only for the group whose utilities were also affected by the experiment. Among those whose utilities were *not* affected, situational anxiety was higher for the few subjects who changed than for those who did not. Unfortunately, the number of subjects did not permit a precise test of this three-way interaction.

Social stimulation for smoking vs. MAS (Appendix XVI-17). There is a fairly strong interaction effect between the level of social stimulation for smoking and Manifest Anxiety scores. The subjects who were most likely to reduce their smoking were those who were low in anxiety, as measured by the MAS, and whose smoking was socially stimulated. However, if they were *high* in MAS scores and in social stimulation for smoking, they were least likely to change. This finding suggests that socially cued smoking may play a different role for anxious and non-anxious subjects; it may be an important source of relief for the tension induced by social contact for the former but not for the latter. If so, it makes sense that anxious subjects for whom smoking is necessary as an icebreaker are unlikely to give it up. This analysis was suggested by Tomkins (1968) as the sole explanation for the social facilitation of smoking. The current finding suggests that this mechanism may operate for some smokers but not for all.

Social closeness: Self-image vs. MAS (Appendix XVI-18). This factor on the Test of Patterns of Support reflects the degree to which smokers identify with others who smoke, feel greater attraction towards groups of smokers than non-smokers, and accept a concept of "self as a smoker" (see Chapter 3). There was a very marked interaction between this factor and manifest anxiety, but only with regressed smoking score as the criterion. The people who changed were either non-anxious and above the average in "Social Self-image," or anxious and below average on this scale. In contrast, the group which was highly anxious and high on the scale was heavily weighted with non-changers. The combination of anxiety and a strong sense of identification as a smoker inhibited change; anxiety in itself, in the absence of self-image as a smoker and a feeling of warmth towards other smokers, did not.

Interactions of Predictors with Experimental Group.

As we noted at the start of the discussion of prediction of change, it certainly was possible that mechanisms of change would differ from one treatment group to another. For example, "doctors" might be more likely to change for cognitive reasons, "patients" because their anxieties were aroused. Since we have found that these two avenues to change were taken by different subjects, it was necessary to determine whether the differences in experimental manipulation were responsible. To test this, we carried out a series of two-by-four analyses of variance with the four experimental groups on one axis and, on the other, dichotomous divisions of the population of subjects on each of the major predictors. If differences in experimental treatment led to differences in the influence of a predictor, interaction effects would have emerged from this treatment. There were none.

In order further to demonstrate that prediction of change was, for all practical purposes, identical in each of the treatment groups, we contrasted the regressed overall SEU scores of changers and non-changers within each of the four study groups (Table 56). The differences between changers and non-changers on the SEU for *continuing* were randomly distributed. In contrast, the scores for stopping and the C–S scores were systematically distributed, with the changers in all four groups showing more positive utilities for stopping and more negative C–S scores than the non-changers. Despite the difference in experiences among the four groups, the relation between change in SEU and change in smoking seemed to be the same. Of course, the groups differed in the relative number of subjects affected by their experiences.

TABLE 56
Comparison of Overall Subjective Expected Utility Scores[†] of Changers and Non-changers within Each Study Group (135 Male College Students)

	Changers			Non-changers		
	Mean	S.D.	N	Mean	S.D.	N
Regressed Continue						
Control	−44	295	6	−93	556	26
Observers	17	347	7	25	443	16
Doctors	243	309	13	−89	492	26
Patients	53	543	5	29	453	36
			31			104
Regressed Stop						
Control	108	453	6	−191	517	26
Observers	144	410	7	− 28	369	16
Doctors	340	573	13	− 16	480	26
Patients	296	520	5	− 47	514	36
			31			104
Regressed Continue minus Stop						
Control	−196	633	6	94	330	26
Observers	−215	291	7	93	213	16
Doctors	−140	492	13	−40	512	26
Patients	−239	864	5	77	396	36
			31			104

[†] *For ranges on pre-experimental SEU, see Table 33 (Chap. 3), on post-experimental SEU see Table 42.*

We did find one difference among the study groups. It has been noted that MAS scores, in conjunction with several other variables, predicted change. Actually, we had expected a curvilinear relation between MAS and change and therefore plotted scattergrams for these two variables. There was no evidence of a curvilinear relation for the subjects as a whole. However, when the subjects were divided according to experimental group, there was a strikingly curvilinear relation for the "doctors," although not for the other groups. Among the "doctors," those who were *moderate* in anxiety showed the greatest change in smoking following the experience of playing the role. To test this statistically, MAS scores were converted into standard scores (z scores) and the absolute values of these z scores of the changers and non-changers were compared. For the "doctors," the changers showed significantly lower absolute standard MAS scores than non-changers ($t = 2.62$, $n = 37$, $p < .01$). In contrast, among the control subjects, the few changers were significantly more anxious, i.e., had higher MAS scores, than the non-changers ($t = 2.62$, $n = 31$, $p < .05$). There was no significant relation between MAS and change within the other two groups.

Summary of Interaction Effects

The many interaction effects found, despite their theoretical interest, should not obscure the main findings of our role-playing study. Most of the change in smoking occurred in subjects who did not have any strong stake in continued smoking and who were confident of their ability to change. Playing the role of "doctor" or observing the role playing led to a desire to change, stimulated by the increase in positive utilities attached to not smoking.

The interaction effects tell us that these changes were potentiated by some ongoing personality characteristics and inhibited by others. They also tell us that for some subjects the determinants of change were not cognitive. That is, the analyses reveal the character of the subjects for whom change occurred despite the failure of SEU to alter appropriately after role playing.

Interactions with SEU. Subjects who were internally oriented changed if there was an increase in the value they assigned to the favorable effects of stopping on health; fatalistic subjects changed despite their temperament if they developed an increased expectation of good health from quitting, and of ill-health from continuing to smoke. Subjects with high scores on the Test of Social Desirability tended to change if their SEU for the hedonic-affective aspects of smoking were altered by role playing. Those with low scores on this test changed if their fears of difficulty in reducing tension decreased following the experiment. The combination of low anxiety levels and an increased SEU for stopping was highly favorable to change; high levels of anxiety inhibited change even among subjects for whom SEU for stopping was affected by the experiment. And SEU for stopping was predictive of change among subjects who were not risk-takers, less predictive among those who were risk-takers.

Interactions with Patterns of Support. While changers were primarily low on Psychological Addiction, it was the combination of this characteristic with low risk-taking tendencies that predicted change. Anxious subjects changed if their smoking was not socially stimulated and if they did not have a sense of social affiliation with other smokers; non-anxious smokers changed even if their smoking *was* highly social.

Lastly, there was evidence that the majority of smokers who changed because of the effect of the role playing on SEU, a cognitive system, were students who were successful in school. The subjects who changed, but whose SEU for stopping was not affected by the experiment, were relatively unsuccessful students in school who were rendered anxious by the experiment.

ANALYSIS OF THE DETERMINANTS OF SITUATIONAL ANXIETY

Although situational anxiety was not predictive of change in smoking, the identification of factors leading to anxious reactions during role playing is still a matter of theoretical interest. Unfortunately, the number of subjects was not large enough to permit an analysis of the effects of situational anxiety within each experimental group. Therefore, the three groups exposed to the role playing were combined for this analysis. Since many observers reported a sense of empathy with the role players, they were added to the "doctors" and "patients."

TABLE 57
Comparison of Subjects Above and Below Mean Situational Anxiety Scores Following Exposure to Role Playing
(103 Male College Students: Experimental Subjects Only)

Variable	Low in Anxiety (N=58)		High in Anxiety (N=45)		
	Mean	S.D.	Mean	S.D.	F
High School Class Standing (deciles)	4.2	1.9	3.3	1.9	6.04**
Value: Stopping, Year	−0.4	3.0	1.0	3.8	3.96*
Expectancy: Stopping Year	26.0	29.0	23.0	28.0	.18
Value: Stopping, Month	−0.5	2.5	−0.7	3.6	3.98*
Expectancy: Stopping, Month	42.0	34.0	33.0	24.0	1.78
MAS	17.2	8.2	21.3	8.2	6.40**
Support for Smoking:					
a) Stimulation	210.3	65.3	238.5	73.9	4.22*
b) Social Stimulation	281.9	60.3	315.6	65.1	7.36**
c) Self-image, Social	211.1	61.7	241.8	52.9	7.08**
d) Tension Reduction	266.6	63.8	300.4	62.7	7.25**
Initial Smoking Level	20.0	9.5	16.0	7.3	5.55**

*$p < .05$, **$p < .01$.

The subjects were divided at the mean of their scores on situational anxiety. The two groups, those high and low in anxious reactions, differ on a number of variables, most of them quite expected (see Table 57). As compared with the subjects who were not upset by the experiment, those who were rendered anxious tended to have had somewhat higher class standing in their high schools, to have higher MAS scores, and to place a higher value on not smoking. They smoked somewhat less initially, but their smoking was more highly supported by the need for tension reduction and stimulation, they smoked more in social contexts, and they accepted for themselves a self-image as a "smoker." They did not have significantly higher expectations of success in stopping. It is apparent that some of the factors which were associated with situational anxiety were also characteristic of the changers (i.e., high value placed on stopping). But in large part the complex of characteristics noted among the subjects who were made anxious seems more like that found among non-changers. The fact that situational anxiety was inversely associated with change among subjects whose utilities were not affected by the experiment (see above) is probably responsible for the similarity between the pattern of variables differentiating anxious from nonanxious subjects and that differentiating changers from non-changers. Note that level of situational anxiety was *not* associated with change in utility and it was the latter which was most closely associated with reduction in smoking for the largest proportion of the changers.

GLOBAL REPORTS OF CHANGE CONTRASTED WITH ESTIMATES OF SMOKING LEVELS

We have referred previously to the item on the post-experimental interview in which subjects were asked whether their smoking levels had changed. A two-way division was carried out in which subjects were classified on one axis according to whether they "said they changed" or "said they were not trying to change" and on the other according to changes in their reported consumption of cigarettes. The group of subjects who "said they changed," but whose reports of smoking levels showed a reduction of less than half a pack or no reduction, were contrasted with the subjects who "said they changed" and whose reports did show reductions of a half a pack or more or cessation (Table 58). Subjects whose global reports were consistent with changes in the count of cigarettes had lower MAS scores, had more negative utilities for smoking, and described less craving for cigarettes. Their levels of situational anxiety were also somewhat lower than those of the other group, but the difference was not significant. This analysis, which adds one more piece of evidence about the role of anxiety in inhibiting change, will be discussed further in the following chapters.

TABLE 58

Comparison of Subjects Who "Said They Changed" and *Did* with Those Who "Said They Changed" and *Did Not* on Follow-up after Role Playing (38 Male College Students: Experimental Subjects Only)

Variable	Said They Changed and *Did* (N=18)		Said They Changed and *Did Not* (N=20)		t
	Mean	S. D.	Mean	S.D.	
MAS	18.2	6.1	22.4	8.0	1.75*
Situational Anxiety	14.5	6.7	16.1	4.7	.81
Psychological Addiction	227.8	60.0	295.0	78.9	2.86**
SEU: Tension Reduction, Pre-exp.	32.3	382.5	495.1	533.4	2.96**
SEU: Mood, Pre-exp.	216.6	501.2	721.6	823.4	2.19**
SEU: Tension Reduct., Post-exp.	−110.0	517.7	335.7	534.2	2.54**
SEU: Self-image, Post-exp.	− 57.7	105.7	14.4	56.1	2.59**

*p < .05 (one-tailed test), **p < .01.*

LONG-RANGE FOLLOW-UP

Approximately six to seven months after the experiment, an attempt was made to reach by telephone the 135 smokers who had participated in the study and the 61 non-smokers who had taken the pre-experimental battery (see Chapter 3). The interview (see Appendix XV) included questions about their current levels of smoking and, for the smokers, their recollections of the experiment, and their experiences with smoking during the interim since the experiment. For the three experimental groups, we also inquired about their reactions to the profile of scores on the Test of Patterns of Support and the associated booklet of hints to smokers.

Of the 135 subjects only seven could not be reached, which gave a return rate of 95%. None of the subjects who were reached refused to answer the questions. The seven experimental subjects who could not be reached consisted of three observers, two "doctors," and two "patients." The interviewers were not given information about the prior smoking status or the treatment group of any of the subjects they called. Of course, during the interview it became apparent whether the subject was a smoker or a non-smoker and, near the end of the interview, into which experimental group he had been placed.

The Non-smokers

Of the 61 non-smokers, 60 were reached. Fifty-five of these reported that they did not smoke cigarettes and never had. Five gave reports contradicting their original statements. Two said they were ex-smokers, three that they were now smoking and had been smoking for over a year. These three may have identified themselves incorrectly as non-smokers at registration (see Chapter 3) because of haste, fear of further questioning, or misinterpretation of the questions. None of the original non-smokers reported that they started to smoke during the 10 months from the administration of the first questionnaire to the time of the follow-up survey.

Results of the Long-range Follow-up

Smoking status. One of the most pressing questions we faced was whether the reductions of smoking levels which occurred shortly after the role-playing experiment would be maintained. The high rate of recidivism among smokers who have cut down or quit is notorious. Unfortunately, a simple description of smoking status at the time of the long-range interview does not give a meaningful picture of the effects of the experiment. We know that some subjects had reduced their smoking immediately after the experiment. Others cut down or stopped at various times between the post-experimental interview and the long-range follow-up. On the other hand, some subjects who had decreased resumed smoking at original or even increased levels. It would be invalid to attribute to the experiment changes in smoking which occurred long after. Our solution was to divide the smokers reached during long-range follow-up on the basis of four categories: those whose smoking remained stable throughout (64%), those who reduced after the experiment but reverted (12%), those who cut down or quit after the post-experimental interview (13%), and those whose reduction immediately after the experiment was maintained (11%). Each of the four groups was subdivided on the basis of the original experimental manipulation (Table 59). Approximately half of the short-range changers in each of the study groups maintained their reduction or cessation after six months except for the "patients." Among the "patients" only one of the five changers reached continued to smoke at a lower level than initially.

TABLE 59
Smoking Status of Subjects in the Four Treatment Groups on Short-range (Five-day) and Long- range (Six-month) Follow-up

Classification of Subjects	Number	%	Con-trols	Observers	Doc-tors	Patients
No Change	82	64	21	12	20	29
Change at Five Days Only	15	12	3	3	5	4
No Change at Five Days, Changed at Six Months	17	13	5	2	5	5
Change at Five Days, Maintained at Six Months	14	11	3	3	7	1
	128[†]	100	32	20	37	39

[†] *Seven of the original 135 subjects could not be reached for the long-range follow-up.*

The four groups, divided on the basis of smoking at the time of the two follow-up interviews, were also compared on each of the subscales of the Test of Patterns of Support and on the overall scores of the measure of Subjective Expected Utility (Table 60). The subjects who initially cut down and then reverted were relatively high on Psychological Addiction, although not as high as the group which did not change at all. They were also highest of the four groups on acceptance of self-image as habitual smokers.

Paradoxically, the subjects who reduced their smoking immediately after the experiment, and then resumed their initial levels, were those on whose utilities the role playing had the most powerful impact. They had markedly higher regressed utilities for stopping, and gave regressed C-S scores which showed a considerable expectation that not smoking would have more favorable effects than smoking. These young men, then, succeeded in changing their smoking behavior immediately after the experiment despite their craving for cigarettes and their use of smoking to define a self-image. However, although the change in SEU was sufficient to induce attempts to eliminate smoking, the craving for cigarettes was too great and the self-image as a smoker too fixed to permit continued success. This impression from the statistical analysis was confirmed by examination of protocols of the long-range interview.

Qualitative Data on Long-range Change

Examination of the interviews corroborates the quantitative analyses cited above. A high proportion of these young men had made some effort to change their smoking behavior, even those in the control group. In answer to the ques-

TABLE 60

Comparison of Mean Values of Scores on Patterns of Support and Subjective Expected Utilities among Groups Differing in Reduction in Smoking Five Days and Six Months After the Experiment (128 Male College Students)

	No Change (N=82)		Change at 5 Days Only (N=15)		No Change at 5 Days, Changed at 6 Months (N=17)		Change at 5 Days Maintained at 6 Months (N=14)		F†
	Mean	S.D.	Mean	S.D.	Mean	S.D.	Mean	S.D.	
Patterns of Support									
Tension Reduction	290	68	267	82	242	59	273	52	2.68*
Pleasure	379	68	330	107	347	87	361	90	2.11
Self-image, Social	230	52	233	78	201	72	196	60	2.33
Self-image, Habit	198	56	214	67	169	41	166	52	3.14*
Social Stimulation	295	65	305	61	288	82	275	49	.58
Psychological Addiction	275	71	260	94	213	77	230	64	4.14**
Stimulation	223	73	222	79	178	47	221	65	1.95
Sensory Motor	230	69	218	101	208	78	188	82	1.41
Total Utilities									
Pre-exp.: Continue	941	701	807	546	1169	803	911	705	.78
Pre-exp.: Stop	1222	693	1389	520	1313	764	1211	658	.32
Pre-exp.: C-S	-281	570	-581	499	-144	697	-301	395	1.70
Post-experimental:									
Regressed Continue	-21	485	78	445	-21	516	144	285	.65
Regressed Stop	-107	473	284	531	150	519	125	450	3.93*
Regressed C-S	92	316	-272	591	-133	660	21	343	4.05**
Absolute Continue	780	685	789	614	936	770	926	626	.38
Absolute Stop	1160	664	1667	648	1480	720	1385	692	3.15*

† df 3,124, *$p < .05$, **$p < .01$.

tion about attempts to change smoking, 54% of the subjects (20 of the 32 control subjects, 14 of the 20 observers, 25 of the 37 "doctors," and 23 of the 39 "patients") indicated that they had made some attempt, even if fleeting, to stop or cut down. Seven subjects gave illness, usually colds, as a reason for the change. Thirteen cited social compacts or personal influence. Other reasons ranged from the cost of smoking to changed circumstances such as the end of the school year or a change in jobs. Twenty of the 103 subjects in the three experimental groups attributed their attempts to reduce or eliminate smoking to their experiences in the experiment. Even taking the test of SEU had some effect; three of the control subjects described their reactions to the test as the trigger for action (see quotations below). Resumption of smoking after attempts to stop were ascribed to the increased tension of school or jobs, to a craving for cigarettes, or, in several instances, to contagion from friends or fellow workers.

The experiences described by the subjects who had cut down or quit are familiar to anyone who has talked with ex-smokers. Twenty-five of them gave the usual accounts of increased health, enjoyment of food, vitality, and freedom from minor illness. On the other hand, 15 of the same subjects also described themselves as being more nervous than before, missing cigarettes, and gaining undesired weight.

We were very interested in the subjects' reactions to the profile of their scores on the Test of Patterns of Support and the booklet of Hints to Smokers which were mailed to all subjects in the three experimental groups about two months after the experiment. Subjects who reported no attempts to change their smoking almost uniformly ridiculed the profile and the accompanying booklet, although a few did say that they found the material interesting and would use it if they ever decided to stop smoking. Among the 62 subjects who had made an effort to change, 21 said that the profile or the hints were interesting and useful, although few of the replies were enthusiastic. Ten of the 62 gave negative evaluations of the profile and booklet; they either rejected the description of their patterns of support or found the hints of little value. The remaining half of those who made an effort to change either found the material irrelevant since they had already stopped or gave neutral statements such as "interesting."

There is no better way of concluding this chapter than to quote some of the actual replies of our subjects during the interview. The following material illustrates many of the points made above and also provides evidence for the interactions of internal factors and social environment described earlier (see Chapter 2).

Control: (How did experience at Beaver affect you?) Found out why average person smokes, what harm it does.

Control: Tests I took made me aware of fact I should cut down my smoking.

Control: About cigarette smoking, how one feels his reactions — the differences between smoker and non-smoker. How healthy non-smokers feel compared to smokers. What the difference is. Thought about what I read.

Observer: Interesting. Made it much more realistic to me. Person playing the doctor was a buddy. Made it much more close than seeing it on TV or something. I cut down to three or four a day right after the survey, felt better, could run better but was more nervous than usual. I have increased now.

Observer: Learned from the book Beaver sent, realized that when I thought about the cigarette I really didn't need it. It was just a habit that I could break. But I went back to it when I got lazy analyzing.

Observer: Mock play; patient being interviewed by a doctor. Impressed me a great deal that cigarettes are hazardous. Made me aware of hazards. Taking action to cut down. Computer . . . pretty accurate. Majority of information seems right but disagree with some. Read over pamphlet a few times but because of school work and everything I more or less brushed it aside.

Observer: Definitely think it made me think more about my smoking.

Observer: It's bad. Cancer and heart disease scared me.
(Profile and hints) Interesting. Found out why I smoked and it helped. I have successfully cut down.

Observer: I placed myself in place of the patient. Didn't like it too much. I'd like to keep my health. Don't want anything to happen.
(Profile and hints) Good. Found out I didn't really want many of the cigarettes I was smoking. So I cut down.

Observer: Results of the tests that made me cut down. My major cause was social and knowing this helped me to cut down.
(Observation of role playing). Yes, I thought about my experiences at Beaver a lot. Made me cut down when I realized the cause of smoking.

Observer: First time I tried cutting down one cigarette each day. Worked until got to 8-9 then started back up. Second time stopped completely but it didn't last. Third time succeeded I think because under no tension, not in school, working instead. Hope and expect not to start again when I go back to school.
(How did you feel when you stopped?) Miserable. I was hard to live with. More mental than physical. Hard to have coffee and not smoke. I switched to milk temporarily.
(Did the experiences at Beaver affect you?) Yes. Made me stop and think. That and will power.
(Profile and hints) I followed some of the suggestions.

Doctor: (Think about your experiences?) Yes, thought it over. Affected my thinking about what it would do to my health and money.

Doctor: Was successful in stopping completely last of July for five and a half days then started when with friends who smoked. Trying all summer to stop or cut down.
(Profile and hints) Surprised! That I was socially stimulated smoker. I tried to avoid friends who smoked. I showed it to other smokers.

Doctor: (Role playing affect you?) Not immediately. But did when I received that thing by mail. Read over material. Didn't take seriously. But remembered about substitution. So substituted orange juice and cigarettes don't taste like anything after orange juice.

Doctor: (Think about experiences at Beaver?) Yes. Gave me initial start. Guilt, started to think about smoking.

(Profile and hints) Read them. Discussed them with my parents. They were helpful in cutting down, making the start.

Doctor: Tried to cut down after the "survey." Stopped immediately after the survey for one month. Then began to smoke again and have gradually increased but not as much as before. Was convinced by interview at Beaver. Interview between doctor and patient seemed convincing for a while but the experience has gradually worn off.

Doctor: (Experience affect you?) Yes. During test and afterwards I stopped smoking for two months. I went out with a girl who smoked and when you are in such close quarters with someone who smokes, you just naturally start smoking.

Doctor: Decided with several friends to stop altogether. Friends of family died of cancer. Stopping as a group helped.

(Experiences at Beaver?) Reinforced fact that smoking is harmful.

(Profile and hints) Not a good idea because emphasis is placed on smoking and ideas associated with smoking when you want to not think of smoking.

Patient: Did think about questionnaires. Thought interview was funny, ridiculous. Questions showed you that it is foolish to smoke, a waste of money.

Patient: (Experiences at Beaver) In long run influenced me to cut down. At first I thought it was research but then realized it could benefit me.

(Profile and hints) No, didn't use them. At same time I read a report of cigarette companies that cancer and cigarettes weren't linked.

Patient: (Effect of experiences at Beaver) Nothing except made me think about it seriously.

Patient: Started to smoke pipe about first of year. Cut down on cigarettes more and more. Had stopped completely in early March. Switched to tea from coffee. Pipe is good after tea, cigarettes after coffee. In late June went back to cigarettes when working. Under pressure as physical therapist at Byberry (a local mental hospital).

(Experiences at Beaver affect you?) Yes. Made me more determined to stop smoking.

8
Discussion of the
Role-Playing Experiment

The role-playing experiment will be discussed within the framework of the hypotheses presented in Chapter 5. In this chapter we will deal with each of the major findings and then, in the following chapter, discuss the more general implications of our studies.

The Impact of Role Playing on Cigarette Smoking: Hypotheses 1 and 2

The first hypothesis stated that subjects who played the role of "doctor" or "patient" in an interaction in which the "doctor" presented evidence to the "patient" of damage to health from smoking would be more likely to reduce smoking than subjects in a control group. There seems little question that the combination of role playing and specific instructions about how to stop was successful in stimulating subjects to decrease their smoking immediately following their experiences in the laboratory. All three groups of subjects exposed to the role-playing situation showed changes in smoking, the preponderance of which were decreases. There was no such pattern among the control subjects who participated in a perceptual experiment. Thus, we were able to confirm the first hypothesis which stated that there would be systematic changes in smoking upon exposure to role playing.

The second hypothesis dealt with our expectations concerning differences among the various experimental groups. On the basis of our pilot study, we predicted a gradient of effect, with the highest level of change expected among the "doctors," moderate change among the "patients," less among the observers, and least among the controls. Our prediction was that "doctors" would be less defensive than "patients" and would, therefore, react more strongly to role playing. The control subjects were expected to provide a baseline indicating the amount of reduction which would occur among male college students exposed to no stronger manipulation than taking tests about smoking. Our observers were the equivalent of the control subjects in the previous role-playing study (Janis & Mann, 1965) after which we modeled our experiment.

Our findings clearly substantiated the hypothesis concerning the potent influence of the experience of playing a doctor's role. However, the "patients" were far less affected than had been anticipated, whereas the observers changed to an unexpected degree. The marked difference in the impact of role playing on those playing "doctor" and "patient" did not appear in our own pilot study (Platt *et al.*, 1969). And the fact that more of our observers than our "patients" reduced or eliminated smoking is not compatible with the findings of Janis and Mann (1965), or those of Himes and his colleagues (Himes, Keutzer & Lichtenstein, unpublished paper).

There are two possible sources of confounding in the comparison of "doctors" to "patients." First, the "doctors" were exposed to the information about the mock laboratory tests twice whereas "patients" were exposed only once. Since the tests were explained to the "doctors" during the briefing by the experimenter, perhaps they were able to learn the material better. In addition, in accordance with Zimbardo's formulation (1965), it is possible that the "doctors" had to engage in a greater effort in connection with the counter-attitudinal material than did the "patients." These explanations are not supported by the unexpectedly high level of change among the observers. Like the "patients," they were exposed to the material of the mock tests only once, and their expenditure of effort was minimal. Of course, the mechanisms of change among "doctors" and observers may have differed, but there is no evidence for this in our data.

There is also a possible source of confounding in the comparison of *all* the experimental groups with the control group. At the close of the experimental session subjects in all three experimental groups were given a pamphlet outlining ways of stopping smoking. This pamphlet did not include any persuasive or exhortatory materials, merely a series of hints about ways and means for reducing or stopping smoking. The control group did not receive such a pamphlet.

Leventhal's work (see Chapter 4) convinced us that few subjects would change their smoking behavior if we did not include suggestions for methods of stopping, and that suggestions alone in the absence of role playing or some other persuasive manipulation, would not have any effect on smoking. We therefore decided to include the suggestions for stopping smoking or cutting down as part of the procedure only for the groups which were to receive some exposure to an anti-smoking experience. However, in interpreting the results of the experiment, it should be noted that the manipulations included not only participation in, or observation of, role playing, but also the receipt of a pamphlet about ways to change smoking behavior.

The observers. We did not anticipate as great an effect on smoking as actually occurred. But someone with a sense of theater might have predicted such an outcome. The observers were seated in a dark laboratory surrounded by amplifying equipment; they focused intently on the drama taking place behind a one-way screen. They listened with earphones and followed every interaction. The observers had a specific task; they were asked to rate both members of the dyad engaged in the role playing. There is no question that most of the observers took this task quite seriously. It is also probable that the level of attention they gave to the content of the interaction was higher than that elicited by a tape recording, as in the Janis and Mann study. Certainly many of the interactions were in themselves rather dramatic. It may be that observers other than college students would show less effect. Possibly college students would take the task of rating behavior more seriously than others in the general population. The value which many of them would place on participating in a scientific investigation may have heightened the intensity with which they attended to the role playing.

We can therefore postualte that the observers were deeply engaged in the events going on behind the one-way screen. There is little objective evidence to support or reject this postulate, but the impressions of the members of the research staff were that the observers were, indeed, deeply involved. This is supported by the vivid recollections many of the observers described during the long-range interview. In both the post-experimental questionnaire and the long-range interview they commented not only on the manner of the role players, but also on the substance of the interaction. A number of them described feelings of identification with the role players. In a sense, the observers may have passed through an Aristotelian catharsis. Among some this led to moderate changes in beliefs and to subsequent changes in behavior.

An additional explanation for change among the observers is that they changed attitudes and behavior somewhat in the way that subjects do in experiments on the effectiveness of overheard communications (Walster & Festinger, 1962). Where defensiveness is high, as is almost universally true with cigarette smokers, an overheard observation is more likely to penetrate defensiveness than a persuasive appeal. It is possible that the observers, deeply involved in rating their fellow students for adequacy of role playing, attended very carefully to the content of the interactions but did not feel that an attempt was being made to influence them. Of the seven subjects in the observer group who changed, six reported that they "thought of themselves" while watching. For example, one said, "I was preoccupied with the idea that I myself might have to be talking to a doctor like that someday." It may be remembered that self-reference among the "patients" was accompanied by a significantly high level of situational anxiety; this was not true for the observers. This may explain the fact that self-reference among observers was associated with change whereas among the "patients" it was not.

Determinants of differences between the two role-playing groups. The "doctors" clearly demonstrated the effectiveness of role playing as a procedure for influencing smokers to change. Had we run the study with "patients" as our only experimental subjects, we might have concluded that role playing was quite ineffective. And yet it was clear as we did the experiment that the "patients" were involved emotionally in the events of the role playing.

There are several alternative explanations for the lack of change in smoking levels among the "patients." The first of these is that the role-playing experience generated so much anxiety among the "patients" that it inhibited change. We have already presented Janis' thesis (see Chapter 5) that high levels of anxiety inhibit change in attitudes, especially where defensiveness also is high. This analysis should apply to behavioral as well as attitudinal change. Thus Janis' argument would lead to the hypothesis that the "patients" in *our* experiment must have become overwhelmingly anxious, and, in an ensuing paralysis, been unable to do anything to reduce their anxiety. There is little evidence from our data to support this hypothesis. In their subjective reports, "patients" did not reveal significantly higher levels of situational anxiety during the experiment than the "doctors." And even if they had, no relation was demonstrated between situational anxiety and change.

A second explanation for the failure of "patients" to change is that by focusing on their own smoking problems they failed to carry out the "review of arguments" which is postulated by Janis as the major element responsible for change following role playing. That is, the "doctors" hammered away at the defenseless experimenter playing the role of "patient" in an effort to persuade him to stop smoking, and thus focused strongly on the arguments in favor of stopping. In contrast, the "patients" were thinking primarily of their own problems with smoking rather than the rationale for giving up. One aspect of the data tends to support this explanation. When we reviewed the relation between changes in subjective expected utilities and change in smoking behavior, it became clear that the component in the measure of values and expectancies most closely related to change in smoking was the SEU for outcomes of stopping rather than that for outcomes of continuing to smoke. It may be that the major difference between the "doctors" and the "patients" was that the role of the "doctor" tended to lead the subject to think about the virtues of stopping, whereas the "patients" were forced to be concerned with the dangers of continuing. The issues raised by this difference in effect on SEU will be discussed further below.

The work of Brehm (1966) suggests another explanation for the "patients'" behavior during and after the experiment. Brehm has found that subjects who feel under external pressure to change opinions respond with a sense of "reactance," i.e., a desire for independence and an emotional rejection of the influencing source. It is possible that the "patients" responded with just such a feeling. They did act as if their own smoking were being discussed; the role playing was more real for them than for the "doctors." They also responded with an outward show of emotionality. The "doctors" had no such reaction since they were less likely to perceive the experiment as one directed towards their own smoking. And it may very well be that the "patients'" covert reaction during the course of the role playing was one of rigid defense. The fact that relatively few of the "patients" changed their utilities following role playing argues that the defense applied not only to the act of cigarette smoking but also to their system of beliefs about cigarette smoking.

An additional fact which supports the notion of covert "reactance" on the part of the "patients" was the frequent discrepancy between their global descriptions of change in smoking levels and their reports of the *number* of cigarettes they had smoked. The presence among the "patients" of a sizable group of subjects whose utilities for smoking did not change but who gave an outwardly ingratiating description of their behavior is certainly compatible with the notion that many of these subjects, although overtly "conforming," were inwardly defiant of the experimenter's influence. While the hypothesis that ascribes the failure of most "patients" to change to "reactance" is certainly tenable, it was developed post hoc and there is relatively little evidence in our own data to permit us to evaluate it.

There is one final consideration about the differences among our three experimental groups. The observers were given the flattering task of assisting in the investigation. The "doctors" had the ego-building experience of pretending to be a member of a prestigious profession and engaging in behavior which was highly dominating. In fact, some of the "doctors" took advantage of the opportunity to bully the experimenter who played the role of "patient" opposite them. We noted that a change in the value of feeling proud of oneself and of being envied was one of the predictors of reduction in smoking. This factor, the regressed SEU: Self-image, was significantly higher for the "doctors" than other groups. It is not far-fetched to propose that the boost to self-esteem which some of the subjects derived from playing the role of doctor or observer might have contributed to the attractiveness of changing their smoking behavior as another ego-building act. For some, at least, this may have been enough to tip the scales of decision.

The Role of Utility: Hypothesis 3

Our third hypothesis stated that those subjects who developed an increase in the negative utility of continuing or the positive utility of stopping would be the most likely to change their behavior. The hypothesis was partially confirmed; the subjects for whom the positive utility of stopping was increased were most likely to decrease their smoking. We found no such consistent relation between changes in the negative utility of continuing to smoke and reduction of smoking. When one examines the character of the script for role playing, this finding may seem surprising. After all, the focus was on the purported danger to the smoker from his continued smoking. One might expect, therefore, that any changes which did occur would be based on the subjects' increased perception of risk. And yet it was the increased perception of benefit from not smoking that predicted change. Actually, there were some aspects of the role playing which would direct the subjects' attention towards the benefits of not smoking. The "doctor" was directed to emphasize the reversibility of the pathological changes in the "patient" if he should stop smoking. And much of the discussion between the two role players after the presentation of the clinical tests centered on the "doctor's" attempts to convince the "patient" that he would not face unsurmountable obstacles if he should try to stop and that he would enjoy an increased sense of pride and well-being if he were successful.

The factor analysis of our measure of SEU revealed the components of patterns of beliefs which were most directly related to change. It was hardly unexpected that the component of SEU dealing with health most strongly predicted change. But despite the fact that the scenario dealt overtly with health, acting it out seems to have affected other areas of belief as well. The subjects for whom the role playing increased the value they placed on "feeling more proud of themselves if they succeeded in changing their smoking behavior" showed more change than those who did not develop this set of beliefs. Note again the importance of the positive aspects of stopping, i.e., "feeling proud of oneself," rather than the negative aspects of continuing to smoke.

Our finding that the subjective expected utility of stopping predicted change in smoking, whereas the measure of utility of continuing did not, may not hold true for all populations. We did, after all, deal with a very narrowly selected group of subjects. They were healthy young men in their late teens or early twenties for whom the prospects of an early death must certainly have been extremely remote. Such young people probably have a strong feeling of invulnerability. It is extremely unlikely that a brief experience in a laboratory could shake this feeling. Possibly a population of middle-aged smokers who were aware of symptoms of ill health attributable to smoking, and for whom mortality was a lively prospect, would be more likely than our young men to react to an increase in negative utility for continuing to smoke.

The Role of Personality: Hypothesis 4

Our fourth hypothesis was that measures of personality would not directly predict change in smoking behavior. This was based on two considerations. The first was that we did not accept the notion that there are traits characterizing "persuasible" or "conforming" personalities. On the contrary, we felt that almost anyone would change attitudes and/or behavior under some circumstances and that there were circumstances in which almost anyone would resist persuasion. Secondly, we felt that the role of personality in smoking varies with beliefs about the effects of smoking and with the patterns of support. Therefore, we predicted that a knowledge of the subjects' personalities in conjunction with the analysis of their subjective expected utilities would lead to increased understanding of the mechanisms of change.

The fourth hypothesis was fully confirmed. Measures of internal/external control, risk-taking tendencies, and "social desirability," did not in themselves predict a tendency to yield to the pressures of the role playing or to resist them. There was some tendency for subjects high in anxiety levels, as measured by the MAS, to fail to change. However, this relation is also accompanied by interaction effects. The finding, therefore, does not invalidate the general thesis that change in smoking behavior cannot be directly predicted from scores on measures of personality. Rather, subjects changed or resisted change in their smoking if the effect of the experiment on their utilities was potentiated either by some characteristic of their personalities or by their pattern of supports for smoking. Thus, fatalism about the possibility of controlling one's own destiny (high I/E) meant that change was unlikely unless the specific content of the role playing led to a strong expectation that continued smoking would make a difference to health. A feeling of control over personal destiny did lead subjects to change, but only when their overall utilities for smoking were affected by the experiment.

Both low and high levels of change occurred among relatively non-anxious subjects. A low level of generalized anxiety (as shown by MAS scores) seemed to potentiate the decision to alter smoking behavior among subjects who became convinced of the virtues of stopping, and to lead to active resistance to alteration among those who were not convinced. The resistance to manipulation is apparent in some of the hostile comments made on the long-range interview by non-anxious subjects who had reacted negatively to their experiences during the experiment.

Change was not restricted to subjects low in anxiety; some changers had relatively high MAS scores; at least five had MAS scores more than 1.5 standard deviations above the mean for the entire group of subjects. Change occurred if the experiment led to an increase in the value placed on controlling one's own destiny, the Self-image component of the test of SEU. Thus, reduction in smoking occurred among both anxious and non-anxious subjects, but the mechanism of change appeared to differ in the two groups.

Analyses which included measures of personality also increased the meaningfulness of relations between scores on the Test of Patterns of Support and change in smoking. The interaction between intrapersonal and environmental factors supporting smoking (see Chapter 2) is exemplified by the relation among anxiety, social factors on the Test of Patterns of Support, and change in smoking. Subjects whose levels of anxiety were low were able to change even if their smoking was socially stimulated and reinforced by a feeling of social identification with other smokers. However, anxious subjects with such a pattern of support rarely changed. This finding is compatible with an instrumental analysis of smoking and of change in smoking. One could assume that non-anxious subjects would be confident that they would be able to maintain friendly relations with their friends who smoke; they might also feel less emotionally dependent on smoking as a source of support for their self-concepts. Anxious subjects did change, but only if they were really convinced that stopping was desirable, and if their smoking was not heavily supported by the fulfillment of social and self-defining needs.

Patterns of Smoking: Hypothesis 5

The fifth hypothesis was that smokers whose use of cigarettes was supported by the fulfillment of important needs would be less likely to alter their smoking than those whose smoking does not fulfill such needs. This was amply confirmed. The score for Psychological Addiction on the Test of Patterns of Support was a potent predictor of reduction or cessation in all of our analyses. That is, those smokers who reported a craving for cigarettes were the least likely to change and, if they did change, the reduction was not maintained. Similarly, most subjects who were high on either Tension Reduction or Pleasure failed to change.

The general finding, then, was that role playing had little effect on subjects whose Test of Patterns of Support indicated that cigarettes fulfilled any one of a number of emotional needs. This is in keeping with data from Study IV (see Chapter 2) and with the findings of McKennell's survey (1968). The implications of this finding will be discussed at length in the final chapter.

The finding that subjects high on Pleasure did not change was somewhat surprising since it was anticipated that subjects who reported cigarettes as pleasurable would find it relatively easy to discover alternative sources of pleasure. Actually, the relation between scores on Pleasure and the amount of reduction in smoking did not survive in the multiple regression analysis. About the same number of changers were above and below the mean for Pleasure, although the subgroup below the mean included several subjects with extremely low scores on this variable. These findings, in addition to the fact that virtually all of the subjects above 300 on Tension Reduction or Psychological Addiction were also above 300 on Pleasure, suggest that the apparent predictive value of scores on Pleasure is specious.

The heavy smokers in our sample were somewhat more likely to change than the light smokers. This is consistent with the results of Graham's work (Mausner & Platt, 1966b, p. 21) with volunteers attending a smoking clinic, although it is not clear whether his proposed explanation is appropriate to our subjects. Graham's heavy smokers changed because they were affected by the impact of smoking on their health; they had symptoms. Our youthful subjects were not likely to be severely ill. However, if they had the same level of symptoms as the young smokers in the British study by Holland and Elliott (1968), many of them probably had noticeable respiratory difficulties. Some did mention coughing and shortness of breath after exertion. It may be that the argument of the role playing was taken more seriously by the heavier smokers not only because of these minimal symptoms but because they could not take refuge in the rationalization that light smoking is unlikely to be harmful. The finding that very light smokers often change readily because they have so little to give up cannot be checked in the current study since we did not include men who smoked less than one-half pack a day.

Self-insight into the Likelihood of Success: Hypothesis 6

The sixth hypothesis predicted that the subjects themselves would be the best source of information about who would and who would not change following the role-playing experiment. This was amply borne out. The subjects' expectation that they would be able to refrain from smoking for varying lengths of time if they should want to, as expressed in the pretest, was a powerful predictor of change. Participation in the role-playing experiment changed the value almost all subjects placed on stopping; this was true for non-changers as well as changers. But even if their attitudes towards smoking were affected, the non-changers did not develop enough confidence in their ability to succeed to be able to make the break. This finding could have important implications for practice. The key to persuading smokers to stop may be the discovery of techniques for encouraging an expectation that not smoking would be beneficial and that success in stopping is likely.

The Effect of Role Playing — A Summary Comment

The foregoing discussion has dealt individually with each of the hypotheses which were tested in the study. In large part our predictions were fulfilled, although there were some surprises. Perhaps the most compelling aspect of the data, however, is their consistency. From the first contact to the last, most of the subjects who were affected by role playing behaved differently from those who were not. On their pretests they revealed greater optimism about the possibility of living without cigarettes. They were willing to say the words, "I will give up smoking" during the role playing. They did not take advantage of the tacit invitation to smoke implied by the presence of ashtrays during the post-tests. Their post-tests clearly showed an increase in the value they placed on not smoking and, for most, in the subjective expected utility of not smoking as well. Thus, the report of lower levels of smoking on the five-day follow-up than on the pretest is not an isolated behavior. But only a minority of our subjects reacted in this manner and the effects, for many, were short-lived. The results of our research still leave many unanswered questions. In the final chapter we will address ourselves to these as well as to the implications of our work for public health practice.

9

Implications for Research
and the Control of Smoking

This volume began with a view of smoking behavior as the final common path for a variety of extrinsic and intrinsic forces. While this formal "ecological" model has been referred to only occasionally, much of the work described in this volume exemplifies the concepts of multiple determination inherent in the model. In the following section we will summarize the contributions provided by our data to an understanding of the complex of environmental and intra-individual factors which determine smoking behavior. We will then discuss the specific implications of our role-playing data for the study of change in smoking and, lastly, will try to apply all of this material to the problem posed by continued smoking to individuals and to society.

THE NATURAL HISTORY OF SMOKING

Environmental Factors

Our work supports the widely held concept that smoking is initiated by forces in the social environment of adolescents. It also presents some evidence for the thesis that smoking throughout life is highly dependent on the social environment. We have little to add to the limited knowledge of physical and biological factors affecting smoking.

The data we have gathered show college students doing a large part of their smoking while with other smokers. But beyond that, they indicate that forces in the social environment interact with individual patterns of support for smoking and with personality traits. For example, we found that anxious students who are under academic stress tend to smoke to relieve tension. Middle-aged men reported that they smoked for tension relief while at work more frequently than in other contexts. And college women chose fellow smokers more frequently than non-smokers to share a variety of activities.

The limited evidence we have gathered emphasizes the need for further and more intensive study, both descriptive and experimental, of interrelations among characteristics of the social environment, individual reactions to that environment, and the use of cigarettes. A full understanding of the character of such interrelations has important theoretical consequences; it provides empirical substance for the abstractions embodied in the general model for the study of behavior presented in our first chapter. Presumably, such confirmation of the model would permit improved prediction of behavior. This would have practical consequences. The control of smoking will depend to a great extent on successful manipulation of the social environment. Persuasive appeals to smokers have reached some people but are clearly not a complete solution to the problem of designing anti-smoking campaigns. Without a subtle understanding of the way in which forces in the social environment affect smoking, the measures taken must of necessity be crude and, possibly, blundering.

It is unlikely that retrospective accounts alone will yield an adequate specification of the interrelation of environmental and intra-individual factors needed to predict the ebb and flow of smoking behavior. The use of diary materials, as seen in Chapter 2, is promising. But they should be supplemented by systematic observations of social groups in which smoking takes place. Hoffman and Boyko's study exemplifies such a technique (unpublished paper). They tested the hypothesis that smokers engaged in playing duplicate bridge would smoke more frequently if someone else at the table was smoking. Duplicate bridge is an ideal setting for such a study since individuals rotate among a variety of partners. Their failure to demonstrate social stimulation to smoking may be due to their lack of information about the patterns of support for smoking of the individuals in their population. It is possible that one could predict whether an individual will light up during a social interaction only if one knew whether the person usually smokes when he is exposed to the smoking of others. Since duplicate bridge, like many other competitive games, is certainly tension producing, it would probably also be helpful to know when the game was generating stress and whether individual players do or do not smoke to relieve tension. In summary, we feel that a combination of information about the individual's pattern of support and the character of the social environment would probably yield good predictions of smoking behavior.

There is no question that both diaries and direct observation make greater demands on the investigator than the use of questionnaires. The cooperation of subjects may be hard to win, especially for the writing of diaries. And the very fact of writing a diary or being observed may affect subjects noticeably. That is, studies using either diaries or direct observation of spontaneous social interactions pose problems because of self-selection of subjects and of the impact of the experimental procedure on the subjects' self-awareness and behavior. Still, both of these techniques, supplemented by questionnaires and by reports of critical incidents involving smoking (as in Studies I and II), would be valuable in delineating the multiple interrelations of environmental and intra-personal determinants of smoking.

Intrinsic Factors in Smoking

Emotional factors in smoking. The importance of emotional rewards from smoking is confirmed by descriptive material (Chapters 2 and 3) and by the results of the role-playing experiment. The components of affective supports for smoking which emerged in our studies are essentially the same as those reported by Horn and his colleagues. Furthermore, we found that the strength of our subjects' emotional gains from smoking predicted the likelihood that they would change their smoking after role playing. Not only were those subjects who reported a high level of pleasure, tension reduction, or craving for cigarettes unlikely to change immediately after role playing, but those who did change, despite emotional dependence, tended to revert.

We found some support for our concept of an affective dimension. That is, pleasure, tension reduction, and craving seemed to form a cumulative dimension rather than the set of mutually exclusive types originally described by Tomkins (see Chapter 3). In the analysis of our role-playing data, however, we treated each subcategory (i.e., Pleasure, Tension Reduction, Psychological Addiction) as an individual variable. In future research an attempt should be made to gather appropriate data so that a cumulative scale could be constructed; such a scale might be a very powerful predictor of spontaneous change as well as of resistance of subjects to persuasive messages.

Social identification and Self-image. We extended the picture of supports for smoking drawn by Horn and Tomkins to include two additional dimensions, social affiliation and role identification. That is, on the basis of descriptive accounts (Mausner, 1966), we postulated that many smokers find rewards from an increase in the sense of affiliation to social groups in which smoking represents a binding force. Furthermore, we postulated that many individuals use not only the fact of smoking but also the gestures of cigarette smoking as a part of the behavior which defines their self-image. We developed supporting evidence for both of these theses. On our Test of Patterns of Support many smokers agreed with items derived from the "Social" and "Self-image" dimensions. However, the clear differentiation of social supports and Self-image as independent dimensions proposed initially (see Chapter 1) was not fully confirmed by factor analysis. Items relating to social cohesion and those indicating that smokers were found to be attractive fell into one factor. A separate factor dealt with the subjects' perception of themselves as being habitual smokers and having the self-image of a "smoker."

The first of these factors (Social-Self-image) was useful, in conjunction with measures of manifest anxiety, in predicting change following role playing (see Chapters 7 and 8). That is, subjects who were anxious and whose smoking was supported by a feeling of social identification with other smokers were exceedingly unlikely to change.

Further research will be needed to see whether the contribution of smoking to a sense of cohesion among smokers is or is not independent of the use of smoking to bolster the individual's concept of himself, his self-image. Most of the data we have reported come from studies of college students, a group among whom problems of identity are notorious. It would be important to study samples of older smokers to determine whether social cohesion and self-image are relevant to the maintenance of smoking in later life.

The cigarette companies seem to feel that both of these factors, if indeed they are separate entities, are important. Their advertisements stress both social affiliation and role definition as major sources of satisfaction from smoking, although their primary *overt* emphasis is on hedonic factors, i.e., the taste of "fine tobacco." It is hard to know whether the television commercials which portray these factors as significant reflect genuine insight into smoking behavior or are themselves the source for the beliefs among smokers that smoking helps bring people closer together, that smokers are admirable folk, and that smoking makes one look and feel like the beautiful people in the television playlets and magazine advertisements.

The administration of tests (i.e., Test of Patterns of Support, diary questionnaires) to large groups of smokers randomly selected from the entire population would give a picture of the presence or absence of beliefs about importance of social and self-image-defining factors to the maintenance of smoking. Whether these beliefs are based on actual mechanisms which support smoking could perhaps best be determined by experimental studies in which groups at the extremes in such verbally expressed beliefs were subjected to experimental manipulations specifically designed to influence the smoking of someone high or low on a given factor. Thus, for example, an attempt could be made to teach cigarette smokers to unlearn the gestures which they use in smoking; this would reduce the degree to which smoking is used to support the social projection of a self-image. Such a procedure should be more effective in changing smoking behavior for subjects among whom the factor of self-image is an important support for smoking, less effective for smokers to whom that factor was largely irrelevant. Similarly, smokers for whom social cohesiveness is an important gain from smoking should change more when they shift into groups of non-smokers than individuals for whom this factor is less important than other patterns of support.

Personality and smoking. The concept that all smokers share a common set of traits (extroversion, neuroticism) is, it seems to us, called into question by the data presented in Chapter 3. Both highly anxious and relatively unanxious people smoke; the former may smoke to reduce tension while the latter do not. Similarly, both gregarious and solitary people smoke, although probably for different reasons. Just as anxious people may smoke to reduce tension, those with strong needs for social affiliation or problems in coping with feelings of anomie might very well use smoking to increase feelings of social identification or to bolster self-image. The general thesis we have presented is that although smokers vary widely in traits of personality, their traits and patterns of support for smoking are lawfully related.

Lastly, the study of single measures of personality in conjunction with individual supports for smoking (e.g., anxiety and the use of smoking for the reduction of tension) should be extended by the use of profiles. With these, the effect of personality and patterns of support on smoking behavior could be examined through the interrelation of arrays of personality traits and complete profiles of patterns of support. The complexity of such designs may very well stagger the imagination, but with multivariate analysis and the capabilities of new generations of computers, it may be possible to study these issues in their full complexity.

IMPLICATIONS OF THE ROLE-PLAYING STUDY

Our work with role playing exemplifies, we believe, an approach to research which is vitally necessary to the continued growth of social psychology. This combines experimental manipulation with extensive measurement of individual variation among subjects.* Such an approach is essential to the healthy growth of a discipline which sits astride the areas of the experimental psychologist, concerned with general laws, and the differential psychologist, interested primarily in individual uniqueness. A study of the sources of individual differences in reaction to persuasive messages can contribute to both areas as well as to experimental social psychology itself.

Attitudinal and Behavioral Change

Notions about the relation between attitudinal and behavioral change have varied all the way from a firm belief that behavioral change must await "change in the minds and hearts of men" to an equally firm rejection of the idea that the two are linked (Festinger, 1964a). The data are mixed. As noted in Chapter 4, studies of smoking have yielded little evidence that change in attitudes towards smoking is necessarily followed by cessation. Some of the findings are reminiscent of the classical studies showing dissociation between bigoted ethnic attitudes and prejudiced behavior.

Rather than deal with "attitudes" as usually measured, we preferred to concentrate on a specific kind of "event in the head," the subjective expected utility of events. SEU is inferred from verbal reports; it is the product of the subjective value placed on an event and perceived likelihood of occurrence of that event. One of our initial hypotheses was that change in subjective expected utilities *would* predict changes in behavior. The fact that this hypothesis was confirmed certainly makes it difficult to accept the thesis that there is no relation between attitudes and behavior.

It seems to us that the most parsimonious concept for handling the systems with which we are dealing is that of McGuire (1968, 1969). He has postulated a chain of events each of which may lead to one of a number of outcomes. The first event is exposure to information; a person may or may not attend. The second is the processing of that information; a person may or may not learn. The third is change in attitudes; these may or may not change. The fourth is retention; the change may or may not be lasting. Last is change in behavior; this may

---

*Our research represents an informal application of the multivariate approach of Cattell and his disciples to the study of attitudinal and behavioral change following social interaction, an area of investigation not represented in their massive handbook (Cattell, 1966).

or may not occur. Mathematically inclined readers may recognize such a series as a Markov chain.

A link which we should like to introduce into this chain of events is an interior process which can only be inferred from verbal descriptions of decision. It is our conclusion that an antecedent to decision is change in the pattern of subjective expected utilities and that, given appropriate environmental and individual factors, alteration of SEU will lead to changed behavior.

We suspect that previous failures to relate attitudinal change to behavioral change occurred because the measures of attitudes were heavily weighted with items dependent on values. In our data, although values play a role in predicting behavioral change, the lawfulness of relations between attitudinal and behavioral measures is largely dependent on the addition of measures of expectation to those of value. Our findings may, therefore, be added to the body of data supporting general models of behavior which include expectation as a major component (e.g., Atkinson, 1964). Examples would be the work of Atkinson, Feather, and their associates with gambling and test taking (Atkinson & Feather, 1966) and Berkowitz' studies of reactions to hostility (Berkowitz, 1960a and b).

The Mechanism of Role Playing

Why does role playing work? The data of the current study demonstrate that role playing works when it leads to changes in subjective expected utility. We can contribute relatively little to the controversy between Janis and Zimbardo (see Chapter 5) over the nature of the forces which lead to changes in attitudes and behavior. We suspect that role playing was effective in our study because it increased the attention paid by subjects to arguments with which they were previously familiar in a general way but which they usually ignored.

All three of the groups exposed to role playing were not subjected to the same pressures towards attending. The "doctor" was most actively involved in working with the content of the interaction. It may be, therefore, that the failure of the "patient's" role to lead to change in a high proportion of subjects was due to lack of attention to the details of the argument, perhaps due to a preoccupation with self. We have suggested two other possible mechanisms for the relative ineffectiveness of the "patient's" role playing. One is the arousal of sufficient anxiety among the "patients" to inhibit change. The other is that "patients" reacted negatively to the sense of pressure exerted by the experimenter in his role as "doctor." The data do not permit us to choose among these hypotheses, although the first is somewhat more fully supported than the other two. In future studies we shall attempt to vary the character of role playing to minimize the "patient's" identification with the role he is playing. This would test the hypothesis that preoccupation with self, induced by identification with the role of patient, inhibits change. Tests of the hypotheses concerning anxiety and reactance should also be carried out, although it is certainly possible that all three mechanisms are engaged and, indeed, may be interrelated.

Our failure to induce much change among "patients" does not seem consonant with the behavior of patients in the real world. We have previously commented on the potency of the physician as a source of influence on the smoking of his patients (see Chapter 5). In fact, one of the premises on which we based the design of the scenario for our study was the expectation that "patients" pretending to see a physician would behave somewhat as real patients do. While we expected that "doctors" in the role playing would show less defensive avoidance than "patients," and thus be more influenced by the role playing, we did hope that a fairly high proportion of the "patients" would be affected by the experience of role playing. And yet most of our "patients" failed to respond by reducing their levels of smoking.

We suspect that some of these young men might have stopped if they had been urged to do so by a real doctor whom they were consulting after they had taken a real series of laboratory tests. Information about actual damage from smoking, especially if accompanied by reassurance that much of it is reversible, would probably be harder to ignore than the make-believe in our experiment. If the "patients" in our study had been forced to pay heed to abnormalities in their *own* vital function tests or sputum cytology reports, a far larger number than responded to the mock tests of the role playing might have reevaluated their utilities for continued smoking and attempted to stop. The thesis is certainly worth testing.

Population and Message as Variables in Role Playing

The population. In our current study we found that changes in SEU for stopping smoking were highly predictive of behavioral change, although changes in SEU for continuing to smoke were not. Some of the young men who participated in the role playing must have been impressed by the fact that they would gain from not smoking; those who were so impressed proceeded to cut down their consumption of cigarettes. It is possible that a middle-aged group of smokers would be more impressed by the possible losses from continuing to smoke, although they might also be unhappy about giving up the gains associated with continuing. For smokers in their forties and fifties the history of reward from smoking is certainly very long. This postulated difference between young and middle-aged smokers in the way in which the utility of stopping or continuing would affect smoking behavior is only one example of variation in the nature of the subjects which might be expected to alter the outcome of a role-playing experiment. Differences in sex, in social class or ethnicity, in level of education, and in exposure to pressures to continue or to stop smoking might very well also be important.

The content of the role playing. Previous studies of role playing as a procedure for influencing cigarette smokers have dwelt on the link between smoking and lung cancer, a horrible and usually fatal disease. Our work revolved around subclinical changes which were presented as relatively harmless in themselves but as warning signals of possible future trouble. It is unclear whether it was the exposure to role playing, either active or passive, or merely exposure to the specific information about smoking which was responsible for the changes in SEU and subsequent changes in smoking. Furthermore, it is unclear whether the amount of exposure to the information is critical. While it is true that the "doctors" were exposed to the content of the charade more fully than the "patients," there was almost as much change among the observers, whose briefing was even more limited than that of the "patients."

To our knowledge the subclinical effects of smoking on healthy young people have not been used previously in experiments testing the impact of role playing on smoking. To evaluate the effect of this specific kind of information, it would be necessary in future studies to add control groups who will learn that information but will neither participate in nor observe the role playing. If the impact of role playing on the observers in our study was due to identification with the role players, as we suspect from their post-experimental reports, then subjects who merely learn the facts without observing should not be affected as much as observers given an opportunity to identify with "patients" or "doctors."

Of course, the particular facts presented in the role-playing scenario may have a different impact on different populations. Our scenario stressed current subclinical changes related to smoking rather than the risk of future disability or death; it seemed likely that young college students would be impressed with such information. Older people might be more responsive to a scenario based on more extensive pathology. Only investigations in which the ages, history of indulgence in smoking, and content of role playing were systematically varied would resolve the questions posed in the previous paragraphs.

Lastly, it has occurred to us recently that the use of a scenario dealing with the dangers of smoking may be a relatively poor way of inducing change. When asked why they continue to smoke, most smokers now stress not their scepticism about the effect of smoking on health, but rather their fears of the consequences of not smoking. And our data show that, somehow, the role playing did lead to a reduction of that fear in some of our subjects, as indicated by the increase in the utility of stopping. Perhaps a more effective procedure than our previous one would be to have smokers role-play being non-smokers. In a way, this would be an application of Leventhal's thesis that precise instructions are needed before an anxiety-inducing message can lead to behavioral change.

IMPLICATIONS FOR THE CONTROL OF SMOKING

The cost of death and disability from smoking is too great to permit the community to wait for the final answers to all the questions about smoking raised in this volume. Therefore, with proper academic caution, we will address ourselves to the professionals in medicine and public health who have the primary responsibility for the fight against smoking.

The results of our study could be the basis for either optimism or pessimism, depending on one's tendency to report a cup as being half full or half empty. Our work confirms what is well known, i.e., the depth of the supports for smoking within individuals and the unwillingness of many, even those convinced of its harmfulness, to give it up. But our work also supports the thesis advanced by McKennell (1968) that there are many smokers who could change relatively easily if they were only convinced of the utility of doing so. We have some insights which could help to identify people who could change relatively easily. These people are probably not fatalistic in general about their ability to control their destinies. They do not find cigarettes an important source either of pleasure or of release from externally-caused tension; they do not crave cigarettes, i.e., they are not psychologically addicted. *And* they have an expectation that they could stay off cigarettes if they wanted to. Since we do not have adequate surveys of the entire population of smokers, we have no idea what proportion of smokers would fit this picture. However, it might be a sizable group, one whose change would make a real dent in the population of smokers. The effect of decreased smoking by this group would be magnified because any reduction in the number of smokers reduces the level of social contagion for other smokers, decreases the legitimacy of smoking, and makes it less likely that children approaching adolescence will model themselves after adults or older children who smoke.

The role-playing procedure as we have used it in the laboratory is not directly applicable to large-scale programs of intervention. But the fact that both "doctors" and observers changed, and that it was the utility of stopping which predicted change, suggests some things about the character of persuasive messages which might be effective in reaching susceptible smokers. First, a persuasive appeal ought to produce identification with the role of a physician or, if there is identification with the patient, it should be relatively impersonal. Second, the appeal should emphasize the benefits of not smoking rather than the horrors of smoking. Third, and most vital, the message should change people's expectation of beneficial outcomes from not smoking, not merely the value they place on these outcomes. Not the least of the expectations to be eliminated is the feeling that success in abstaining from cigarettes is difficult if not impossible to attain.

Marshal McLuhan (1964) has described television as a "cool" medium. If it really is, then TV ought to be an ideal vehicle for promoting the apparently paradoxical disinterested identification which we have suggested as a desirable characteristic of programs of persuasion addressed to cigarette smokers. It may be that the television camera could function as the eye of the observer in such a way that he really "becomes" the doctor explaining to a patient the damage done by smoking and the benefits of stopping. It may be that the kinds of impressions reported so vividly by our observers (see the close of Chapter 7) could be generated in a mass audience. If even a fraction of the viewers determined to change their smoking behavior, the results would be well worth the effort.

Programs of Assistance to Smokers

The results of our study would probably be useful in face-to-face contacts with smokers or in work with small groups as well as in the planning of programs of mass persuasion. Two areas of application are immediately apparent. The first deals with techniques for increasing for all smokers the initial expectation that abstention is a possible goal. The second deals with differentiated approaches to smokers with varying patterns of support for smoking.

Feather and his colleagues (Atkinson & Feather, 1966) have reported experimental investigations in which subjects' expectations of success in gambling and in a variety of academic exercises were enhanced by manipulations which emphasized the rewards of success and which generated high levels of achievement drive and a moderate level of "motivation anxiety." The techniques of behavior therapy might be used in parallel efforts to Feather's work to increase expectations of success in abstaining from cigarettes. Schedules of reinforced abstention might be used to give smokers a set of experiences which would strengthen the belief that they really could abstain, a belief which might lead to continued efforts towards that goal. Such applications of behavior therapy might be more successful in affecting smoking than the more usual aversive conditioning.

We would like to support the notion presented by Horn and others that a diagnosis of the pattern of supports for smoking should be used to determine the advice given to smokers. Appendix XIV gives the best insights which were available to us for a differentiated set of suggestions to smokers who vary in the strength of one or another of the supports. Unhappily, we have little evidence that any of these suggestions is really effective. But they do seem reasonable, in that they represent the application of the kind of guidance which has been effective in other contexts for the control of other undesirable behavioral patterns.

Finally, we should like to comment on the question of ongoing support for smokers attempting to stop. Our subjects' reports confirmed the general belief that recidivism occurs when smokers are subjected to external stress, or when social supports for smoking are too hard to resist. It may be that a continuing relation between an anti-smoking counselor who is familiar with the smoker's pattern of supports and the character of his environment would enable the counselor to warn the smoker of threats to his continued abstention or reduction. We continue to feel (Mausner & Mausner, 1968) that the most powerful persuasive force in changing the behavior of smokers is probably the individual physician. It is he who carries the weight of authority, who can induce the smoker to see the utility of not smoking, whose guidance in matters of health is usually accepted with little question. If doctors, real doctors, would take smoking in healthy adults as seriously as it deserves to be taken, they might find themselves talking about it with virtually all of their patients who smoke. Then the insights about smokers developed by psychological research might be useful in helping them to a more subtle view of smoking than they now hold and might assist them to work out detailed regimens based on the needs of individual patients.

SOME GENERAL COMMENTS

At many points throughout our discussion we have commented on the number of unanswered questions left by our own research and by the comparison of our work with that of others. If we were describing the state of any other area of research in the sciences, the same unfinished character would undoubtedly be evident. Unanswered questions are not, in themselves, reasons for dismay. If anything, the health of a growing area of investigation is demonstrated by the number of lines of research which open within it. The problem posed by the continuation of cigarette smoking is not, however, one which may be safely left to the slow progress of academic research in the social sciences. For one thing, the social losses are too great and the inadequacies of current programs for control too limiting. For another, the number of variables which affect the behavior of subjects in experiments on the modification of smoking requires that large-scale investigations be undertaken to provide answers to some very complex questions. A massive social commitment would be needed for a comprehensive experimental program which could examine the sources of social and intra-individual support for continued smoking. Further, this program could evaluate the relative effectiveness of the available persuasive techniques and test the combination of different methods of persuasion with a variety of procedures for helping smokers who try to stop.

There would be many problems in the implementation of a truly comprehensive program of basic research, in recruiting scholars willing to participate, and in arranging for the housing and conduct of the work in appropriate settings. If the social decision were taken, however, that the current slow progress is incompatible with the needs of the community, then an attack on smoking would require the kind of mobilization of social forces and expenditure of resources which has been characteristic in the past of military ventures rather than searches for ways of improving public health or the quality of human life.

Social and Individual Decision

It would take another volume to attack the question of the perception of threat at the societal rather than individual level, of the determinants of social decision, and of the factors which lead to a community's response to threat. In a sense, the present volume is preliminary to that discussion. The decisions of a society are, in large part, a consequence of the needs of its individual members. We have clearly demonstrated that smoking is an enormously rewarding act to many of the individuals who engage in it. One can only suspect that society as a whole, as well as the individual smoker, now sees the benefits of smoking as more important than its presumed hazards and that it appears unlikely that cigarette smoking will be effectively controlled in the near future. That suspicion is supported by the fact that society has not taken the threat posed by cigarette smoking sufficiently seriously to assign high priority to opposing it. The picture we drew in Chapter 1 of the history of legislation and governmental action makes it clear that most of the important power centers in our community fail to take the threat seriously at all. Even the medical profession, which should lead, is ambivalent. True, a large proportion of physicians do not themselves any longer smoke. But organized medicine, as represented by the American Medical Association, has accepted large sums of money from the tobacco industry for its program of research on smoking and has failed, as late as December 1969, to support the systematic, nationwide action against smoking proposed by experts in preventive medicine (AMA News, Dec. 15, 1969).

It should be made clear that we are not proposing the prohibition of cigarettes. The futility of such a move is demonstrated not only by the history of the twenties but by the current campaign against marijuana. It is, in a sense, astonishing that marijuana, for which relatively little harm has been clearly demonstrated, should rouse such intense emotion while the use of tobacco is viewed with relative calm. The fact that cigarette smoking, as we have described it in this volume, is an important aid to Americans in their attempts to cope with the demands of society while marijuana is a symbol of withdrawal may account for the difference in the way in which they are treated. In any event, no practical man would propose banning an activity which is valued by almost half the adult population. In the end, the problem of smoking remains one of individual decision.

It is very easy to formulate this problem as one of rationality vs. irrationality. If one makes the assumption that being physically ill is bad, and dying prematurely is even worse, then no rational human being could possibly continue to smoke. But even rational people might be willing to accept cigarette smoking as a social necessity in a civilization which faces its members with overwhelming needs for precisely the kinds of effects generated by smoking. When one sees modern Western man trapped in a traffic jam, struggling with bureaucracy, fighting deadlines, soaked in boredom, and threatened with alienation, then the descriptions in the earlier part of the volume of the rewards from cigarette smoking make it clear that the cigarette or some substitute may, indeed, be a social necessity. For, it reduces tension, provides a source of fellowship, and creates a sense of individual identity. Each smoker must decide whether these advantages are worth the risk of illness and premature death.

One wonders whether, in fact, individual smokers do so decide or whether they merely drift through life, fatalistically enjoying the rewards of smoking without ever casting up the odds. Of course, many individuals would be unable to behave "rationally," i.e., would not follow the direction suggested by the comparison of utilities, even if they did assess the utility of alternatives. But one can wish that every smoker could be forced to carry on a rational examination of alternatives. If all those who could give up their smoking with skilled assistance were to stop, this would hasten the day when an ashtray becomes an historical curiosity and the community no longer has to bear the burden of illness and death which is the price of smoking.

References

Allen, W. A. & Fackler, W. A. An exploratory survey and smoking control program conducted among parents of Philadelphia school children. In S. V. Zagona (Ed.), *Studies and issues in smoking behavior.* Tucson: University of Arizona Press, 1967. Pp. 63-65.

Allport, G. W. *Pattern and growth in personality.* New York: Holt, Rinehart & Winston, 1961.

Allport, G. W. *Personality.* New York: Holt, 1937.

American Medical Association. *American Medical News,* December 15, 1969.

Atkinson, J. W. *An introduction to motivation.* Princeton: Van Nostrand, 1964.

Atkinson, J. W. & Feather, N. T. (Eds.) *A theory of achievement motivation.* New York: Wiley, 1966.

Bandura, A. & Walters, R. *Social learning and personality development.* New York: Holt, Rinehart & Winston, 1963.

Barker, R. G. & Wright, H. F. *One boy's day: A specimen record of behavior.* New York: Harper, 1951.

Berglund, E. *A follow-up study of thirteen Norwegian tobacco withdrawal clinics. The five-day plan.* Oslo, Norway: Landsforeningen Mot Kreft, The Norwegian Cancer Society, 1969.

Berkowitz, L. Repeated frustrations and expectations in hostility arousal. *Journal of Abnormal and Social Psychology,* 1960, **60**, 422-429. (a)

Berkowitz, L. Some factors affecting the reduction of overt hostility. *Journal of Abnormal and Social Psychology,* 1960, **60**, 14-21. (b)

Bernstein, D. A. Modification of smoking behavior: An evaluative review. *Psychological Bulletin,* 1969, **71** (6), 418-440.

Borgatta, E. F. & Evans, R. R. (Eds.) *Smoking, health, and behavior.* Chicago: Aldine, 1968.

Brehm, J. W. *A theory of psychological reactance.* New York: Academic Press, 1966.

Brehm, J. & Cohen, A. *Explorations in cognitive dissonance.* New York: Wiley, 1962.

Briney, K. L. Relation of knowledge of effects of cigarette smoking to the practice of smoking among high school seniors. *California School Health,* 1966, 2, 17-21.

Brock, T. C. Commitment to exposure as a determinant in information receptivity. *Journal of Personality and Social Psychology,* 1965, 2, 10-19.

Brock, T. C. & Balloun, J. L. Behavioral receptivity to dissonant information. *Journal of Personality and Social Psychology,* 1967, 6 413-428.

Cattell, R. B. (Ed.) *Handbook of multivariate experimental psychology.* Chicago: Rand McNally, 1966.

Clyde, D. J., Cramer, E. M., & Sherin, R. J. *Multivariate Statistical Programs.* Coral Gables: University of Miami, 1966.

Cofer, C. N. & Appley, M. H. *Motivation: Theory and research.* New York: Wiley, 1964.

Creswell, W. H., Jr., Huffman, W. J., Stone, D. B., Merki, D. J., & Newman, I. M. A replication of the Horn study on youth smoking in 1967. Paper presented at the American Public Health Association, Miami Beach, October 1967.

Crowne, D. & Marlow, D. *The approval motive: Studies in evaluative dependence.* New York: Wiley, 1964.

Crutchfield, R. S. Conformity and character. *American Psychologist,* 1955, **10,** 191-198.

Dabbs, J. M. & Leventhal, H. Effects of varying the recommendations in a fear-arousing communication. *Journal of Personality and Social Psychology,* 1966, **4,** 525-531.

Dixon, W. J. (Ed.) *BMD Biomedical computer programs.* Health Sciences Computing Facility, Department of Preventive Medicine and Public Health, School of Medicine, University of California, Los Angeles, 1965.

Edwards, W. Behavioral decision theory. In P. R. Farnsworth *et al.* (Ed.), *Annual Review of Psychology.* Palo Alto, Calif.: Banta, 1961, **12,** 473-498.

Edwards, W., Lindman, H., & Phillips, L. D. Emerging technologies for making decisions. In F. Barron *et al. New directions in psychology II.* New York: Holt, Rinehart & Winston, 1965.

Ejrup, B. The role of nicotine in smoking pleasure, nicotinism, treatment. *Tobacco Alkaloids and Related Compounds.* Proceedings of the 4th International Symposium, Stockholm, February 1964. New York: Pergamon Press, 1965. Pp. 333-345.

Elms, A. C. Role playing, incentive, and dissonance. *Psychological Bulletin,* 1967, **68,** 132-148.

Eysenck, H. J. *Smoking, health and personality.* New York: Basic Books, 1965.

Eysenck, H. J., Tauant, M., Woolf, M., & England, L. Smoking and personality. *British Medical Journal,* 1960, **1,** 1456-1460.

Feather, N. T. Cigarette smoking and lung cancer: A study of cognitive dissonance. *Australian Journal of Psychology,* 1962, **14,** 55-64.

Federal Trade Commission. Report to Congress pursuant to the Federal cigarette labeling and advertising act, June 1968.

Festinger, L. *A theory of cognitive dissonance.* Stanford: Stanford University Press, 1957.

Festinger, L. Behavioral support for opinion change. *Public Opinion Quarterly,* 1964, **28,** 404-417. (a)

Festinger, L. *Conflict, decision and dissonance.* Stanford: Stanford University Press, 1964. (b)

Fisher, R. A. *Smoking: The cancer controversy.* London: Oliver & Boyd, 1959.

Flanagan, J. C. The critical incident technique. *Psychological Bulletin,* 1954, **51,** 327-358.

Fletcher, C. M. Cigarettes and respiratory disease. In *World conference on smoking and health: A summary of the proceedings.* September 11-13, 1967. Sponsored by the National Interagency Council on Smoking and Health.

Forrest, D. W. Attitudes of undergraduate women to smoking. *Psychological Reports,* 1966, **19,** 83-87.

Fredrickson, D. T. *New York City smoking withdrawal clinic.* Smoking Control Program, New York City Department of Health, 1967.

Fritschler, A. L. *Smoking and politics: Policymaking and the federal bureaucracy.* New York: Appleton-Century-Crofts, 1969.

Graff, H., Hammet, V. B. O., Bash, N., Fackler, W., Yanovski, A., & Goldman, A. Results of four antismoking therapy methods. *Pennsylvania Medical Journal,* 1966, **69**, 39-43.

Graham, S. In B. Mausner and E. S. Platt (Eds.), Behavioral aspects of smoking: A conference report. *Health Education Monographs,* Supplement No. 2. New York: Society of Public Health Educators, 1966, p. 21.

Gross, A. Smoking: Why you do it and how not to suffer when you stop. *Mademoiselle,* October 1969, 166-167, 213-215.

Guilford, J. P. *Fundamental statistics in psychology and education.* (3rd ed.) New York: McGraw-Hill, 1956.

Heider, F. *The psychology of interpersonal relations.* New York: Wiley, 1958.

Hersey, R. B. Periodic emotional changes in male workers. *Personnel Journal,* 1929, **7**, 459-463.

Hersey, R. B. Emotional cycles in man. *Journal of Mental Science,* 1931, **77**, 151-169.

Hersey, R. B. Rate of production and emotional states. *Personnel Journal,* 1932, **10**, 355-364.

Herzberg, F. *Work and the nature of man.* Cleveland: World, 1966.

Herzberg, F., Mausner, B., & Snyderman, B. *Motivation to work.* New York: Wiley, 1959.

Higgins, M. W., Kjelsberg, M., & Metzner, H. Characteristics of smokers and non-smokers in Tecumseh, Michigan, I. The distribution of smoking habits and their relationship to social characteristics. *American Journal of Epidemiology,* 1967, **86**, 45-59.

Himes, K. H., Keutzer, C. S., & Lichtenstein, E. Emotional role-playing and smoking: Some procedural refinements. Unpublished paper, University of Oregon.

Hochbaum, G. M. Public participation in medical screening programs: A socio-psychological study. Washington, D. C.: U. S. Government Printing Office, 1958.

Hochbaum, G. M. Behavior in response to health threats. Paper presented at the Annual Meeting of the American Psychological Association, Chicago, 1960.

Hoffman, D. T. & Boyko, E. P. Cigarette smoking by tournament bridge game participants. Unpublished paper, University of Bridgeport.

Holland, W. W. & Elliott, A. Cigarette smoking, respiratory symptoms, and antismoking propaganda. *The Lancet,* 1968, 41-43.

Horn, D. Modifying smoking habits in high school students. *Child,* 1960, **7**, 63-65.

Horn, D. Behavioral aspects of cigarette smoking. *Journal of Chronic Diseases,* 1963, **16**, 383-95.

Horn, D. Closing remarks. In B. Mausner and E. S. Platt (Eds.), Behavioral aspects of smoking: A conference report. *Health Education Monographs,* Supplement No. 2. New York: Society of Public Health Educators. 1966. Pp. 49-55. (a)

Horn, D. Cigarette smoking in the high schools. *California School Health,* 1966, **2**, 17-21. (b)

Horn, D. Some factors in smoking and its cessation. In E. F. Borgatta and R. R. Evans (Eds.), *Smoking, health, and behavior.* Chicago: Aldine, 1968. Pp. 12-21. (a)

Horn, D. Factors affecting the cessation of cigarette smoking: A prospective study. Paper presented at the meeting of the Eastern Psychological Association, Washington, D. C., April 1968. (b)

Horn, D. Smoker's self-testing kit. Public Health Service Publication No. 1904, Part 1. Washington, D. C.: U. S. Department of Health, Education, and Welfare, 1969.

Horn, D., Courts, F. A., Taylor, R. M., & Solomon, E. S. Cigarette smoking among high school students. *American Journal of Public Health,* 1959, **49**, 1497-1511.

Horn, D. & Waingrow, S. Some dimensions of a model for smoking behavior change. In From epidemiology to ecology—A panel discussion, smoking and health in transition. *American Journal of Public Health and the Nation's Health,* **56**, 21-26, Supplement to December 1966. (a)

Horn D. & Waingrow, S. Smoking behavior change. Research report presented at National Research Conference on Smoking Behavior, University of Arizona, March 30-April 1, 1966. (b)

Hovland, C. I. & Janis, I. L. (Eds.) *Personality and persuasibility.* Vol. 2:*Yale studies in attitude and communication.* New Haven: Yale University Press, 1959.

Ianni, F. A. & Beck, W. A study of the relationship between motor accidents and certain characteristics of drivers. Unpublished manuscript, Russell Sage College, 1958.

James, W. H., Woodruff, A. B., & Werner, W. Effect of internal and external control upon changes in smoking behavior. *Journal of Consulting Psychology,* 1965, **29**, 184-186.

Janis, I. L. Effects of fear arousal on attitude change: Recent developments in theory and experimental research. In L. Berkowitz (Ed.), *Advances in experimental social psychology.* Vol. 3. New York: Academic Press, 1967. Pp. 166-224.

Janis, I. L. & Gilmore, J. B. The influence of incentive conditions on the success of role playing in modifying attitudes. *Journal of Personality and Social Psychology,* 1965, **1**, 17-27.

Janis, I. L. & Hovland, C. I. An overview of persuasibility research. In C. I. Hovland and I. L. Janis (Eds.), *Personality and persuasibility.* Vol. 2. *Yale studies in attitude and communication.* New Haven: Yale University Press, 1959. Pp. 1-26.

Janis, I. L. & King, B. T. The influence of role-playing on opinion change. *Journal of Abnormal and Social Psychology,* 1954, **49**, 211-218.

Janis, I. L. & Mann, L. A conflict-theory approach to attitude change and decision making. In A. G. Greenwald, T. C. Brock, and T. M. Ostrom (Eds.), *Psychological foundations of attitudes.* New York: Academic Press, 1968. Pp. 327-360.

Janis, I. L. & Mann, L. Effectiveness of emotional role playing in modifying smoking habits and attitudes. *Journal of Experimental Research in Personality.* 1965, **1**, 84-90.

Kennedy, R. F. Address to World Conference on Smoking and Health. *World conference on smoking and health: A summary of the proceedings.* September 11-13, 1967. Sponsored by the National Interagency Council on Smoking and Health. Pp. 4-13.

Keutzer, C. S. Behavior modification of smoking: The experimental investigation of diverse techniques. *Behaviour Research and Therapy,* 1968, **6**, 137-157.

Keutzer, C. S., Lichtenstein, E., & Mees, H. L. Modification of smoking behavior: A review. *Psychological Bulletin,* 1968, **70**, 520-533.

King, B. T. & Janis, I. L. Comparison of the effectiveness of improvised vs. non-improvised role playing in producing opinion change. *Human Relations,* 1956, **9**, 177-186.

Kline, M. V. *The use of extended group hypnotherapy sessions in controlling cigarette habituation.* Unpublished manuscript, The Institute for Research in Hypnosis, New York City, 1969.

Knapp, P. H., Bliss, C. M., & Wells, H. Addictive aspects in heavy cigarette smoking. *The American Journal of Psychiatry,* 1963, **119**, 966-972.

Kogan, N. & Wallach, M. A. *Risk taking.* New York: Holt, Rinehart & Winston, 1964.

Kogan, N. & Wallach, M. A. Group risk taking as a function of members' anxiety and defensiveness levels. *Journal of Personality,* **35**, No. 1, March 1967.

Krasner, L. & Ullman, L. P. *Research in behavior modification.* New York: Holt, Rinehart & Winston, 1965.

Lampert, K. J. Social correlates of smoking among youth: A study of smoking among Missoula, Montana, students. Unpublished paper, University of Pittsburgh, 1965.

Leventhal, H. Experimental studies of anti-smoking communications. In E. F. Borgatta and R. R. Evans (Eds.), *Smoking, health, and behavior.* Chicago: Aldine, 1968. Pp. 95-121.

Leventhal, H. Findings and theory in the study of fear communications. In L. Berkowitz, (Ed.), *Advances in experimental social psychology.* Vol. 5. New York: Academic Press, 1970.

Leventhal, H. & Niles, P. A field experiment on fear arousal with data on the validity of questionnaire measures. *Journal of Personality,* 1964, **32**, 459-479.

Leventhal, H., Singer, R. P., & Jones, S. Effects of fear and specificity of recommendation upon attitudes and behavior. *Journal of Personality and Social Psychology,* 1965, **2**, 20-29.

Leventhal, H. & Trembly, G. Negative emotions and persuasion. Unpublished manuscript, University of Wisconsin, 1968.

Leventhal, H. & Watts, J. C. Sources of resistance to fear arousing communications on smoking and lung cancer. *Journal of Personality,* 1966, **34**, 155-175.

Leventhal, H., Watts, J. C., & Pagano, F. Effects of fear and instructions on how to cope with danger. Unpublished paper, Yale University, 1965.

Lichtenstein, E. Smoking attitudes and intentions of college students and their relation to cognitive dissonance. *Psychological Reports,* 1967, **21,** 425-430.

Lichtenstein, E., Poussaint, A. F., & Bergman, S. H. A further report on the effects of the physician's treating of smoking by placebo. *Diseases of the Nervous System,* 1967, **28,** 754-755.

Lieberman Research, Inc. *The teenager looks at cigarette smoking.* Unpublished report of a study conducted for the American Cancer Society. November 1969.

Lindzey, G. & Aronson, E. (Eds.). *The handbook of social psychology.* Vol. 3. *The individual in a social context.* (2nd ed.). Reading, Mass.: Addison-Wesley, 1969.

MacMahon, B., Pugh, T. F., & Ipsen, J. *Epidemiologic methods.* Boston: Little, Brown, 1960.

Mann, L. & Janis, I. L. A follow-up study on the long term effects of emotional role playing. *Journal of Personality and Social Psychology,* 1968, **8,** 339-342.

Matarazzo, J. D. & Saslow, G. Psychological and related characteristics of smokers and non-smokers. *Psychological Bulletin,* 1960, **57,** 493-513.

Mausner, B. A decisional model for the study of the interrelationship of attitudinal and behavioral change. Paper presented at the meeting of the Eastern Psychological Association, New York, 1966. (a)

Mausner, B. Report on a smoking clinic. *American Psychologist,* 1966, **21,** 251-255. (b)

Mausner, B. & Mischler, J. B. Cigarette smoking among junior high school students. *Journal of Special Education,* 1967, **1,** 61-66.

Mausner, B. & Platt, E. S. Knowledge, attitudes and behavior: Studies in smoking. Final report to U. S. Public Health Service, September 1966. (a)

Mausner, B. & Platt, E. S. (Eds.) Behavioral aspects of smoking: A conference report. *Health Education Monographs,* Supplement No. 2. New York: Society of Public Health Educators, 1966. (b)

Mausner, J. S. Smoking in medical students: A survey of attitudes, information and smoking habits. *Archives of Environmental Health,* 1966, **13,** 51.

Mausner, J. S. & Mausner, B. The physician and the control of smoking. (editorial) *Annals of Internal Medicine,* 1968, **68,** 1359-1362.

Mausner, J. S., Mausner, B., & Rial, W. Y. The influence of a physician on the smoking of his patients. *American Journal of Public Health,* 1968, **58,** 46-53.

McGuire, W. J. Personality and attitude change: An information-processing theory. In A. G. Greenwald *et al.* (Eds.), *Psychological foundations of attitudes.* New York: Academic Press, 1968. Pp. 171-196.

McGuire, W. J. Nature of attitudes and attitude change. In G. Lindzey and E. Aronson (Eds.), *The handbook of social psychology.* Vol 3. (2nd ed.). *The individual in a social context.* Reading, Mass.: Addison-Wesley, 1969. P. 206.

McKennell, A. C. British research into smoking behavior. In E. F. Borgatta and R. R. Evans (Eds.), *Smoking, health, and behavior.* Chicago: Aldine, 1968. Pp. 140-164.

McLuhan, H. M. *Understanding media: The extensions of man.* New York: McGraw-Hill, 1964.

Morison, J. B., Medovy, H., & MacDonell, G. T. Health education and cigarette smoking: A report on a three-year program in the Winnipeg School Division, 1960-1963. *The Canadian Medical Association Journal,* 1964, **91**, 49-56.

Neuberger, M. B. *Smoke screen: Tobacco and the public welfare.* Englewood Cliffs, N. J.: Prentice-Hall, 1963.

Niles, P. Two personality measures associated with responsiveness to fear-arousing communications. Unpublished doctoral dissertation, Yale University, 1964.

Osgood, E. C. & Tannenbaum, P. H. The principle of congruity in the prediction of attitude change. *Psychological Review,* 1955, **62**, 42-55.

Pervin, L. A. & Dalrymple, W. Undergraduate smoking habits and related behavior, Part I. Familial smoking behavior and health difficulties. *Journal of the American College Health Association,* 1965, **13**, 242-249. (a)

Pervin, L. A. & Dalrymple, W. Undergraduate smoking habits and related behavior, Part II. Attitudes toward the smoking-cancer relationship and personality traits. *Journal of the American College Health Association,* 1965, **13**, 379-389. (b)

Pervin, L. A. & Yatko, R. J. Cigarette smoking and alternative methods of reducing dissonance. *Journal of Personality and Social Psychology,* 1965, **2**, 30-36.

Platt, E. S., Krassen, E., & Mausner, B. Individual variation in behavioral change following role playing. *Psychological Reports,* 1969, **24**, 155-170.

Poussaint, A. F., Bergman, S. H., & Lichtenstein, E. The effects of physician's smoking on the treatment of smokers. *Diseases of the Nervous System,* 1966, **27**, 539-543.

Pumroy, D. K. Cigarette smoking, academic achievement and driving behavior among teenagers. Paper presented at the meeting of the Eastern Psychological Association, Philadelphia, 1964.

Pumroy, D. K. & March, B. A. The evaluation of a cigarette smoking reduction method. Paper presented at the meeting of the Eastern Psychological Association, 1966.

Robbins, W. T. & Lichlyter, M. W. Bronchial epithelium in cigarette-smoking college students. *Journal of the American College Health Association,* 1968, **16**, 384-385.

Rosenberg, M. J. An analysis of affective-cognitive consistency. In M. J. Rosenberg, C. I. Hovland, W. J. McGuire, R. P. Ableson, and J. W. Brehm, *Attitude organization and change: An analysis of consistency among attitude components.* Vol. 3. *Yale studies in attitude and communication.* New Haven: Yale University Press, 1960. Pp. 16-64.

Rosenberg, M. J. & Abelson, R. P. An analysis of cognitive balancing. In M. J. Rosenberg, C. I. Hovland, W. J. McGuire, R. P. Abelson, and J. W. Brehm, *Attitude organization and change: An analysis of consistency among attitude components.* Vol. 3. *Yale studies in attitude and communication.* New Haven: Yale University Press, 1960. Pp. 112-163.

Rosenblatt, D. & Allen, H. Use of group therapy in smoking cessation. In E. F. Borgatta and R. R. Evans (Eds.), *Smoking, health, and behavior.* Chicago: Aldine, 1968. Pp. 122-127.

Rotter, J. B. Generalized expectancies for internal versus external control of reinforcement. *Psychological Monographs,* 1966, **80**, (1, Whole No. 609).

Salber, E. J. & Abelin, T. Smoking behavior of Newton school children — five-year follow-up. *Pediatrics,* 1967, **40**, 363-372.

Salber, E. J. & MacMahon, B. Cigarette smoking among high school students; related to social class and parental smoking habits. *American Journal of Public Health,* 1961, **51**, 1780-1789.

Salber, E. J., MacMahon, B., & Welsh, B. Smoking habits of high school students related to intelligence and achievement. *Pediatrics,* 1962, **29**, 780-787.

Salber, E. J. & Rochman, J. E. Personality differences between smokers and non-smokers. *Archives of Environmental Health,* 1964, **8**, 459-465.

Salber, E. J., Welsh, B., & Taylor, S. V. Reasons for smoking given by secondary school children. *Journal of Health and Human Behavior,* 1963, **4**, 118-129.

Sarason, S. B. & Mandler, G. Some correlates of test anxiety. *Journal of Abnormal and Social Psychology,* 1952, **47**, 810-817.

Schonbar, R. A. Some manifest characteristics of recallers and nonrecallers of dreams. *Journal of Consulting Psychology,* 1959, **23**, 414-418.

Schwartz, J. L. & Dubitzky, M. Changes in anxiety, mood, and self-esteem resulting from an attempt to stop smoking. *American Journal of Psychiatry,* 1968, **124**, 1580-1584. (a)

Schwartz, J. L. & Dubitzky, M. One-year follow-up results of a smoking cessation program. *Canadian Journal of Public Health,* 1968, **59**, 161-165. (b)

Schwartz, J. L. & Dubitzky, M. *Psycho-social factors involved in cigarette smoking and cessation.* Final Report of the Smoking Control Research Project, July 1, 1964-June 1968. Berkeley: Institute for Health Research, 1968. (c)

Schwartz, J. L. & Dubitzky, M. Smoking habits of an adult male population. *Journal of Occupational Medicine,* 1968, **10**, 233-237. (d)

Scott, W. A. Attitude measurement. In G. Lindzey and E. Aronson (Eds.), *The handbook of social psychology. Research methods.* (2nd ed.) Vol. 2. Reading, Mass.: Addison-Wesley, 1968.

Selltiz, C., Jahoda, M., Deutsch, M., & Cooks, S. W. *Research methods in social relations.* New York: Holt, 1959.

Shields, J. E. (Ed.) Controversy over cigarette advertising. *Congressional Digest,* June-July 1969, **48**, 163-192.

Singer, J. L. *Daydreaming.* New York: Random House, 1966.

Skinner, B. F. The science of learning and the art of teaching. In W. I. Smith and J. W. Moore (Eds.), *Programmed learning: Theory and research.* Princeton, N. J.: Van Nostrand, 1962. Pp. 18-33.

Spelman, M. S. & Levy, P. Knowledge of lung cancer and smoking habits. *British Journal of Social and Clinical Psychology,* 1966, **5**, 207-210.

Stewart, L. & Livson, N. Smoking and rebelliousness: A longitudinal study from childhood to maturity. *Journal of Consulting Psychology,* 1966, **30**, 225-229.

Straits, B. C. Sociological and psychological correlates of adoption and discontinuation of cigarette smoking. Report to The Council for Tobacco Research, U. S. A. Grant #354. Unpublished progress report. University of Chicago, 1965.

Straits, B. C. The discontinuation of cigarette smoking: A multiple discriminate analysis. In S. V. Zagona (Ed.), *Studies and issues in smoking behavior.* Tucson: The University of Arizona Press, 1967. Pp. 79-81. (a)

Straits, B. C. Resume of the Chicago study of smoking behavior. In S. V. Zagona (Ed.), *Studies and issues in smoking behavior.* Tucson: The University of Arizona Press, 1967. Pp. 73-78. (b)

Straits, B. C. & Sechrest, L. Further support of some findings about the characteristics of smokers and non-smokers. *Journal of Consulting Psychology,* 1963, **27**, 282.

Taylor, J. A personality scale of manifest anxiety. *Journal of Abnormal and Social Psychology,* 1953, **48**, 285-290.

Thompson, D. S. & Wilson, T. R. Discontinuance of cigarette smoking: "Natural" and with "therapy." *Journal of the American Medical Association,* 1966, **196**, 1048-1052.

Tomkins, S. Psychological model for smoking behavior. *American Journal of Public Health,* 1966, **56**, 17-20. (a)

Tomkins, S. Theoretical implications and guidelines to future research. In B. Mausner and E. Platt, Behavioral aspects of smoking: A conference report. *Health Education Monographs,* Supplement No. 2. New York: Society of Public Health Educators, 1966. Pp. 35-48. (b)

Tomkins, S. A modified model of smoking behavior. In E. F. Borgatta and R. R. Evans (Eds.), *Smoking, health, and behavior.* Chicago: Aldine, 1968. Pp. 165-186.

U. S. Public Health Service. *Smoking and health.* Report of the Advisory Committee to the Surgeon General of the Public Health Service. Washington, D. C.: U. S. Department of Health, Education, and Welfare, Public Health Service Publication No. 1103, 1964.

U. S. Public Health Service. *Use of tobacco. Practices, attitudes, knowledge, and beliefs. United States – Fall 1964 and Spring 1966.* U. S. Department of Health, Education, and Welfare, Public Health Service, National Clearinghouse for Smoking and Health, 1969.

U. S. Public Health Service. *The health consequences of smoking. A public health service review: 1967.* U. S. Department of Health, Education, and Welfare, Public Health Service Publication No. 1696.

U. S. Public Health Service. *The health consequences of smoking.* 1968 Supplement to the 1967 Public Health Service Review. U. S. Department of Health, Education, and Welfare, Public Health Service Publication No. 1696.

Vitz, P. & Johnston, D. Masculinity of smokers and the masculinity of cigarette images. *Journal of Applied Psychology,* 1965, **49**, 155.

Wakefield, J. (Ed.) *Influencing smoking behaviour.* A Report of the Committee for Research in Smoking Habits appointed by The Norwegian Cancer Society. Geneva: 1969.

Walster, E. & Festinger, L. The effectiveness of "overheard" persuasive communications. *Journal of Abnormal and Social Psychology,* 1962, **65**, 395-402.

Watne, A. L., Montgomery, R. L., & Pettit, W. W. A cigarette information program. *Journal of the American Medical Association,* 1964, **188**, 872-874.

Watts, J. C. The role of vulnerability in resistance to fear-arousing communications. Unpublished doctoral dissertation, Bryn Mawr College, 1966.

Weatherly, D. Some personality correlates of the ability to stop smoking cigarettes. *Journal of Consulting Psychology,* 1965, **29**, 483-485.

Webb, E. J., Campbell, D. T., Schwartz, R. D., & Sechrest, L. *Unobtrusive measures: Nonreactive research in the social sciences.* Chicago: Rand McNally, 1966.

Weir, J. M. Male student perceptions of smokers. In S. V. Zagona (Ed.), *Studies and issues in smoking behavior.* Tucson: University of Arizona Press, 1967. Pp. 147-155.

Wolitzky, D. L. Cognitive control and cognitive dissonance. *Journal of Personality and Social Psychology,* 1967, **5**, 486-490.

Wolpe, J. S. *Conditioning therapies.* New York: Holt, Rinehart & Winston, 1964.

World Conference on Smoking and Health: A summary of the proceedings. September 11-13, 1967. Sponsored by the National Interagency Council on Smoking and Health.

Zagona, S. V. Studies and issues in smoking behavior. Tucson: University of Arizona Press, 1967.

Zimbardo, P. G. The effect of effort and improvisation on self-persuasion produced by role-playing. *Journal of Experimental Social Psychology,* 1965, **1**, 103-120.

Appendices

Appendix I

Interview Questionnaire   (high school students)

Rate each cigarette that you remember having smoked according to how much you think you wanted it.

| Wanted Cigarette Very Much | Wanted Cigarette Very Little | Time |

```
|____|____|____|____|____|____|____|
  1    2    3    4    5    6    7          _____

|____|____|____|____|____|____|____|
  1    2    3    4    5    6    7          _____

|____|____|____|____|____|____|____|
  1    2    3    4    5    6    7          _____

|____|____|____|____|____|____|____|
  1    2    3    4    5    6    7          _____

|____|____|____|____|____|____|____|
  1    2    3    4    5    6    7          _____

|____|____|____|____|____|____|____|
  1    2    3    4    5    6    7          _____

|____|____|____|____|____|____|____|
  1    2    3    4    5    6    7          _____

|____|____|____|____|____|____|____|
  1    2    3    4    5    6    7          _____

|____|____|____|____|____|____|____|
  1    2    3    4    5    6    7          _____

|____|____|____|____|____|____|____|
  1    2    3    4    5    6    7          _____

|____|____|____|____|____|____|____|
  1    2    3    4    5    6    7          _____

|____|____|____|____|____|____|____|
  1    2    3    4    5    6    7          _____

|____|____|____|____|____|____|____|
  1    2    3    4    5    6    7          _____
```

Appendix I (cont.)

1. What was happening at the time you smoked the cigarette?
2. Was there anything about this situation that led you to take the cigarette?
3. What was your mood before taking the cigarette?
4. Did the cigarette change this mood?
5. How did you feel after finishing the cigarette?
6. What did you expect to get from the cigarette?
7. Were your expectations fulfilled?
8. How do you think you would have felt if you had not been allowed to smoke that cigarette?
9. Comments:

This questionnaire was completed three times with reference to the cigarette wanted most, wanted moderately, and wanted least, respectively.

Appendix II

Questionnaire (adult males)

Approximately how many cigarettes did you smoke yesterday? _____

Try to recall each of these cigarettes. Like most smokers you will probably realize that you wanted some of these cigarettes very much, some of them moderately, and some very little. Approximately how many of the cigarettes that you smoked yesterday did you want:

Very much _____ Moderately _____ Very little _____

Now choose as many as 5 cigarettes that you *wanted very much.* On each of the following lines fill in the approximate time that you smoked the cigarette, what you were doing at the time you smoked the cigarette, and what made you want the cigarette so much. If you wanted all of yesterday's cigarettes only moderately or very little, *do not fill in the form below.* (Same form used for cigarettes *wanted moderately,* and for those *wanted very little.*)

	Approx. Hr. Smoked	What were you doing at this time?	What made you want the cigarette so much?
Cig. # 1			
Cig. # 2			
Cig. # 3			
Cig. # 4			
Cig. # 5			

Appendix III

Questionnaire (adult males)

INSTRUCTIONS: Place an "X" in the space that best describes your feelings about each statement.

3. If someone were to take a candid snapshot of you holding a drink, how closely would it picture the "real you"?

L					J
completely	almost com- pletely	moderately	weakly	not at all	

4. If someone were to take a candid snapshot of you *not* holding a drink, how closely would it picture the "real you"?

L					
completely	almost com- pletely	moderately	weakly	not at all	

5. If someone were to take a candid snapshot of you behind the wheel of a car, how closely would it picture the "real you"?

L					
completely	almost com- pletely	moderately	weakly	not at all	

6. If someone were to take a candid snapshot of you with a cigarette in your hand, how closely would it picture the "real you"?

L					
completely	almost com- pletely	moderately	weakly	not at all	

7. If someone were to take a candid snapshot of you *without* a cigarette in your hand, how closely would it picture the "real you"?

L					
completely	almost com- pletely	moderately	weakly	not at all	

8. If someone were to take a candid snapshot of you with a hat on your head, how closely would it picture the "real you"?

L					
completely	almost com- pletely	moderately	weakly	not at all	

9. If someone were to take a candid snapshot of you *without* a hat on your head, how closely would it picture the "real you"?

L					
completely	almost com- pletely	moderately	weakly	not at all	

Appendix IV

Post-Diary Interview

1.   How did doing the diary affect your smoking?
2.   Did you have any problems filling out the diary?
3.   Was there anything unusual about the days on which you filled out the diary?
4.   Now that you have thought about your smoking, is there anything you can tell us that doesn't come out in the diary or in the questions we asked?
5.   We have developed the idea that there are three different kinds of factors which support people's smoking. Could you tell us how your own pattern of smoking fits these?

    5.1   Smoking as affiliative behavior (describe briefly). (Ask subject to place herself on the scale below.) Why do you feel this way?

1	2	3	4	5	6	7
Group Irrelevant			Group a Little Relevant			Group Very Relevant

    5.2   Smoking as role-defining behavior. Could you tell us how this fits?

1	2	3	4	5	6	7
Role Irrelevant			Role a Little Relevant			Role Very Relevant

    5.3   Smoking as an affective problem. Check each one that applies to you. Why did you check the ones you checked?

    HABIT (little or no affect)

1	2	3	4	5	6	7
Habit Irrelevant			Habit a Little Relevant			Habit Very Relevant

ENJOY SMOKING: It is pleasant. (increase positive affect)

1	2	3	4	5	6	7
Enjoyment Irrelevant			Enjoyment a Little Relevant			Enjoyment Very Relevant

Appendix IV (cont.)

TENSION RELEASE: It makes me relax when I am nervous. (Decrease negative affect)

1	2	3	4	5	6	7
Tension Irrelevant			Tension a Little Relevant			Tension Very Relevant

ADDICTIVE: I crave cigarettes when I don't have them.

1	2	3	4	5	6	7
Addiction Irrelevant			Addiction a Little Relevant			Addiction Very Relevant

6. Do you plan to change your smoking in the near future?

_____ yes   _____ no

If yes, will doing the diaries make any difference?

Appendix V

List of Adjectives Suggested in Diary Given to 31 College Women

aggressive	anxious	pleasure-seeking	timid
informal	inhibited	rugged	daring
restless	meek	self-pitying	shy
frank	hasty	emotional	conventional
interests narrow	feminine	awkward	energetic
curious	sophisticated	sexy	broad-minded
masculine	touchy	mature	show-off
unexcitable	sociable	dominant	individualistic
sensitive	eager	friendly	sulky
reckless	temperamental	quiet	formal
weak	enthusiastic	adventurous	good-natured
unemotional	unfriendly	calm	interests wide
generous	poised	uninhibited	warm
self-confident	irritable	efficient	infantile
religious	immature	unstable	moody
active	high-strung	rebellious	suggestible
easy-going	dynamic	pleasant	irresponsible
moralistic	responsible	gentle	artistic
nervous	neurotic	independent	submissive
relaxed	tense	self-controlled	dignified

Appendix VI

Values-Expectancies Test — Sample Item

28. How much do you care about coughing a lot in the mornings?

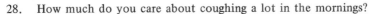

−5   −4   −3   −2   −1   0   +1   +2   +3   +4   +5

DON'T want it to happen   Don't care   DO want it to happen

If you STOPPED smoking, what do you think are your chances that you would cough a lot in the mornings?

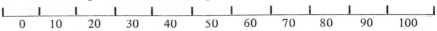

0   10   20   30   40   50   60   70   80   90   100

If you CONTINUED to smoke, what do you think are your chances that you would cough a lot in the mornings?

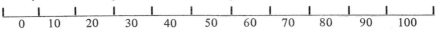

0   10   20   30   40   50   60   70   80   90   100

Items:

1.   How much do you care about being nervous?
2.   How much do you care about living longer than the average man?
3.   How much do you care about enjoying coffee?
4.   How much do you care about feeling depressed or blue?
5.   How much do you care that any new friends you make would be non-smokers?
6.   How much do you care about feeling proud of yourself?
7.   How much do you care about being energetic?
8.   How much do you care about having something to calm you down when you are tense or angry?
9.   How much do you care about being irritable with people?
10. How much do you care about other smokers being envious of you?
11. How much do you care about concentrating well?
12. How much do you care about non-smokers respecting you?
13. How much do you care about being tolerant of other people's smoking?
14. How much do you care about having something to do with your hands?
15. How much do you care about getting along with your friends?
16. How much do you care about becoming short of breath?
17. How much do you care about feeling close to those friends of yours who are smokers?
18. How much do you care about getting lung cancer?
19. How much do you care about enjoying your meals?
20. How much do you care about having something to perk you up?
21. How much do you care about getting heart disease?

Appendix VI (cont.)

22. How much do you care about having your clothes stay in good condition?
23. How much do you care about your home having a pleasant odor?
24. How much do you care about having your teeth and fingers stained?
25. How much do you care about having a good appetite?
26. How much do you care about looking "wrong" to your friends?
27. How much do you care about getting bronchitis?
28. How much do you care about coughing a lot in the mornings?
29. If you ever have children, how much would you care if they became smokers?
30. How much do you care about having something to relieve short periods of boredom?
31. How much do you care about having a good taste in your mouth?
32. How much do you care about feeling really good when you first get up in the morning?
33. How much do you care about studying well?
34. How much do you care about feeling like "yourself"?
35. How much do you care about becoming upset easily?
36. How much do you care about having a good sense of smell?
37. How much do you care about having enough pocket money?
38. How much do you care about gaining a noticeable amount of weight?
39. How much do you care about being a slave to a habit?
40. How much do you care about enjoying an alcoholic beverage?
41. How much do you care about staying away from cigarettes for a week?
42. How much do you care about staying away from cigarettes for a month?
43. How much do you care about staying away from cigarettes for a year?

Appendix VII-A

Spirometer Record Used as a Prop in the Role-Playing Study
(1) Report on Spirometer Record

Weight: ....160...... lbs.

Name:.........................

Body surface area .... sq. m.

Height:. 5' 10". inches   Date: · · · · · ·

Temperature of
expired air ....

Age: . 48. . Race: W. Sex: ...M....
Occupation (previous if retired):.....

....

SOURCE OF REFERRAL: HME........Physician... X ... Other ....

REASON FOR REFERRAL:......Health maintenance...........................

I. History: Smoking   Amount per day   Years

..X.. cough   ..X... cigarettes   30   35

..X.. sputum   ...... cigars   ....

..no. hemoptysis ...... pipes   ....

..no. chest pain

..X.. wheeze   Stopped smoking (year) ....

..X.. dyspnea: on exertion .... X ..... at rest ....

II. Past Chest Disease: none

III. Chest X-ray Report: negative

IV. Ventilatory Studies:

	Predicted	Observed	% of Predicted
Forced Expiratory Volume (FEV) − cc	4300	2800	65
Forced Expiratory Volume-one second (FEV$_{1.0}$)−cc	3400	1400	41
Maximal Voluntary Ventilation (MVV)−liters/min.			

Impression: Both valves are low, especially the FEV$_{1.0}$. This indicates mild restriction of ventilation and marked obstruction to expiration probably due to smoking.

Thank you for the opportunity to study this patient.

Sincerely,

William Weiss, M.D.
Department of Preventive Medicine

Appendix VII-A

Spirometer Record Used as a Prop in the Role-Playing Study
(2) Spirometer Record

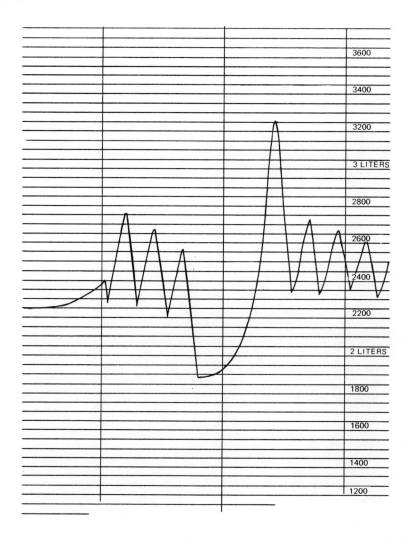

Appendix VII-A

(3) Overlay of a "Normal" Spirometer Record

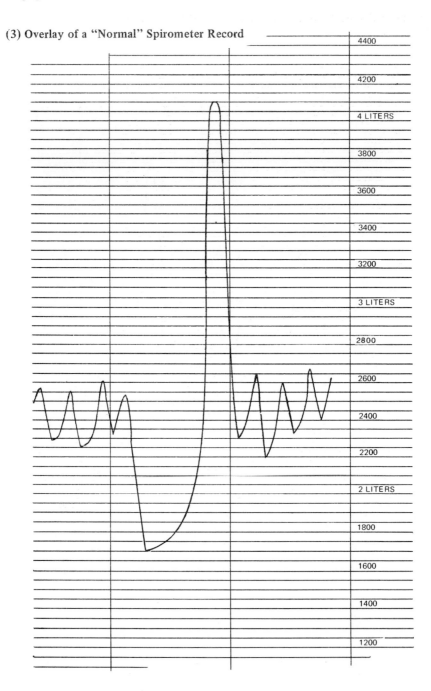

Appendix VII-B

Sputum Cytology Report Used as a Prop in the Role-Playing Study

Please type or print

(Last name	first	middle)
(Clinic No.)	(Street Address)	
(City	State	Zip No.)

PREVIOUS SMEAR NO.   EX. CYT. LAB. ONCOLOGY

Dr.

Age

Date   Jan., 1968

Prov. Diag.   Hormonal Rx   L.M.P.

Source of Material   X-Ray Rx   Menopause

Cl. Resume

Comments:

Report: Slide No. _____

Is the patient a smoker?

☐ CLASS I   No evidence of malignancy
☐ CLASS II   Atypical but no evidence of malignancy
☐ CLASS III   Suspicious cells present (dysplasia or CA in situ)
☐ CLASS IV   Cells consistent with malignancy
☐ CLASS V   Strong probability of malignancy
☐ PLEASE REPEAT

HOSPITAL OF THE   OF PA.

Examined by

Date

EXFOLIATIVE CYTOLOGY   Cat. 73   Rev. 8-64

Appendix VIII

Rating Sheet Used by Observer in the Role-Playing Study

Observer's Code # _____

Role Player's Code # _____

OBSERVER'S EVALUATION SHEET DURING ROLE PLAYING

Beaver College 1968

1. How well did the doctor play the role?

Very poorly 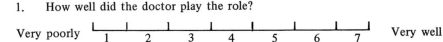 Very well

2. How well did the patient play the role?

Very poorly 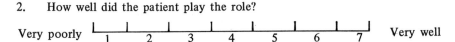 Very well

3. How friendly are you with the doctor?

Not at all 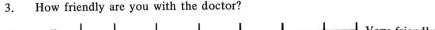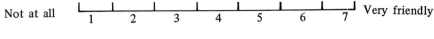 Very friendly

4. How friendly are you with the patient?

Not at all 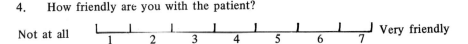 Very friendly

Appendix IX-A

Test of Situational Anxiety Used by Doctors and Patients
Role-Playing Study

Now go through the following five items. Please place an X in the space above the number that you think best describes how you felt during the role-playing situation.

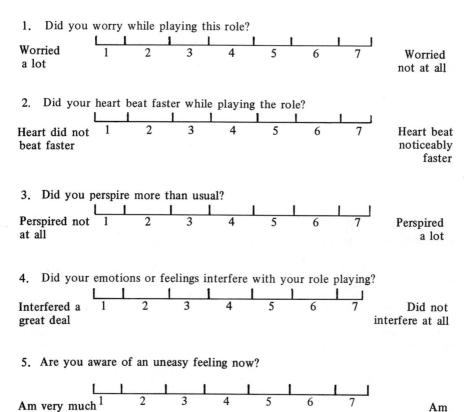

1. Did you worry while playing this role?

Worried   1   2   3   4   5   6   7   Worried
a lot   not at all

2. Did your heart beat faster while playing the role?

Heart did not   1   2   3   4   5   6   7   Heart beat
beat faster   noticeably
                                   faster

3. Did you perspire more than usual?

Perspired not   1   2   3   4   5   6   7   Perspired
at all   a lot

4. Did your emotions or feelings interfere with your role playing?

Interfered a   1   2   3   4   5   6   7   Did not
great deal   interfere at all

5. Are you aware of an uneasy feeling now?

Am very much   1   2   3   4   5   6   7   Am
aware of it   not aware
                                   of it at all

Appendix IX-B

Test of Situational Anxiety Used by Observers

Role-Playing Study

CODE # _____

Now go through the following five items. Please place an X in the space above the number that you think best describes how you felt during the role-playing situation.

1. Did you worry while watching the doctor and patient playing this role?

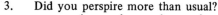

Worried   1   2   3   4   5   6   7   Worried
a lot   not at all

2. Did your heart beat faster while watching the doctor and patient?

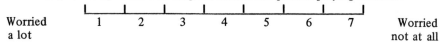

Heart did not   1   2   3   4   5   6   7   Heart beat
beat faster   noticeably faster

3. Did you perspire more than usual?

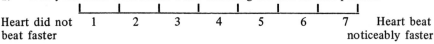

Perspired not   1   2   3   4   5   6   7   Perspired
at all   a lot

4. Did your emotions or feelings interfere with your judgments of role playing?

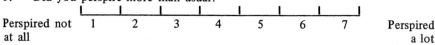

Interfered a   1   2   3   4   5   6   7   Did not
great deal   interfere at all

5. Are you aware of an uneasy feeling now?

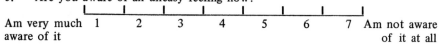

Am very much   1   2   3   4   5   6   7   Am not aware
aware of it   of it at all

Appendix X

Post Experimental Questionnaire
Role-Playing Study

CODE # _____

1. Did you watch the National Smoking Test on CBS TV 10 on Tuesday evening, Jan. 16, at 10 P. M.?_____

2. How much of the program did you see (which segment)?_____

3. Did you take the test?_____

4. What did you learn about your smoking from the program?

5. What were you thinking of during the role playing here today?

6. Are you planning to do anything about your smoking?_____
    If yes, what?

Appendix XI

Material Distributed to Experimental Group Subjects
Immediately After the Role-Playing Experiment

HOW TO BREAK THE SMOKING HABIT*

We recognize that it is not easy to give up a strongly ingrained habit. To help you we have listed on the following pages a number of suggestions which should help you to stop smoking with the least discomfort and effort, and with the greatest possibility of success. As you read this, try to translate our general suggestions into specific actions most appropriate to your smoking patterns.

Step 1 — Preparation

Make a list of the things you think make you smoke. Compare this list to a second list which gives all the reasons *why you might want to stop*. In particular, search for ways to counter the first list. For example, suppose the main reason you smoke is:

Reason: "It's a habit — too difficult to break."
Counterattack: REMEMBER — You can in fact change your habits. A habit such as smoking consists of many smaller parts such as buying cigarettes, carrying the pack, reaching for it, opening, lighting, etc. The failure to execute any step in the chain means that you won't smoke! Since smoking involves the integration of such a complex set of reactions you can disrupt the habit at any point, and so stop smoking.

Reason: "It's relaxing. If I didn't smoke, I'd be a nervous wreck."
Counterattack: REMEMBER — The relaxing effect of smoking is mainly due to its function as a pace-breaker. This relaxation can be easily achieved by other pace-breakers which are not harmful. You can go out for a walk; get up and stretch; take a few deep breaths; take a drink; chew gum.

Reason: "I just enjoy smoking."
Counterattack: REMEMBER — Smoking is not pleasant until you have accustomed your body to its effects — the harsh taste, giddy feeling, nausea.

REMEMBER — The "side effects" of smoking — increased nervousness, loss of energy, respiratory trouble, lung cancer — are far from being pleasant.

REMEMBER — Giving up smoking isn't all self-denial. Food will taste better; things will smell better; you'll feel more energetic and less nervous.

Step II — Stop Smoking Day *(For smokers who have decided to STOP)*

Select a specific day within this week as your STOP SMOKING DAY. On that day and from then on:

1. *Avoid the conditions which tend to get you to smoke.*
    - If you are a "social smoker," don't eat with friends who are smoking.
    - You may find it easier not to tell other smokers you are stopping.
    - Make up an excuse to decline cigarettes well in advance of any offers from friends. Say you left your own at home and that you are now smoking brand z.
    - Prepare a further dodge in case you are pressed: e.g., "I never smoke right after eating," or "My throat is a bit irritated."

---

*The material in this report is based upon information now being used in a project of the New York City Department of Health. Our thanks are extended to A. Blum, M.D., Project Director, for making the material available.

Appendix XI (cont.)

2. *Change your way of doing ordinary things associated with smoking. The key to success is to have new actions to substitute for those that are part of your habit-patterns.*
    - If you have cigarettes, throw them out. Don't carry matches with you. In the process of hunting for both you will disrupt the habit.
    - If you buy cigarettes from a machine, don't carry change or keep your change in a wallet so as to make it harder to reach the money.
    - Think ahead! Keep in mind specific items which you could buy in place of cigarettes. Spend the money, and if necessary a little extra, on a magazine, mints, coffee, or some other items which you enjoy.
    - Carry gum or some other substitute which can be reached for and opened. Keep it where you used to keep your cigarettes.
    - If you feel like smoking, do something else appropriate to the time and place.
      For example:
    - If you are studying in your room, get up and pace about for a moment.
      Take a deep breath, or go to the library (where smoking isn't permitted) instead.
    - If you are on the street, take a deep breath, or walk more briskly.
      Try to do more walking. It's fun and good for you.
    - At the dinner table, substitute a drink of water, milk, or coffee for a cigarette.

3. *Anti-smoking drugs.*
    You may want to supplement the techniques described above by using an anti-smoking drug. One such drug often prescribed by doctors is Lobeline. It is a non-habit-forming nicotine substitute which is extremely effective because it produces the same effects on the body as does smoking. It satisfies whatever physiological or psychological need is associated with the smoking habit but, at the same time, it helps to break the habit chain by *eliminating the act of smoking*.

    Presently Lobeline is available at your druggist in at least two brand-name tablets, *Bantron* and *Nikoban*. The instructions for use of these products require you to take one tablet after each meal for 4 days, and then a tablet a day for as long as the desire to smoke continues.

    Many people have used Lobeline preparations while trying to stop smoking. The drug is probably only effective when used in conjunction with procedures such as those outlined above. The use of the drug by itself may be inadequate to prevent *resumption* of the smoking habit.

    Caution: Although the tablets containing Lobeline are sold without prescription, we advise you to see your doctor before using them as some persons (e.g., those with heart problems or ulcers) may experience undesirable side effects.

Step II – (For smokers who have decided to cut down)
One way of trying to stop smoking is to go about it gradually. Most people find that they want some cigarettes more than others. It is easy to start by cutting out the cigarettes you don't really want. In order to find out about your own smoking habits you can use the sheets we will give you to rate each cigarette you smoke. Each cigarette is rated on a scale ranging from *1* to *5* like this:

Appendix XI (cont.)

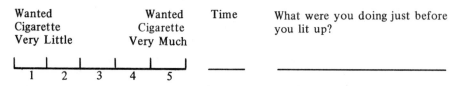

| Wanted Cigarette Very Little | Wanted Cigarette Very Much | Time | What were you doing just before you lit up? |

Rate every cigarette you smoke for the next couple of days. You will probably discover that you tend to smoke at about the same times every day. Some of the cigarettes are smokes you really want; and you rate them "5" or "4." Others are cigarettes you want a little but not too much; you rate them "2" or "3." Others are cigarettes you want very little and you rate them "1."

If you really want to try to stop smoking, you can use these ratings in a way worked out by Professor Pumroy of the University of Maryland. Begin by cutting out the cigarettes you wanted the least, the "1" and "2" cigarettes. Each day cut down by a few cigarettes. Then go on to cut out the cigarettes you want a little more, the "3" and "4" cigarettes. After a while you will find that you are down to the few cigarettes you really want.

If you keep up with this scheme, you should find that you will want fewer and fewer cigarettes, and eventually that you don't have to smoke at all.

You might find that something comes up that will make you want to smoke more than usual. Don't worry about it. After the need has passed, start again to cut down. You will notice that you will begin to feel better. You won't be short of breath as much as you might have been. You may be eating a little more because your appetite is improving. You may have to watch your diet for a while. Try to avoid rich, spicy foods. If coffee makes you want to smoke, try to cut down on coffee for a while. Drink lots of water; in fact, if you find yourself wanting a cigarette take a glass of water instead. If you normally take a break where everybody smokes, try to find a place where people don't smoke.

Step III – Culmination

If you have followed steps I and II then by now you will have broken the back of the habit; the worst is over. But your craving for "just one" cigarette may still be pretty strong. So:

- Don't test your strength by having the trial cigarette.
- When the urge does hit you: Take 6 deep breaths; get up and move about or stretch; take a drink or a nibble.
- When stressful situations arise practice relaxing techniques. Remember why you undertook to stop smoking in the first place. And, at all times, keep the upper hand. Good luck!

Appendix XI (cont.)

Rate each cigarette that you smoke according to how much you wanted it.

Wanted Cigarette Very Little			Wanted Cigarette Very Much		Time	What were you doing just before you lit up?
1	2	3	4	5	____	_____
1	2	3	4	5	____	_____
1	2	3	4	5	____	_____
1	2	3	4	5	____	_____
1	2	3	4	5	____	_____
1	2	3	4	5	____	_____
1	2	3	4	5	____	_____
1	2	3	4	5	____	_____
1	2	3	4	5	____	_____
1	2	3	4	5	____	_____
1	2	3	4	5	____	_____
1	2	3	4	5	____	_____
1	2	3	4	5	____	_____

Appendix XII

Telephone Interview Form Used for the Initial Follow-up
Role-Playing Study

NAME _____ **CODE NO.** _____

PHONE _____ Dates a. _____ b. _____

1. How many cigarettes did you smoke yesterday? _____

2. Is that a typical day? _____ If not, why not? _____

_____

3. How many cigarettes do you usually smoke a day? _____

4. Has anything happened recently to change your smoking? _____

    If so, what? _____

Appendix XIII

Computer Output Showing an Individual Smoker's Profile
Of Factor Scores on the Test of Patterns of Support For Smoking

FACTOR SCORES OUTPUT

Subject Number 30

0   100   200   300   400   500

Reduce Negative
Feelings

Pleasure

Self-Concept:
Social Role

Self-Concept:
Habitual Smoker

Smoking Socially
Stimulated

Psychological
Addiction

Stimulation

Sensual Feeling

LISTING OF DATA IN ORDER OF APPEARANCE ON GRAPH

(1) 260   (2) 400   (3) 329   (4) 257   (5) 375   (6) 350   (7) 300   (8) 300

Appendix XIV

Pamphlet Mailed to Smokers Two Months After Role Playing

HINTS TO SMOKERS
BEAVER COLLEGE HEALTH EDUCATION PROJECT
Glenside, Pa.

Eight factors were identified as supports for smoking on the questionnaire given recently to groups of smokers. The graph enclosed with this pamphlet has *your own* score on these factors. Each factor summarizes several of the items on the survey. For example, the first factor, "Reduce Negative Feelings," is based on agreement with five items:

4. When I feel "blue" or want to take my mind off cares and worries, I smoke cigarettes.
12. When I feel uncomfortable or upset about something, I light up a cigarette.
19. I light up a cigarette when I feel angry about something.
25. When I feel ashamed or embarrassed about something, I light up a cigarette.
33. Few things help better than cigarettes when I'm feeling upset.

The score was obtained by adding 5 if you checked *Always* on an item, 4 if you checked *Frequently,* 3 if you checked *Occasionally,* 2 if you checked *Seldom,* and 1 if you checked *Never.* The sum was then multiplied by 100 and divided by the number of items, in this instance five. Thus, if you had checked *Always* for all five items your score on the factor would be 500; if you checked *Occasionally* on all five items, your score would be 300. The labels for the factors are self-explanatory. By looking at the graph you can see what you yourself reported as the pattern of forces which, in part, support your continuing to smoke.

If you have decided to try to cut down or stop smoking, you may find the picture of your own smoking pattern helpful. This pamphlet contains some ideas related to each of the supports for smoking. The suggestions are based in part on the experiences of people who have been working with smokers and in part on the application of principles developed in other areas with similar problems.

Different people smoke for different reasons. Because of this, the problems faced by a smoker who is trying to stop may depend on many things – his background and life situation, his temperament, and his pattern of smoking. Obviously, we cannot advise you about the particular circumstances of your life or about your psychological problems. But we can suggest ways in which people should attack their smoking in terms of their own smoking pattern.

Step I:

After you have looked at your graph, identify all the factors with scores over *300*. If none of the factors have scores as high as 300, use the one or two with the highest scores. Read the paragraphs below devoted to those factors. You may want to read the entire pamphlet but pay special attention to the sections devoted to the factors on which you had high scores.

Step II:

Now you are ready to attack your smoking systematically. Nobody really has the last word on how to stop smoking. Each individual has to work out his

Appendix XIV (cont.)

own procedure. But knowing what *you yourself* saw as the factors which support your smoking may help you work out ways of doing without these supports.

Reduce negative feelings. If you have a high score on this factor, you indicated that you smoke to cut tension, to make you feel better when you are upset. You could try to recognize the signs in yourself of mounting tension, the cues that usually make you reach for a cigarette. Can you learn how to face your trouble? This *is* the best way. If you can't do without something to cut the tension, try to find something other than cigarettes to make you feel better when you are low. For some people the answer is food, but there is a danger of becoming overweight. For some it may be a quick workout or a short walk. A change of pace, if you have the kind of situation which permits it, will sometimes help. You have to make a strenuous effort to eliminate the cigarettes you smoke to calm you down, the very ones you seem to need the most. If smoking makes you feel better when you are upset, taking a cigarette after an upsetting incident strengthens or reinforces your tendency to continue to smoke. If you want to eliminate an act, then you must try actively to avoid continuing to reinforce it.

Pleasure. If you have a high score on this factor, you find cigarettes pleasant and relaxing. You should try to make smoking less pleasant for yourself. Carry a little reminder about the nasty consequences of smoking; force yourself to look at it each time you smoke. If you can't make the act of smoking unpleasant, you don't have much of a chance. You might even try smoking too much. After six or eight cigarettes in a row, the pleasure is considerably diminished.

Are there alternate sources of pleasure you can substitute for the cigarettes you enjoy? Since tastes differ we can't suggest particulars, but you should be able to examine your life pattern to find an act which *you* would enjoy as a substitute. If the pleasure you get from smoking, however, comes from the reduction of tension then you have a more complex problem than those who merely enjoy the cigarette itself. You should look at the section headed "Reduce Negative Feelings."

Self-concept: social role. You told us that you think of yourself as a "smoker," that you like and admire other people who smoke, that you enjoy smoking with other people whom you like. This is a tough one to break. It is hard for people to change their concepts about themselves. Can you convince yourself that many admirable people don't smoke? Can you find people on whom you would like to model yourself who are either non-smokers or ex-smokers? Do you admire bright and successful people? If so, remember that the further up you go in the income and educational scale the fewer smokers there are. Over 100,000 doctors have stopped smoking cigarettes. Do you admire athletes? Very few of them smoke even when they aren't in training.

Self-concept: habitual smoker. You think of yourself as a smoker who smokes without being aware of it. You are the kind of person who "finds a cigarette in my mouth and didn't remember putting it there." First think about whether you want to be someone who has no control over himself, who does things that might harm him without even thinking about it. Then concentrate on breaking the chain of habit. Avoid the cues which set off automatic smoking. For example, if coffee is always a cue for a cigarette, switch to tea. Don't keep cigarettes in the usual place. Don't carry matches. If you do find yourself with a cigarette in your mouth without knowing how it got there, don't finish smoking it. Make it necessary to go through a complicated ritual in order to get a cigarette. Try to condition yourself to think, "Smoking makes me sick today and may kill me

Appendix XIV (cont.)

tomorrow," whenever you enter into a situation where you usually smoke. For example, if you smoke while you drive, train yourself to think about the ill effects of smoking as soon as you see or feel the ignition key. Remember that smokers miss twice as many days of work as non-smokers.

Smoking socially stimulated. You said that you tended to smoke more when you were with people who smoke, and less when you were with people who didn't smoke. We can't suggest that you make new friends, but wherever possible try to avoid the company of smokers unless they are close friends. Don't go to a table at a cafeteria if others are smoking. Don't take a break where people smoke. Don't go to a smoking lounge or study. Avoid the smoking cars of trains. Be wary; for you the smoking of others is highly contagious.

Psychological addiction. You have a craving for cigarettes that comes solely because you don't have a cigarette. A well-known psychologist named Silvan Tomkins talks about his own feelings for cigarettes as being analogous to love sickness. When he stopped smoking, he engaged in a kind of mourning; the sense of loss was as keen as if he had broken with someone he cared about greatly. He says he didn't really enjoy smoking but was miserable without it. The only way he was able to quit was by spending three days in a movie theater where smoking was not permitted. Although he got very tired of the movie, it was distracting enough so that he could spend long periods of time without even thinking about smoking. For a truly addicted smoker stopping is sheer hell, but once he makes it through he never will smoke again because he can't face the prospect of having to break with smoking again. Do you have the courage to quit cold? It won't be much fun, but if Tomkins is right, once you have gone through the misery of the first couple of weeks you will be cured for life.

Stimulation. You said that you smoke because it gives you a lift, perks you up, keeps you from slowing down. You have to find alternative ways of keeping yourself from feeling draggy or tired, and you have to work at avoiding the use of cigarettes to perk you up. Mildly stimulating drinks like Coke or Pepsi might work. If you have a weight problem, the diet drinks would probably be useful. Breathing deeply might work, so might a short period of exercise. Your need for stimulation is certainly legitimate, but you should try to find some other way than smoking to satisfy it.

Sensual feeling. This title may sound a little odd, but it merely means that you told us that you enjoy handling the cigarette and watching the smoke. You probably like having something to do with your hands. Can you find a substitute? People have used rubbing stones, marble eggs, key chains, hippie beads, silly putty. They get phoney cigarettes which they can keep in their mouths or hands and which give a menthol taste.

* * * * * *

Lastly, if you feel the need of help, talk with your doctor about the use of one of the anti-smoking drugs. They contain a substance called Lobeline which is similar in action to nicotine. It doesn't require a prescription. If your doctor tells you that using these drugs is acceptable for you, and if having a medicine helps you think of your smoking as a disease you want to get rid of, then the Lobeline drugs are worth trying. Of course, if you have any problems with your health we must urge you to see your doctor.

GOOD LUCK

NOTES

Appendix XV

Six-Month Telephone Interview Form
Role-Playing Study

SIX-MONTH FOLLOW-UP — OGONTZ

S No. _____

Name _____   Phone _____

Do you smoke cigarettes? _____

IF NO:

Did you ever smoke as much as half a pack a day? _____

If so, when did you stop? _____

What made you stop? _____

For how long had you smoked half a pack a day? _____

IF YES:

How long ago did you start smoking? _____

How many cigarettes did you smoke yesterday? _____

How many cigarettes a day do you usually smoke? _____

If you did not smoke the usual number yesterday, why was yesterday different? _____

Has anything happened in the last six months to change your smoking

in any way? If so, what? _____

Appendix XV (cont.)

Six-Month Telephone Interview Form
Role-Playing Study (continued)

S#_____

Interviewer _____

(probe) Have you tried to cut down
your smoking or stop smoking
during the past six months? _____

NOTE TO INTERVIEWER: IF YES TO ABOVE QUESTION, continue ...

IF NO, go to Question 3 next page ....

Check questions you asked to
elicit answers — see below.

1._____A. Can you tell me about your
experiences?

_____B. What happened?

_____C. How did you go about it?

_____D. What did you do?

_____E. Can you tell me a little more
about it?

2._____A. How did you feel when you
stopped (or cut down)?

_____B. How did it affect you?

_____C. What else can you tell me
about it?

Appendix XV (cont.)

Six-Month Telephone Interview Form
Role-Playing Study (continued)

3. A.   Did you come to Beaver College last winter for an experiment?
         IF YES, CONTINUE ....

    B.   What was it about? _____

4. A.   Did you think about your experiences at Beaver afterwards?

    B.   Did they affect you in any way?

5.   Did you receive any materials from Beaver afterwards? _____ IF YES

    A.   What did you think of them?

    B.   Did you make any use of them?

    C.   How?

Appendix XVI

Interaction Effects on Multiple Analysis of Variance
Personality vs. SEU Factor Scores on Patterns of Support for Smoking

1. Criterion: Regressed Smoking Score, Cigarettes Smoked Yesterday

Post-experimental Value x	Internal/External Control		
Expectancy: Ill-Health	low	high	interaction
low	−2.83	1.39	F = 4.613
high	1.28	0.38	$p < .03$
			df = 1,131

2. Criterion: Regressed Smoking Score, Cigarettes Smoked Yesterday

	Internal/External Control		
Regressed Value: Ill-Health	low	high	interaction
low	−3.78	0.98	F = 5.433
high	1.61	0.66	$p < .02$
			df = 1,124

3. Criterion: Regressed Smoking Score, Cigarettes Usually Smoked

Regressed expectancy C–S	Internal/External Control		
Ill-Health	low	high	interaction
low	−0.14	2.24	F = 4.713
high	−0.23	−3.08	$p < .03$
			df = 1,124

4. Criterion: Absolute Change in Number of Cigarettes Usually Smoked

Regressed expectancy C–S Ill-Health	Internal/External Control		
	low	high	interaction
low	−3.41	−1.84	F = 4.924
high	−3.56	−8.26	$p < .03$
			df = 1,124

Appendix XVI (cont.)

5. Criterion: Regressed Smoking Score, Cigarettes Smoked Yesterday
Social Desirability

Regressed Expectancy: Tension Reduction C–S	low	high	interaction
low	−1.50	1.10	F = 3.897
high	1.30	−1.09	p < .05
			df = 1,124

6. Criterion: Regressed Smoking Score, Cigarettes Smoked Yesterday
Social Desirability

Value x Expectancy: Tension Reduction	low	high	interaction
low	0.32	−1.73	F = 4.177
high	−0.16	3.07	p < .04
			df = 1,124

7. Criterion: Absolute Change in Number of Cigarettes Usually Smoked
Social Desirability

Regressed Value: Mood	low	high	interaction
low	−2.54	−6.53	F = 3.765
high	−4.30	−2.70	p < .06
			df = 1,124

8. Criterion: Regressed Smoking Score, Cigarettes Usually Smoked
Social Desirability

Regressed Value: Mood	low	high	interaction
low	0.91	−2.04	F = 3.918
high	−0.56	1.33	p < .05
			df = 1,124

9. Criterion: Regressed Smoking Score, Cigarettes Smoked Yesterday
Manifest Anxiety

Regressed SEU for Stopping	low	high	interaction
low	0.96	0.65	F = 4.581
high	−2.41	2.72	p < .03
			df = 1,124

10. Criterion: Absolute Change in Number of Cigarettes Usually Smoked
Manifest Anxiety

Regressed Expectancy: Self-image C–S	low	high	interaction
low	−6.97	−1.53	F = 4.160
high	−3.10	−3.69	p < .04
			df = 1,124

Appendix XVI (cont.)

11. Criterion: Regressed Smoking Score, Cigarettes Smoked Yesterday

	Manifest Anxiety		
Regressed Expectancy: Self-image	low	high	interaction
low	−2.76	3.95	F = 7.738
high	0.40	0.07	p < .01
			df = 1,124

12. Criterion: Regressed Smoking Score, Cigarettes Usually Smoked

	Manifest Anxiety		
Regressed Expectancy: Self-image	low	high	interaction
low	−2.75	2.47	F = 3.474
high	0.17	0.73	p < .07
			df = 1,124

13. Criterion: Absolute Change in Number of Cigarettes Usually Smoked

Post-experimental SEU for Stopping	Risk		
	low	high	interaction
low	−9.31	−5.70	F = 4.235
high	−5.32	−4.21	p < .04
			df = 1,124

14. Criterion: Absolute Change in Number of Cigarettes Usually Smoked

Regressed SEU for Stopping	Risk		
	low	high	interaction
low	− 1.22	−5.93	F = 4.173
high	−5.25	−4.13	p < .04
			df = 1,124

15. Criterion: Absolute Change in Number of Cigarettes Usually Smoked

Psychological Addiction	Risk		
	low	high	interaction
low	−3.70	−9.04	F = 4.416
high	−3.42	−2.00	p < .04
			df = 1,99

16. Criterion: Absolute Change in Number of Cigarettes Usually Smoked

Tension Reduction	Situational Anxiety		
	low	high	interaction
low	−7.13	−2.70	F = 3.611
high	−1.89	−3.80	p < .06
			df = 1,99

Appendix XVI (cont.)

17. Criterion: Regressed Smoking Score, Cigarettes Usually Smoked

Social Stimulation for Smoking	Manifest Anxiety		interaction
	low	high	
low	0.87	0.27	F = 4.229
high	3.24	1.27	$p < .04$
			df = 199

18. Criterion: Regressed Smoking Score, Cigarettes Usually Smoked

Social closeness — Self-image	Manifest Anxiety		interaction
	low	high	
low	−0.53	−2.79	F = 5.967
high	−2.15	2.29	$p < .02$
			df = 1,99

Author Index

Abelin, T. 7, 8
Abelson, R. P. 91
Allen, H. 103
Allen, W. A. 103
Allport, G. W. 12, 13, 29
American Cancer Society 5-6
American Medical Association 181-182
Appley, M. H. 9
Aronson, E. 26, 61
Atkinson, J. W. 176-180

Balloun, J. L. 93
Bandura, A. 7
Banzhoff, J. F., III 3
Barker, R. G. 8
Bash, N. 104
Beck, W. 6
Berglund, E. 103
Bergman, S. H. 107
Berkowitz, L. 176
Bernstein, D. A. 96
Bliss, C. M. 11
Borgatta, E.F. 183
Boyko, E. P. 172
Brehm, J. W. 91, 95, 164
Briney, K. L. 90
Brock, T. C. 93

Campbell, D. T. 117
Cattell, R. B. 175
Clyde, D. J. 124
Cofer, C. N. 9
Cohen, A. 95
Cook, S.W. 47
Courts, F. A. 7
Cramer, E. M. 124
Creswell, W. H. 9, 87, 90-91
Crowne, D. 56, 68, 69, 116, 147
Crutchfield, R. S. 114, 116

Dabbs, J. M. 100
Dalrymple, W. 7
Deutsch, M. 47
Dixon, W. J. 124
Dubitzky, M. 14, 98, 101, 103, 113

Edwards, W. 97
Ejrup, B. 85
Elliott, A. 168
Elms, A. C. 108
England, L. 55
Evans, R.R. 183
Eysenck, H. J. 6, 55, 92

Fackler, W. A. 103, 104
Feather, N. T. 92, 176, 180
Federal Communications Commission 3
Federal Trade Commission 2
Festinger, L. 91-92, 93, 95, 163, 175
Fisher, R. A. 6
Flanagan, J. C. 18
Fletcher, C. M. 11
Forrest, D. W. 12
Fredrickson, D. T. 122
Fritschler, A. L. 3

Gallup, G. 2-3
Gilmore, J. B. 108
Goldman, A. 104
Graff, H. 104
Graham, S. 168
Gross, A. 48
Guilford, J. P. 141

Hammet, V. B. O. 104
Heider, F. 91
Hersey, R. B. 29

Stone, D. B. 9, 87, 90-91
Straits, B. C. 7, 51, 55, 97, 101

Tannenbaum, P. H. 91
Tauant, M. 55
Taylor, J. 56, 69, 79ff.
Taylor, R. M. 7
Taylor, S. V. 8, 9
Thompson, D. S. 103
Tomkins, S. 10, 13-14, 15, 18-19, 48, 62,
    78, 79, 104, 113, 122, 173
Trembly, G. 100

Ullman, L. P. 104
United States Public Health Service 1, 92,
    98, 101, 109

Vitz, P. 12

Waingrow, S. 15, 31, 33, 57, 75, 86, 98-99
Wakefield, J. 102
Wallach, M. A. 56, 68, 115, 116, 149

Walster, E. 163
Walters, R. 7
Watne, A. L. 102
Watts, J. C. 99, 100
Weatherly, D. 101
Webb, E. J. 117
Weir, J. M. 12
Wells, H. 11
Welsh, B. 8, 93
Werner, W. 101
Wilson, T. R. 103
Wolitzky, D. L. 93, 94
Wolpe, J. S. 104
Woodruff, A. B. 101
Woolf, M. 55
World Conference on Smoking and Health
    2, 11
Wright, H. F. 8

Yanovski, A. 104
Yatko, R. J. 94

Zagona, S. V. 8
Zimbardo, P. G. 108, 162, 176

Subject Index